A Game Enjoyed

A Game Enjoyed

An Autobiography

Peter May
with Michael Melford

Stanley Paul
LONDON MELBOURNE SYDNEY AUCKLAND
JOHANNESBURG

Stanley Paul & Co Ltd
An imprint of Century Hutchinson Ltd
17–21 Conway Street, London W1P 6JD

Hutchinson Publishing Group (Australia) Pty Ltd
PO Box 496, Hawthorn, Melbourne, Victoria 3122

Hutchinson Group (NZ) Ltd
PO Box 40–086, Glenfield 10, Auckland

Hutchinson Group (SA) Pty Ltd
PO Box 337, Bergvlei, 2012 South Africa

First published 1985
© Peter May 1985

Set in Sabon by Input Typesetting Ltd,
London, SW19 8DR
Printed and bound in Great Britain by
Anchor Brendon Ltd, Tiptree, Essex

ISBN 0 09 162260 3

Contents

Acknowledgements

I have read again with much interest several books on tours: *West Indian Adventure* by E. W. Swanton, Museum Press, 1954; *The Ashes* by Ian Peebles, Hodder and Stoughton, 1955; *Report from South Africa* by E. W. Swanton, Robert Hale, 1957; and *Four Chukkas to Australia* by Jack Fingleton, Heinemann, 1959.

I am most grateful to John Warr for his foreword. His wit, wisdom and good nature mean that he is subjected to countless calls on his oratory and writing and even an old friend approached him with diffidence.

I owe thanks, too, to Donald Carr for checking my references to the laws and the often-changed playing conditions of the post-war years; to Freddie Brown for reading the two chapters on the tours on which he and I were manager and captain; to Tony Wreford-Brown for refreshing my recollections of my schooldays; and to my five equestrian advisers at home who know my limitations when it comes to describing the horse and his ailments.

Foreword

BY J. J. WARR

Peter May, in collaboration with Michael Melford, has given us a true and fascinating picture of the cricket world in a vintage period in its history. As someone who played in sixty-six Test matches, as captain in forty-one, which fell mostly between 1951 and 1958 when England were undefeated in a series home or away, and as a vital ingredient in a Surrey side which won the championship seven consecutive years, twice under his captaincy, Peter is uniquely placed to give his version of events from the centre of the stage.

Those of us lucky enough to have played with him know that the story will have no recriminations against authority, no insensitive knocking at contemporaries and, above all, no bitterness towards the game itself. As someone who has occupied three of the hottest seats in sport – as captain of the England cricket team, as President of MCC and as chairman of England's cricket selectors – he has, you could suppose, a masochistic streak in him, but the title of the book says it all.

He had a great stroke of luck as a schoolboy at Charterhouse in being coached by George Geary. Here was a great bowler and no mean bat who had played with and against all the great prewar masters and had studied their technique from the front line. He instilled the basics of balance, footwork and head position into a schoolboy prodigy, basics which stayed with him all his career. The immediate product was an extraordinary last year at Charterhouse in which Peter made 100 against each of Eton, Harrow and the Old Carthusians, followed at Lord's by 148 for the Southern Schools against the Rest and 146 for the Public Schools against the Combined Services (next highest score 18).

For those interested in technique, the nearest player in modern cricket to Peter May is Vivian Richards. They both have appeared to favour the onside but in fact any bowler who tried attacking them on or outside the off stump would find plenty of strokes in the repertoire in that area. They both have had the unerring foot movement to position themselves for the intended shot, keeping batsmanship as one-dimensional as possible. They also have both had that extra sixth sense which seems to anticipate where the ball is going to be bowled. Peter, possibly, punched the ball with wrist and forearm more than Vivian Richards, who is more a swinger of the bat.

However, one important difference lies in the pitches on which they played. Pitches were not covered until 1959 and many of the county matches were played on rain-affected wickets on which spin bowlers could really turn the ball. A glance at any *Wisden* of the period will show quite emphatically that P.B.H. was head and shoulders above his contemporaries on such pitches. It was not uncommon at the Oval for sides to be bowled out for less than Peter scored himself.

There was once a barmy theory that he was vulnerable against leg spin. It is not a view that I have heard expressed by the best leg spinners of the period.

In Test matches he seemed to be like Horatius on the bridge keeping the foe at bay single-handed. He would arrive at the crease time after time with a crisis either on hand or impending. It has always been a mystery to me how, with his ice-cold temperament, he failed to do himself justice in the Varsity match in which he played three times. After my year as captain the choice of my successor lay between Peter and David Sheppard. Undergraduates tend to be swayed by considerations of success or failure on what they considered the big day and the choice fell on the future Bishop of Liverpool.

As it turned out, Peter's career, both as captain of his country and his county, was not blighted. Indeed, in a wider sense his two mentors in the art of captaincy were Stuart Surridge and Sir Len Hutton who represented different ends of the captaincy spectrum. Stuart was the enthusiastic, extrovert, buccaneering risk-taker who pushed and prodded his players into whole-hearted effort. Len was the deep-thinking introvert whose attitudes were supremely, cautiously, professional, who drew on his Yorkshire roots to give nothing away with bat or ball. Peter's approach lay somewhere between the two, being slightly inclined to Len's when captaining England and more to Stuart when at the helm for Surrey.

Another very important difference between first-class cricket in that era and today was the distinction between amateur and professional. Peter was the true blue amateur and it was not always easy in that role to gain the fullest respect and admiration of your professional colleagues who were inclined to see you as a threat to their livelihood. What is remarkable is that if there were not a Saint Peter already, all the Surrey professionals who played with Peter May would press for his instant canonization. They would unashamedly class themselves as hard-bitten and difficult to impress with cricketing performances, but their admiration and respect for P.B.H. are unanimous and unbounded.

It must be said that he never played 'instant' one-day cricket which started in earnest in 1963. My own feeling is that it would be like asking

Artur Rubinstein to play honky-tonk or persuading Sir Thomas Beecham
to conduct the Rolling Stones. Cricket is now clearly divided into
classical and pop and whilst I have the greatest admiration for the good
'pop artists' who bring in money and crowds to modern-day cricket, I
am enough of a purist to think that Peter May should be remembered
as a great performer in the classical tradition.

But Peter's life has by no means been confined to cricket. A devoted
family man whose wife and four daughters are dedicated to the esoteric
world of three-day eventing, he has plenty on his plate acting as chief
bottlewasher and cheerleader. He is as keen for them to win on a horse
as he was himself to win on the cricket field more than twenty years
ago. He mentions in the book that he does not ride himself but the real
reason for that came in his cryptic reply to me when I queried his lack
of horsemanship. 'Easy, J.J.' he said. 'No brakes.'

Pictures of people and events tend to get blurred and even distorted
with time. But nobody who saw Peter May at his peak in the fifties and
early sixties will forget that sight. A tall willowy figure with a slightly
disjointed way of running between the wickets, he was the supreme
professional in the ranks of the amateurs just as Denis Compton was
the supreme amateur in the ranks of the professionals. Peter easily joins
the distinguished band of all-time great batsmen. Like Sir Jack Hobbs
before him, a modest man who was almost embarrassed and weighed
down by the limelight, he has taken a long time to tell his story but it
has been well worth the wait.

Introduction

Most cricket followers of the 1980s probably know me as the chairman of selectors and therefore as one of the most vulnerable sporting Aunt Sallies of the day. An old friend wondered why on earth I wanted to take on this job after being closely involved with cricket for over thirty years as player, captain, selector and administrator. I was, he said, a certain loser before I reached the starting stalls and it was not as if I had nothing else to do. When the appointment was announced, I was still only halfway through my year of office as President of MCC. My friend clearly thought that I was a glutton for punishment.

I suppose that I could have given him the well-tried but none the less sincere reason that I had an obligation to the game to put something back into it. There is certainly truth in that and I was mindful too of the immense amount that my great friend Alec Bedser had put into a job which has become increasingly responsible and timeconsuming.

But the basic reason for continuing my close association with cricket was the sheer enjoyment which I have derived from it since I first began to play. There may have been times when I did not perhaps look as if I was having great fun. I am well aware that although I was an amateur – and a genuine one unsupported by sponsors or advertisers – I did not always play in the obviously lighthearted way which had been associated with some amateurs in the past. I considered Test cricket a hard game and the captaincy of England and Surrey a highly responsible job. As a young captain in first-class cricket I always had to remember that even if I did not earn my living from the game, most of those playing under me did. But that did not detract from the intense enjoyment which cricket provided for me then – and ever since. Sport gives many things to many people. To me cricket has given immense pleasure.

I recognize that I have been lucky to have a job outside cricket, so that the game has always been a game for me and not a business. I am lucky too to have a family whose main life is with horses but who do not allow that to stop them from taking an enthusiastic interest in cricket. I am not short of advice from my daughters on whom to pick.

In early 1980 Billy Griffith rang me up and to my astonishment asked me if he might nominate me as his successor as President of MCC. I was staggered. I was only fifty, which seemed to be no age at all for such an office. Billy left me to talk it over with the family.

In something of a daze I put the telephone down and broke the news to my wife, Virginia. 'Come on,' she said at once. 'Let's do it. You may not be asked again. Let's enjoy it while we can.'

We did. This may surprise some other recent Presidents who in their year of office have run up against a Packer affair or some international crisis. But I can only say that I look back on the year not only as an honour but a pleasure. So does Virginia, who was a tremendous help in entertaining in the President's box. For many distinguished visitors the only sight of cricket in the year may be from the President's box at Lord's and the President has to do his best to see that they get the right impression.

Not everything in the game is as I would like it to be but too much emphasis is usually put on what is wrong with it. It was the realization that, having experienced the rigours of being both a modern President of MCC and the chairman of selectors, I still enjoyed the game, which prompted me to write this book.

I am very grateful to Michael Melford for jogging my memory, checking the recollections of more than thirty years and putting things in order. I am particularly glad that he was able to help me, not only because he is an old friend, a fellow Carthusian and for long a much respected cricket writer for the *Daily Telegraph* and *Sunday Telegraph*, but because without his assistance I might not have had my years in first-class cricket.

In the summer of 1952 I was in my last term at Cambridge but had no job in sight, certainly no job which would allow me to play cricket regularly. One day Michael, while clipping his parents' hedge in St John's Wood, fell into conversation with their next-door neighbour, Ian McKechnie, a member of Lloyds, who happened to ask what I was going to do for a job.

Michael said that he had not heard that I had anything lined up, at which Ian McKechnie thought a bit and said, 'Ask him if he's interested in Lloyds.' Knowing that Ian was not one to make suggestions lightly, Michael drove via Cambridge next day on his way to Sheffield. It was a Sunday evening and he caught me in my rooms in Pembroke just as I was going into Hall for dinner.

A meeting with Ian McKechnie was arranged and through Ian's kind offices I joined the insurance-broking firm of E. R. Wood which was most generous in allowing me time off to play for Surrey and to go on tours. In the 1970s I moved on to Willis, Faber and Dumas, which has been as indulgent with an ageing selector as E. R. Wood was with a young player.

My memory is pretty good and I have a lot of records of my playing days but inevitably Michael and I spent a lot of time checking facts and figures in *Wisden*. I hope that the present editor of *Wisden*, John Woodcock, whose admirable writings in *The Times* I have read with appreciation for over thirty years, will accept this acknowledgement of the help obtained from recent editions of the *Almanack* and from those produced by his predecessor, the late Norman Preston. No other game can have as valuable and comprehensive a work of reference as *Wisden*.

Selborne   Peter May
February 1985

I
Charterhouse and Cambridge

If I am to begin at the beginning – or before the beginning – I can do no better than quote Ben Travers. It must have been at about the time I first played for England that I met him.

'I take considerable credit for your success,' he said. 'I was a good enough instructor to keep your father alive to produce you.'

In the First World War, before he became famous as the author of the Aldwych farces, Ben was in the Royal Naval Air Service and it was then that he taught my father to fly Sopwith Camels and Pups. We also had Charterhouse in common and he remained a valued friend into his last years when still a very active ninety-year-old.

I doubt if the RNAS had a large complement in those days and it is a strange coincidence that Virginia's father, Harold Gilligan, also served in it.

My father subsequently ran the family contracting business in Reading and my brother John and I grew up there. John is nearly three years younger than I am but he was always a fine games player and we spent hours together on the family's hard tennis court with a ball. Any sort of ball. Tennis ball, football, cricket ball. The wire netting bowed from being hit a thousand times at roughly the same level. We did have stumps which we put into a wooden block and I can certainly appreciate now the value of learning on a true surface. But cricket was just one game that we played in its season.

My mother was a very good tennis player and she was the one who really encouraged our interest in ball games. Very sadly, she died when I was sixteen. My father had never played cricket, at least, not since his schooldays, but he took the keenest interest in our games playing and lived on throughout my time as captain of England.

I first played organized games at Marlborough House School, after which I went on to Leighton Park junior school when war broke out. Bob Relf, formerly of Sussex, was then coaching at Leighton Park, and although I did not come across him much I suppose that he must have passed the word on to Charterhouse where he had previously been the coach. But I remember little about early coaching. I did not like nets. I never did like them subsequently. I would use a net if I wanted to correct a fault or was out of form. Otherwise, it seemed to me that it encouraged a looseness of method which would be found out in competitive cricket.

But until I was sixteen cricket, as I have said, was just one of several games, each to be played in its season and not to be given a lot of thought at other times.

I was still only twelve when I went to Charterhouse in September 1942 and in the following summer came under the wing of George Geary who had succeeded Bob Relf as coach. I was undoubtedly very lucky. George was then fifty but he had been playing in Test matches against Australia only nine years before and had only played his last season for Leicestershire in 1938, when incidentally he averaged 40 with the bat. People forget that he was a good enough all-rounder to make two 50s against Australia batting at number eight.

Thus he numbered among his many admirable qualities the fact that he was still a fine bowler. In the nets he would pitch his off break exactly where he wanted. If he thought a boy suspect against a particular type of ball, then he would bowl it until the correct stroke was played. Large hands are said to be an aid to a bowler. George had the largest hands that I had seen until I met Alec and Eric Bedser.

'Coach' is probably not quite the right description of George in those days. He was more of a guide and adviser, having the innate gift of recognizing the natural ability of a boy and encouraging it. He liked a young batsman to play straight but did not discourage one who played slightly across the line if it was generally done with safety. His reasoning was that overall the runs were worth the risk. It made sense to me and still does.

He spoke simply and not too much. I always felt that to be one of his great attributes. Too much advice can either confuse boys or, if taken, make them all the same. He used to say in later years that he taught me nothing. That was kind of him and flattering but untrue. I may have found batting easier than most boys of my age but I had plenty to learn.

'There are basics,' he would say. 'Keep your head still. Stand still as long as you can. When you move your feet, move quickly, but the longer you stand still, the later you'll play the shot.' I still look for this in a batsman. Vivian Richards and Greg Chappell are two prime examples of modern batsmen who stayed wonderfully still until the last moment.

Footwork probably comes less naturally to a tallish batsman than to the small compact nimble type but after George's groundwork it never worried me. When I was out of form in later years, I would often say to myself, 'Move your feet.' George gave me confidence, instilled determination and made me realize the value of patience and of what is nowadays called 'building' an innings.

Apart from what we learned from George on the technical side, we had the great joy of listening to him talk. We sat there on wet afternoons and listened to tales of Australia in 1928–29, of the fourteen Tests he played between 1924 and 1936, of the great players of those years, of characters like George Brown of Hampshire, of hospitality from maharajas on tours of India, of ever bigger elephants and tigers there. Some of the stories may have been improved with age but, with their fascinating glimpses of an exotic outside world, they taught us a lot about cricket and what it stood for.

I am very pleased that as a memorial to George we now have a seat at Charterhouse from which people can watch the cricket on Green. From the fund launched in his memory there is also a George Geary annual award of bat and pads for the most promising under-sixteen cricketer of the year.

However gifted, a coach needs support. Similarly, one cricket master at a school cannot do it all on his own. So we were also fortunate to have several very good cricketers on the staff at Charterhouse, the number growing as several more were demobilized late in 1945.

Wilfred Timms was responsible for the First XI at the time I appeared. W. W. Timms had been a familiar name in Northamptonshire teams during the school holidays until the early 1930s. He had a lot of first-class experience as an amateur in what must have been the tough school of Northamptonshire cricket in those days. A neat competent batsman, he knew a lot about the game. We respected this. Boys listen all the more eagerly to someone who has done it. The sight of a county cap or sweater in itself commands respect.

There was always the wisdom of Bob Arrowsmith, the master in charge of cricket and now very properly renowned as one of the game's great historians. He was an excellent leg-spinner who gave the ball plenty of air, so much in fact that he would sometimes hit the crosspiece which covered some nets and the ball would flop down on the pitch.

Tommy Garnett, later Master of Marlborough and headmaster of Geelong Grammar School in Prince Charles's time, and Tony Wreford-Brown returned in 1945, both of them fine cricketers with first-class experience. Garnett had been an outstanding schoolboy cricketer at Charterhouse and in 1933 had made 1000 runs in school matches and 1000 runs in house matches. John Marriott, now keeper of the royal stamp collection, was another good cricketer on the staff and subsequently played for Hertfordshire.

With this encouragement and with the help of wonderfully true pitches, I had every chance. I must have taken it fairly early, for in that first summer of 1943 the headmaster, Robert Birley, who was also my housemaster, was called on to decide whether a boy in his first year should be allowed to play in the First XI. He decided that in everybody's interests I should wait. I was not really aware of this at the time. Boys are not great thinkers about matters outside their immediate interests and I was simply interested in playing. For whom I played was of no great moment.

However, in 1944, when I was fourteen, I played in the First XI and made my first 100 against Harrow. My main recollection of this is of Alistair McCorquodale bowling very fast and having me caught in the gully. Considering that only four years later he was fourth in the Olympic 100 metres and being referred to as 'the fastest white man in the world', he must have been a formidable sight rushing up to the crease. I think I accepted this at the time as the norm and was more intrigued by the fact that he wore a scarf.

In 1945 I was picked for the Public Schools against the Combined Services at Lord's. There were some good players in the side. Peter Blake, later captain of Oxford, and Ian Campbell, an immensely powerful schoolboy cricketer and a still better hockey and rugby player, made 127 in an hour before I went in at number three. My contributions were 0 and 1 and I could only console myself with the thought that I was bowled by Trevor Bailey in one innings and was lbw to Freddie Brown in the other.

In 1946 we had a very good side at Charterhouse including Tony Rimell, the captain, and Oliver Popplewell. Four years later we were all three in the same Cambridge side. We also had a remarkable schoolboy cricketer in Bob Whitby, who attracted much public interest later, not on the cricket field but as Prince Charles's housemaster at Gordonstoun. He had a good high action, moved the ball a lot at a lively fast-medium and took a huge number of wickets including 8 for 16 against Winchester.

Charterhouse's successes against Winchester, as against Harrow, were rare things. Eton gave us singularly little trouble. In 1946, however, we beat Winchester, Whitby having bowled them out for 90. It was not easy even then. I was dropped at slip and survived to make 34. Oliver Popplewell steered us home by 4 wickets.

Amongst those present was Field Marshal Lord Montgomery. One of his favourite sayings was 'In every battle there is a crisis. In every battle a turning point.' He said that my being dropped was the turning point in this battle.

Years later when I was captain of England Monty came to our dressing room during a Test match. He still referred to the match as a battle and grilled me on how my troops prepared for it.

'I suppose they don't smoke,' he said. I fended that one off.

'Must go to bed early too, I expect,' he added. He then turned to the nearest player. 'Do *you* go to bed early?' he asked.

Of all people, he had picked on Godfrey Evans whose sleeping hours were notoriously unconventional. Godfrey managed to satisfy the Field Marshal somehow while the rest of us watched with a fiendish glee.

Bob Whitby played for the Public Schools at Lord's in both 1946 and 1947 but I was left out in 1946, though I was top scorer for the Southern Schools against the Rest in the preliminary match. I accepted that there were a lot of good players about and was not aware of any other reason for my omission, but I read in next year's *Wisden* that it was because of my poor fielding. I was no greyhound in the field but there had been no complaints that I had heard. As the general standard of fielding was said to be low I was mildly surprised by this revelation. But by then we were into the sunny season of 1947.

I was now captain of Charterhouse. Popplewell and Rimell had left and we had a less strong side that year but I was delighted to be able to give my brother John his colours. I suppose our main success was in beating Eton by 169 runs. We lost to Winchester by 11 runs. It was a glorious summer, I batted on some wonderful pitches – and made a lot of runs. I finished with two 100s at Lord's.

Of my contemporaries, I have already mentioned Whitby's mighty contributions – a boy who takes wickets as he did is a tremendous asset in school cricket – and Tony Rimell, a fine left-hander and off-spin bowler. The learned High Court judge of today, Sir Oliver Popplewell, was a wicketkeeper-batsman who was to be in three Cambridge sides and to sire the spirited Somerset all-rounder of the 1980s. Jim Prior was in the cricket XI in his last year but was a much better footballer, a wing half who contributed a lot later on to winning Arthur Dunn sides.

Jim and I were in the same house and in the same college at Cambridge – Pembroke. I have often been asked whether it was suspected then that we had a future senior minister of the Crown in our midst. The answer is that we certainly knew that he was bright. He got a First in agriculture. And I remember the day when we were discussing what we were going to do when we left university. Jim said, 'I want to go into politics.' I am afraid that we must have seemed surprised, not because of any doubts of his ability but because to those present it seemed an extraordinary thing to want to do.

Simon Raven, the author, was in the Charterhouse XI in my early years. William Rees-Mogg, later editor of *The Times*, was a diligent scorer for the First XI. Dick Taverne, forerunner of the SDP, was head of the school and in the cricket XI in his and my last year.

Thereafter we all went our different ways. Mine led into the Navy and then, after a two-year break in my academic life, to Cambridge.

I should at once remove any idea that I went up to Cambridge just to play cricket and that the college authorities connived at this. It was rather the opposite. Pembroke had had a reputation as a college for games players and in the late 1940s was trying to break away from the sporting tradition.

When I was interviewed by the senior tutor, who seemed to have heard of my cricket interests, he left me in no doubt that Pembroke would not stand for work being subordinated to cricket. 'Where is Fenners?' he asked, not through any search for knowledge but by way of impressing on me his idea of my priorities.

In fact, I succeeded in getting through three seasons at Cambridge without having to take a match off for work. Reading history and economics, I tried to do the work in the winter and use the summer for revising. Luckily I have a good memory. Anyhow I satisfied the examiners and took a 2.2.

It was unquestionably a help to my cricket that I went up to Cambridge when there were a lot of good cricketers there, not only players of budding talent but of experience with first-class counties. Like myself, they had done national service and came up two years older than the modern undergraduate. Hubert Doggart, a marvellous all-round games player who was that year's conscientious and enthusiastic captain, John Dewes, John Warr and David Sheppard were four who were all immensely successful in 1950.

The universities today still produce some top-class players, but although they remain a valuable source of Test cricketers their sides are less mature. The better players, especially the bowlers, are less obviously effective because they usually lack support. Oxford in particular have problems in putting anything near their best side in the field during the term.

In all three summers we had a strong, well-balanced side. Yet if the ultimate object of a Cambridge season is to beat Oxford, we failed dismally. Betwen 1950 and 1952 Cambridge fielded six players at Lord's who had already played Test cricket and two others who were to do so later. Yet we drew two of the University matches and lost the other in 1951 when we did ourselves less than justice and Oxford played at their very best, fielding brilliantly. This in a year when four of the Cambridge side were considered good enough to play for the Gentlemen at Lord's a few days later.

I am afraid that our approach to the University match was wrong. In those days the match was still watched by big crowds and there was a lot of tension. We allowed the importance of it to upset our judgement. Certainly most of the batsmen, myself included, did not play the bowling on its merits as we did against the counties – often when up against some of the best bowlers in the country. At Lord's we let the bowlers dictate. There were exceptions, but it remains a disappointment to me that in years when I was averaging over 60 for Cambridge my highest score in five innings against Oxford was 39.

Hubert Doggart, who was not much more successful in the University match than I was, rectified the matter in later years when playing for Sussex. I believe he received a telegram from Jim Swanton: 'Congratulations on your runs against Oxford. Better late than never!'

Though some of us in the early 1950s may have allowed the occasion to overawe us, I hate the idea of the University match declining in stature and in 1982, as chairman of selectors, I gave Derek Pringle, then captain of Cambridge, every opportunity to play in it rather than in a Test match against India with which it clashed. He had played in the First Test of the series and I told him that we would quite understand it if he wished to captain his side in the University match, which he would never have the chance to do again. It would in no way affect his position in the Test side.

In my day it would have been accepted that an undergraduate, especially a captain, had a first duty to his university during his brief residence there. As recently as 1971 Majid Khan, then Cambridge captain, played in the University match rather than for Pakistan in a Test match at Headingley.

However, Pringle chose to play for England and I realized that this was compatible with the change in the cricketing world. For one thing, he was hoping to make a living out of cricket. I noted, too, that the other members of the Cambridge team, which would be considerably weakened by his absence, fully supported his decision, indeed looked on it primarily as a boost for Cambridge cricket. I hope that clashes between the University match and Test matches will always be avoided whenever possible and that other players will not have to make the choice. But fixture planning in the era of limited-over cricket, of six Tests instead of five and in a short English summer, is an unenviable job.

Having said that it would be a great pity if the University match lost stature, I must add that I welcome the less grim approach of recent years when it has been played more like an ordinary first-class match between two counties and without the same determination to avoid defeat. Given a good pitch, it is bound to be difficult to finish in three days a match between two sides who are always likely to have stronger batting than bowling. It is easier to be a productive batsman at twenty than a penetrative bowler. So, with the qualification that its character and tradition are not allowed to be too far undermined, I welcome University matches such as the one in 1982 which, after the loss of nearly all the first day's play, was revived by declarations, Cambridge eventually winning on one. It would not have happened in 1950.

My first taste of the beautiful batting pitches produced for so long at Fenners by Cyril Coote was highly favourable. This was against Sussex. David Sheppard, another freshman, who had been a remarkably late developer at Sherborne, made 100 and he and I shared in a stand of 153. We scored over 350 before Hubert declared.

A batsman who made hundreds of runs for Cambridgeshire over the years, Cyril Coote was a sound judge of the game and always ready with advice if asked for it. Countless Cambridge bowlers as well as batsmen must have profited from playing in their developing years on the true pitches which Cyril turned out so consistently.

The pitch on which we played West Indies in the fourth match of 1950 must have been one of the truest Cyril ever produced. Michael Melford says that he remembers an ominous moment in the second over of that remarkable match when John Dewes hit Prior Jones like a bullet along the ground through the covers without moving his feet at all. It was that sort of pitch. By tea the opening partnership of Dewes and Sheppard was worth nearly 300. I went to the wicket at a quarter to seven with the score 487 for 2.

It was an amazing day's batting to look back on. The ball seemed to hit the middle of the bat and nowhere else all day. Yet the bowlers – Johnson, Jones, Worrell, Ramadhin and Valentine – were those who two months later were beating England. The snag, of course, was that anything we could do the West Indian batsmen were likely to do better and they duly replied with 730 for 3, Everton Weekes making 304 not out with all the dazzlingly quick strokes with which one associated him.

There was a lot of waiting with pads on to be done in those days. While Hubert Doggart was away playing in the First Test at Old Trafford, I was lucky enough to get in at number three against Hampshire on one of Cyril Coote's best products and passed 200 for the first time. John Dewes and Mike Stevenson also made 100s. Against West Indies Dewes and Sheppard had made 343 together, yet this was not their best of the season. Against Sussex at Hove their opening stand was 349. They were a fine contrasting pair – Dewes a sturdily built left-hander with immensely strong forearms, Sheppard a tall handsome driver of the ball.

We found batting at Lord's in the University match much more testing and a fairly even match interrupted by rain was drawn. But I had a lot of pleasure from a match at Lord's a month later when my brother John was chosen for the Public Schools against the Combined Services. While Colin Cowdrey was making 100, John scored 44 out of a stand of 66 with him.

Under the astute and never dull captaincy of J. J. Warr, which I rated highly, Cambridge had a pretty good season in 1951 with a melancholy end when Oxford beat us in a dour match at Lord's. For a university side we had had remarkably little trouble in bowling opponents out, for the formidable combination of Warr and Wait took nearly 100 wickets, J.J.'s share being 51 at 13 apiece.

There was a lot of rain during the term and we played on some damp pitches but J.J. was already a very good bowler, swinging the ball away from the bat late. Even then, he was able to spot a batsman's weaknesses more quickly than most. He had doubtless benefited from bowling in unrewarding conditions in Australia during the previous winter and I always thought that he was underestimated as a bowler. He was too often judged on his record when picked prematurely for a relatively weak bowling side in Australia. In the later 1950s I found him as hard as any to play but by that time many other good bowlers were on the scene – Statham, Tyson, Trueman, Bailey, Loader, Moss among them – and J.J. was never given another chance.

David Sheppard had also profited from the winter in Australia but, having to catch up on two terms' lost work, he played only one match before June – against the South Africans, when he batted soundly for three hours.

When he came into the side he was soon in tremendous form and we shared some useful stands, beginning with one of 215 against Middlesex when David made 100 in each innings.

On tour we beat Worcestershire, Sussex and MCC. Warr, Wait and sometimes Marlar bowled sides out and our only setback was against Hampshire. We declared on taking a first-innings lead with only 6 wickets down but in the last innings the ball turned and Charles Knott bowled us out – 8 for 26. He was a very useful off-spinner with plenty of flight, a genuine amateur if ever there was one. He was in the fish business and would have spent several hours at the docks before he arrived on the ground, sometimes only just before the start of play. In the 1980s he has still been serving Hampshire cricket as chairman of the cricket committee, a job which has become no easier in days both of economies and of greater rewards for players.

We finished our tour with a two-day match at Sandhurst against the Army. That, of course, was not to be taken lightly in those days of national service – indeed, the opposition included a Test player in Signalman Brian Close, who made 100 – but two of our middle batsmen also made 100s, Raman Subba Row and the Australian Bill Hayward, and we should have gone to Lord's brimming over with confidence. Oxford had beaten only the Free Foresters.

With only 750 runs scored in three full days, the University match of

1951 must have been hard work to watch. But it was close enough to
sustain interest, it had a tense climax on the last day and there was some
good cricket played, mostly by Oxford. Their fielding saved many more
than the 21 runs by which they won.

Murray Hofmeyr, the Oxford captain, was not as gifted a cricketer
as he was a rugby footballer but he applied himself with 100 per cent
concentration and his fighting spirit was reflected in everything his side
did. I can remember Donald Carr making runs quite freely in both
innings but what really thwarted us was Brian Boobbyer's dogged 80 in
the second innings. This must have lasted five hours and it meant that
we needed 219 in the last innings in about four and half hours.

By then the ball was turning. In fact, it turned a bit on the first day
when Robin Marlar took 5 wickets. Boobbyer and Carr played him well
in the second innings but Raman Subba Row, whose leg spin had not
often been needed that summer, took 5 for 21 and it was clear that we
had lost the advantage which on paper the fast bowling of John Warr
and John Wait gave us.

Oxford's fast bowling may have been limited but they had two repu-
table spinners in 'Buck' Divecha, who toured England in the following
season with the Indians, and the left-arm John Bartlett. Buck especially
was very hard to score off on this sort of pitch. There were no leg-side
restrictions then and he could have several short legs and an outer ring.
To Oxford's credit, they cast an added gloom over the batsman by
giving the impression that anything which left the ground would be
caught.

Our innings started promisingly. David Sheppard and Pat Mathews
made 44 for the first wicket but we were 75 for 4 with May still there,
if not exactly in command. At this point I was joined, to my great
surprise, by John Warr who had promoted himself some three places in
the order. He left no doubt that he did not care for the way in which
we had been playing and was prepared to take a more positive line
himself. 'You hold on, leave the strokes to me' was roughly the theme.

Anyhow J.J. at once hit Divecha twice back over his head and we
battled away for an hour. At 127 for 4 with several useful batsmen to
come, including Subba Row, it looked just possible that J.J.'s unor-
thodox approach to spin might be going to do the trick. But after tea I
was caught at the wicket off Bartlett, Warr was bowled by Divecha and
eventually Oxford won with fifteen minutes to spare.

It was not a contest on which I look back with unqualified pride and
pleasure but it was a classic example of what keen and athletic fielding
can do. They made us fight for every run in both innings.

That month of July 1951 was one of sharp contrasts for me. I had
done little in the University match but ten days later I made 100 for the

Gentlemen against a Players attack of Bedser, Statham, Tattersall, Hilton, Compton and Ikin. I made another 100 against Middlesex at Lord's and before the end of the month was making another at Headingley against South Africa in my first Test match.

In 1952 under David Sheppard's captaincy we had the players to make us one of the most successful university sides on record. Warr and Wait were still up, though John Wait played in only a few matches. There was a formidable replacement for him in the tall, almost gangling Cuan McCarthy, who had toured with the 1951 South Africans and must have been about the fastest bowler in the country at the time, even if there were doubts about his action. Robin Marlar was becoming one of the best off-spinners in the country. For one of only medium height he had a very deceptive looping flight. He spun the ball and was, I thought, unlucky not to be picked for the tour of West Indies in 1953–54 instead of one of the fast bowlers. A first-class wicketkeeper-batsman had arrived in Gerry Alexander, later to captain West Indies. Mike Bushby, a freshman, was a batsman of much promise.

Yet although we started well, watched by some remarkably big crowds for Fenners, we never quite produced the results. The way in which Oxford saved the University match, having been largely outplayed, was somehow typical of the whole season.

David Sheppard was in form throughout. I made three 100s in May and over successive weekends we declared at 375 for 6 against Yorkshire and 329 for 4 against Lancashire. Both were at full strength and in those days were looked on by university sides with greater awe than most counties. But Leicestershire's last pair held out against us, we were only a few runs short of beating Essex with wickets in hand and rain prevented a finish in several other matches.

In the whole season we lost only twice – to Sussex after we had declared twice at Hove and to Surrey when we were below strength at the Oval. But we beat only one county, Worcestershire, when the captain made 239 not out in the last innings out of 376 and we won by 6 wickets. Even that win at Worcester had a cloud over it, for Cuan McCarthy was no-balled for throwing by Paddy Corrall.

For two and a half days the University match went quite well for us. We kept Oxford to 233 for 6 on the first day and Marlar was in his fiftieth over when they were all out for 272 well into the second day. By that evening we were just ahead with 4 wickets standing, David having made a very good 127. He declared at one o'clock next day when Raman Subba Row and the later batsmen had extended the lead to 136.

McCarthy soon fired out Oxford's opening batsmen and when they were 19 for 3 and 86 for 6 with a lot of time left, we looked like winning.

We stuck against Alan Dowding and the lower half of the order. The pitch was dry and slightly uneven. Batting against McCarthy and indeed Warr took some courage. But Oxford resisted stoutly and their number nine, Coxon, played an innings which I expect is remembered by all who saw it. Aiming a lot of unusual strokes at the fast bowlers, he was hit on the head by McCarthy but was totally unconcerned and went on hurling the bat at the ball with abandon until the match was safe.

Thus ended my university career. Against a very modest Oxford bowling side I had again not produced the runs expected of me. The next weekend at the Oval I made 100 against Kent with relatively little trouble – and it was not as if that was an occasion for relaxing, as Surrey were engaged in what was to be a successful campaign for the first of their seven successive championships.

My winters had not been wholly spent in the lecture room and at the books. I had played a lot of soccer, three times against Oxford and I was captain in my last year.

I played a few matches for Pegasus including a tough one away to Crook Town in the Amateur Cup. We drew that but I was not required for the replay. I rather think that Donald Carr played instead. He was a more polished and quicker inside forward than I was. I was not really good enough at that level. I also played a few matches for the Corinthian Casuals.

I played hockey once for the university but I was rather better at Eton fives which I also played away from Cambridge with my brother as partner. In fact, John and I won the championship, the Kinnaird Cup, three times. We retired undefeated – indeed, it was only in the last final that we conceded a game. We had had two outstanding tutors at Charterhouse in Tony Wreford-Brown and Tommy Garnett, former winners of the Kinnaird Cup themselves.

I loved fives. It is a marvellous game with just the one drawback. It is not suited to singles.

2

First Years with Surrey

My association with Surrey began long before I played in a first-class match for them, which was in the second half of 1950. It was a fairly natural development in that I was at school in Surrey, which gave me one of the qualifications for registration, and the county of my birth and residence, Berkshire, was not a first-class one. There was also a link between Berkshire and Surrey, for the Bedsers also came from Reading. Ken Barrington was to follow. Geoff Kirby, our reserve wicketkeeper, was also Reading born.

In the school holidays I had played a little for Berkshire under D. W. Stokes, a great stalwart of the county, but Harry Lewis, the secretary, a much respected friend and counsellor of cricketers in those parts and an even greater force in the hockey world, was entirely sympathetic when Surrey approached me.

The approach came from Brian Castor, the secretary of Surrey and one of the most active and influential county secretaries of the postwar years. The public perhaps knew him best for those booming interventions over the loudspeaker aimed at some long-established frequenters of the Oval outfield: 'Go away, you pigeons. Go to Lord's!'

Brian was a great friend of my future father-in-law, Harold Gilligan, and he became a great friend to me too; indeed, he made the speech at my wedding. He was a marvellous secretary who really got things done. In fact, he would personally see to it that they were done.

Just occasionally this caused him embarrassing moments. Once Dennis Cox, the very worthy fast-medium bowler who used to come into the side when Alec Bedser was away, limped off the field. Within a minute or two Brian was on the phone to Sandy Tait, our masseur, in the dressing room.

'Tait?'

'Yes, Mr Castor.'

'What's the matter with Cox?'

'He's got a bad knee, sir.'

'Tell him to run it off.'

Next day Dennis Cox had his cartilege out. But, of course, having established that something really was wrong, Brian would be kindliness itself.

He had been secretary of Essex before the war but since then he had been a prisoner of the Japanese for three years. When he came home he brought his considerable ability to bear on rebuilding Surrey cricket and repairing the Oval, which had not only been laid out as a prisoner-of-war camp but had suffered bomb damage. A delayed centenary appeal was launched – the year should have been 1945 – and a number of matches were played by a Surrey XI in aid of the appeal. One, in 1947, was at Farncombe, just down the hill from Charterhouse.

I was in my last year at Charterhouse and was invited to play in the Surrey XI which included most of the Oval heroes of the day – Errol Holmes, Laurie Fishlock, Stan Squires, Eddie Watts and the Bedsers. Brian Castor also played and Alan Melville, captain of the touring South Africans, came to watch.

I doubt if the Farncombe bowling was very taxing but I was scoring a lot of runs at the time and played well enough to make Brian write to me a few days later to ask me to throw in my lot with Surrey. I was flattered and delighted. I learned many years later that he consulted Errol Holmes and Stan Squires, who both said that I reminded them of Douglas Jardine in build and method. I have a photograph of the two sides which shows me seated on the ground looking suspiciously at the camera. If any one had told me then that only four years later Alec Bedser and I would be travelling up to Leeds together to play in a Test match, I should have thought it a wild fantasy. Looking back, I find it even more remarkable. Four years now seems such a short time.

There my association with Surrey rested until the second half of 1950 except for a Second XI match which I played at Norwich in 1948 while on leave from the Navy.

I had already been accepted for Pembroke College, Cambridge. Robert Birley wanted me to go to Oxford but although I sat a scholarship exam there, I was not offered a place. First, however, came two years' national service.

I had had no firm ideas about which of the services should be inflicted with May but while I was playing for the Public Schools against the Combined Services at Lord's, Captain John Ellerton, secretary of the Royal Navy Cricket Club, put forward the attractions of the Navy.

It seemed a good idea and I applied to the local recruiting office in Reading. There were apparently not many lads with seafaring ambitions in those parts and I was in due course admitted to the senior service.

Obviously I hoped to have the chance of playing cricket and football during my two years but I looked on that as a bonus and for some time they played a relatively small part in my life. Writer P. B. H. May had his initial training at H.M.S. *Royal Arthur* at Corsham, near Chippenham, before being posted to H.M.S. *Ceres* at Wetherby for instruction in the supply and secretarial branch.

I was there during the 1948 cricket season but with limited opportunities. I might have had more if I had accepted an invitation to play for Harrogate in the Yorkshire League but I felt that I had a prior loyalty to *Ceres*, which played in the more modest Harrogate and District League. I enjoyed the cricket there and met a number of very interesting people through it. To talk about cricket with that lovely character, Maurice Leyland, was a wonderful experience for a young man of eighteen.

I was picked for the Combined Services in June and played my first first-class match against Hampshire on a turning pitch at Aldershot. Neither then nor later in the inter-services matches at Lord's did I distinguish myself. I suppose that that summer was a letdown after my last season on the perfect pitches at Charterhouse in the glorious summer of 1947, but it made an invaluable steppingstone to a higher level of cricket. The services were then well stocked with good young players, some of them already on county staffs. I was out to Gunner Tony Lock of Surrey in the match against the Army at Lord's, caught incidentally by a major general.

The next summer was completely different. By then I had been moved down to Chatham to the office of the Commander-in-Chief, Nore. I remained Writer May, which seemed to suit every one, my duties being clerical with strong cricketing interludes. No commissions were open to national servicemen at the time, even if I had had the qualifications. If I had wanted a commission, I should have had to have stayed on in the Navy and, as I had a place booked at Cambridge, the matter did not arise.

'Writer May' puzzled a lot of people, especially when it was abbreviated on score cards, as at Lord's, to 'Wtr'. I actually heard two MCC members trying to work it out as I walked through the Long Room to have a net. Suddenly the light dawned on one of them. 'Waiter,' he said triumphantly. 'Chap's the mess waiter.'

I played a lot more cricket that summer of 1949 and began making runs almost at once – 50 for the Navy against Hampshire at Portsmouth in early May followed by another against Kent in the second innings at Gillingham. I found it a very interesting experience playing against Doug Wright who, despite a bitter east wind on that exposed ground, took 13 wickets in the match, including mine in the first innings for nought. When he was pitching it and making the ball bounce unusually high

at a far greater pace than the normal leg-spinner, Doug could be devastating. He was not far off doing me first ball in the second innings. It
pitched middle and leg and I was pretty sure that it was a googly, so I
took a swing at it. It went for 4. If I had been wrong I should have
recorded a 'pair' very early in my career instead of waiting another
twelve years for what was, in fact, my only 'pair'. Ron Hooker's medium
pace and Fred Titmus's off spin were too much for me at Lord's when
we played Middlesex in 1961 in the match before my last Test against
Australia.

I have pointed out to John Warr that, after all the years we played
against each other, it was curious that this happened in the first season
after he retired. He was equal to it. 'I softened you up for them,' he
said. He hit back even harder a year or so ago when, as a silver wedding
present, he gave us two pear trees – in memory of my 'pair' against
Middlesex, he said – and he named them Ron and Fred.

As the 1949 season progressed the counties put out less strong sides
against us and we made plenty of runs. I had only mixed fortunes at
Lord's – more than 200 runs without being out against the RAF, 5
against the Army (bowled by Signalman Tyson), not many more for the
Services against the Public Schools when in the second innings I was
caught and bowled Cowdrey. I clearly underestimated his guile.

It was all splendid and largely unexpected experience with a somewhat
embarrassing climax when the final first-class averages appeared. These
have sometimes included irregular players, perhaps Irish or Scottish,
who have taken just enough wickets or played just enough innings to
qualify. In that year, 1949, the freak was May whose name, on the
strength of twelve first-class innings, lay in third place behind the illustrious ones of Hardstaff and Hutton.

And so, in October 1949, to Cambridge and, after the following
summer's University match, to Surrey and my first championship match
at Bristol. Somebody had to drop out for me and it is a measure of how
I was treated by every one at the Oval from the start that, if all the
batsmen were fit and in form, the two senior professionals, Laurie Fishlock and Jack Parker, would take it in turns to stand down for me. This
was just one of their kindnesses in my early years with Surrey.

I did not exactly make a prolific start when on a turning pitch at
Bristol I mustered 2 runs, 1 in each innings. I was bowled in the first
innings by Tom Goddard, who, Desmond Eagar once told me, had
seemed an awesome figure to him as far back as 1935 when Desmond,
as a schoolboy at Cheltenham, played his first match for Gloucestershire.

Tom Goddard had a similar physique to George Geary, with what looked like the same huge hands. He turned the ball a prodigious amount. On this one meeting I shouldered arms to a ball far outside the off stump and was bowled in front of my pads. He was in his fiftieth year and, as it turned out, in his last full season, although he showed no signs of retiring, for that year he took 137 wickets at under 20 apiece. Unfortunately, he was taken ill in 1951 and did not finish the season.

Coming into the Surrey side in July 1950 carried extra responsibilities, for they were well enough placed in the table to have hopes of bringing the championship to the Oval for the first time since 1914. We beat Gloucestershire at Bristol but the next match at the Oval was a much more difficult proposition against Yorkshire, who had been joint champions with Middlesex the year before.

It proved to be just as difficult as expected. We were bowled out twice on a wet pitch for around 100 and lost by 7 wickets. I made 0 and 5, bowled by Appleyard in the first innings and lbw to Wardle in the second.

That proved to be the nadir of Surrey's fortunes, for we won our next seven championship matches, beginning at Worcester. I had made runs at Worcester before and that was where my own fortunes changed. Having been dropped twice early on, I made my first 100 for Surrey. It was none too soon. Indulgent though they were, they would not have been able to go on playing me indefinitely while I was not even reaching double figures.

The pitch at Worcester took a little spin, as had those in my first two championship matches. The frequency with which one batted then against good spinners able to turn the ball is in tremendous contrast, it seems to me, with the modern game in which batsmen may go for weeks without seeing the ball turn. If it does turn, it usually does it too slowly to do much harm. Worcestershire in those days had the leg spin of Roly Jenkins and the left-arm spin of Dick Howorth. The ebullient Jenkins used to accuse me of being just an on-side player. I had to put that right occasionally.

My fourth match for Surrey, against Middlesex at the Oval, was a memorable one not only because it was Laurie Fishlock's benefit but because it was Denis Compton's first first-class match since an operation on his knee two months before. This was the first time I played with Denis, though he had been one of my heroes. I still marvel at his method, a model to any young batsman because he played so straight – and not only in defence. His genius was that he had so many improvisations on a basic soundness.

One of the things I noticed when I was at school was that Denis held his bat in his left hand as he walked to the wicket. He was, of course, left-handed in some things and no doubt did it naturally. But as one was always told that more emphasis should be put on the left, or top, hand when batting, it made sense to me to hold the bat in the left hand on my way to the wicket and I decided that this was one of the requirements.

Nearly 50,000 watched the match over the three days and almost everything went right for us. I was bowled by Jim Sims, that wily old leg-spinner talking away out of the side of his mouth, but Laurie himself made a hard-working and highly important 100. So did Denis, who had a habit of returning after a long absence and playing brilliantly. We won by 10 wickets with Laurie, very suitably, at the wicket. He was a fine left-hander, a marvellous player of leg spin and most unlucky that on both his tours of Australia in 1936–37 and 1946–47 he broke a bone in his hand in Adelaide.

Laurie had been out in the first innings from a hard drive to mid-on where John Warr held a splendid catch right-handed. A few months later J.J.'s fallibility in catching and indeed his way of shaping up to a catch were under severe scrutiny in Australia, but it was a spectacular catch at the Oval. He professes not to remember it, but when I have asked him in later years how he would have liked to have had himself fielding in the slips to his own bowling, he says that at least he would have been paying attention, which is more than some did. He also claims to have held some of his best catches at midwicket off Denis Compton's bowling – 'when the long hop happened to be the googly'. He says that most of them came with the speed of an Exocet missile.

Towards the end of the 1950s I remember being out quite a few times to J.J., then a very good fast-medium out-swinger, but in my early matches against Middlesex I always seemed to get out to Jack Young. I believe it was eight times running. He was a well-read, whimsical student of life, a friendly and unusual character, who retired soon after the sequence was broken, being then well into his forties. He had a flat, nagging flight with the knack of holding a ball back by a good variation in length. Sometimes you went to drive and were not quite there.

As we continued that winning run in 1950 I gathered confidence, learning a lot about the professional approach from partnerships with Laurie Fishlock and Jack Parker and in numerous other ways. Eventually we came to our last match but one of the season which was against Lancashire, by then our only rivals for the championship.

This was a match which neither side intended to lose. In fact, first-innings lead was of prime importance because the 4 points from this, Lancashire's last match, would put them clear of us and give them the championship. It was therefore a grimly fought contest and no great spectacle, although it was pretty tense as we worked our way up to their 221 and past.

Lancashire had left out Bob Berry, who was in the MCC team about to leave for Australia, and played a young amateur called Dickinson from Manchester University, a fast bowler who had played only once before. Brian Statham had only come on the scene in the second half of that season but they both bowled tremendously well. I had to put my head down and battle it out. I batted for nearly five hours, and although I did not make 100 I took satisfaction from being able to play an innings of this sort against good bowling, and when it mattered.

Tattersall and Hilton were also among the Lancashire bowlers – there were few better off-spinners and left-arm spinners in the country at the time – but I remember finding Dickinson as difficult to score off as any of them. He did, in fact, bowl 26 overs for 38 runs and 1 wicket, which was a remarkable effort at the age of nineteen. One would have thought then that he had a very bright future in the game but he scarcely played any first-class cricket afterwards. By contrast his partner, Brian Statham, went on to play in seventy Test matches and to become one of the most important members of England sides in the next ten years.

'George' Statham had a lovely temperament. It never mattered what you asked him to do, whether it was to come on for a few overs, to bowl until lunch, to bowl uphill or upwind. Whatever it was, he would take the ball and do it. He had that amazing accuracy on and around the off stump which undoubtedly provoked batsmen whom he tied down into taking liberties at the other end. He must have got a lot of wickets for whoever bowled with him.

He really hit the bat hard, and although he usually bowled a full length there were times when, if the ball missed the bat, you suffered. Once, at Old Trafford, he brought a ball back to hit me inside the right thigh where there was no protection. The pain went right through me. It was the last ball of an over and I stood there determined not to show that I had been hurt. I then noticed George half down the pitch, hands on hips, looking at me with a half-smile.

'Go on, skipper. Rub it,' he said. 'I know it hurts.' There was a touch of sympathy in it. He bowled without a trace of animosity.

To my complete surprise, after the match against Lancashire in 1950, only my eleventh first-class match for Surrey, I was given my county cap. Knowing how long many players have to wait to be capped, I considered it a wonderful compliment.

The draw meant that if we beat Leicestershire in our last match at the Oval we shared the championship with Lancashire. Leicestershire were having a poor season and our main concern proved to be the weather. Rain caused interruptions on each of the first two days. The third was fine and, Laurie Fishlock having made 100 and Alec Bedser having taken 12 wickets, we won by 10 wickets.

To a county which had not known such success for thirty-six years, half a championship was glory indeed. I was delighted to have played a small part in it. For most of the next decade a halved championship would have been something of a disappointment but none of us in 1950 could have guessed what was to follow and we were far from blasé then.

In my second season with Surrey, that of 1951, I could only play in seven championship matches and one of those, at Taunton, was almost washed out. After the University match I had one of those happy periods when you not only run into form but into a succession of splendid batting pitches. Having made 100 for the Gentlemen, I was picked that weekend for my first Test match and on the Monday made another 100 at Lord's against Middlesex in my first match for Surrey in 1951. The Test match and another 100 followed and it was the August bank holiday weekend before I played my second match of the season for Surrey.

This year Surrey had made too poor a start to have any chance of the championship which was won very easily by Warwickshire under Tom Dollery, another native of Reading. We missed Alec Bedser who because of Test matches played in only fifteen out of twenty-eight matches. Rain interfered with quite a few and Surrey won only once at the Oval where in fine weather the bowlers did not have a lot of help. That, of course, was to change!

I went on showing what I like to think was a suitable appreciation of good pitches – 80 odd against both Nottinghamshire and Middlesex at the Oval, 100 in each innings against Essex at Southend – but was stopped in my tracks by Glamorgan at Cardiff. Wilf Wooller used to delight in making things difficult for the Test batsmen of the day and, with the help of Don Shepherd and Jim McConnon, did so successfully for many years. I think that even Denis Compton found runs hard to make against Glamorgan in that era.

This was the last of Michael Barton's three seasons as captain. He was a quiet, thoughtful captain who had the respect of the players. He started the era of success with the half-championship of 1950 and laid some of the foundations for the subsequent triumphs under Stuart Surridge. As a batsman he obviously did very well to bridge the long gap in his first-class cricket between leaving Oxford in 1937 and taking on the captaincy of Surrey in 1949. He had an impressive record for Oxford, and although mainly an on-side player made many useful runs for us. He retained his links with Surrey and has been president in the 1980s.

*

I had enjoyed my two short periods of cricket with Surrey and felt that I had learned a lot from them. It had also been a great experience for me to meet former players who had previously just been legendary names.

Our scorer was the famous wicketkeeper, Herbert Strudwick – Mr Strud, we called him. He was always happy to talk to us and to advise. In his scoring he was always meticulous and was terribly upset on the only occasion he was caught out which was by a leg-pull. We had to bat for two overs one evening at Old Trafford and Stuart Surridge decided to go in himself with Alec Bedser. Eric Bedser, who usually opened, always wore a cap. Alec did not. On this occasion Alec not only put on a cap but a Surrey sweater, which he seldom wore. He was out and Mr Strud duly recorded E. A. Bedser c and b Tattersall o.

Our coach was Andrew Sandham. He would not say a lot, but when I was not satisfied with how I was playing I would ask him to stand behind the net. He would watch a few balls and come up with the solution. 'You've opened your stance' or 'You're moving before the ball's bowled.' A lot of our success was due to him.

We saw a little of Jack Hobbs. I remember seeing him once walking in through the Hobbs Gates and, as usual, I mentally stood to attention. It seemed to me very sad that the boys with the autograph books paid him not the slightest notice. The fleeting nature of fame was impressed on me. He was a dear, kindly man.

I have already mentioned another rich character, Sandy Tait, our masseur. I realize that I use the word 'masseur' at some peril now but Sandy was a rubber; he rubbed very effectively and I doubt if he or any of us had heard of physiotherapists.

One of the nice things about Surrey – and, no doubt, other counties – has been the way in which old players have involved themselves so much in the administration. Here lies my big argument against the signing of overseas players. They come, they earn a lot of money, they do their county well, they entertain. But, with very few exceptions, when they have finished they go home and have nothing more to offer.

3
An Undergraduate in Test Cricket

Without being immodest I can say that selection for my first Test match in 1951 did not exactly come as a total surprise. There had been the painful preliminary of the Test trial at Bradford the year before.

Four of us from Cambridge were chosen – Hubert Doggart, John Dewes, David Sheppard and myself. John Dewes was an old hand at disasters, for in his only Test match to date, against Australia at the Oval in 1948, England had been bowled out for 52. But he had a stroke of luck this time. He was chosen on the England side and did not have to face Jim Laker.

It was an honour to be included among the best players in the country and at that time I did not think of Test trials as being as pointless as I later did. There may be a justification for a trial when a number of established players have just retired and the selectors want to see possible replacements all together. There was obviously a case for a Test trial after the war when the selectors had to look at players with a reputation from wartime cricket in competition with those left over from prewar first-class cricket.

But a Test trial is hard to fit into an already congested programme. The evidence of just one match is not necessarily reliable and may force the selectors to pick a player whom they know in their hearts will not be as successful in the long run as another. If they go against the evidence of a Test trial, they will be asked what the point of staging it was. There is also something alien to the spirit of cricket in a match in which players are blatantly promoting their own interests rather than those of their side.

These arguments against Test trials seem to me strong enough if the match is played on a perfect pitch which gives a chance to batsmen and bowlers alike. But no one can rely on that being provided early in an English season and on the pitch at Bradford at the end of May 1950 the trial was the very height of futility. It was over before lunch on the second day by which time 30 wickets had fallen for 369 runs.

The Rest were put in on the first morning by Norman Yardley and were bowled out for 27 by Jim Laker who took his famous 8 for 2. One of the 2 runs which he conceded was scored by Eric Bedser who, as a

Surrey colleague, was given one to get him off the mark! We were a young and inexperienced side, including Donald Carr from Oxford as well as the Cambridge representatives. He and I contributed the identical scores, 0 and 2. We needed the best possible conditions to do ourselves justice against Bedser, Trevor Bailey, Laker and Hollies. Against the turning, lifting ball and Jim's accuracy and powers of spin, we were out of our depth.

The match certainly confirmed that, even allowing for the heaven-sent conditions, Jim Laker was an off-spinner of the highest class. But that was known already. It showed that Len Hutton, who made 85, was a great batsman. But that, too, was not exactly news.

As for the undergraduates, they returned chastened to their seats of learning. To those of us at Cambridge, who had been making 594 for 5 against West Indies at Fenners two weeks before and who made 467 for 4 against Hampshire on return from the north, it was a nightmare to be forgotten as soon as possible. It had not even had a useful educational value. The conditions had been too extreme and the experience too brief.

Even the most calamitous cricket matches have an element of humour about them. England at that time were on the lookout for possible captains. Norman Yardley, captain against Australia in 1948, had been followed in South Africa by George Mann, who was followed, after the first two Tests of 1949, by Freddie Brown, who had just returned to first-class cricket as captain of Northamptonshire. Now, in 1950, George was no longer available. Freddie was thought by many, erroneously, to be too old at forty and Norman was back captaining England in the Test trial. The captaincy of the Rest was given to Hubert Doggart, that year's Cambridge captain.

The captain was never born who could have saved the Rest from their shattering defeat on that pitch, but Hubert was understandably distraught. In the course of a conversation with the Bedser twins conducted with his mind half on other things, he asked Alec where he was born.

'In Reading,' said Alec.

'What about you, Eric?' Hubert asked, still far away.

'Reading too,' said Eric. 'My mother didn't have a bicycle in those days.'

There was humour for the rest of us in the experience of David Sheppard who did not go north again until six weeks later when he was summoned by Sussex to play at Old Trafford on the day after the University match. By the time our drawn match at Lord's had ended and we had had our meeting at which David was elected secretary for the following season, he had missed the last train and was given a lift

CAMBRIDGE UNIVERSITY v WEST INDIES, Fenners

Match Drawn

CAMBRIDGE UNIVERSITY

J. G. Dewes c Weekes b Goddard	....	183
D. S. Sheppard c Trestrail b Williams	....	227
†G. H. G. Doggart c and b Williams	....	71
P. B. H. May not out	....	44
A. G. J. Rimell c Christiani b Goddard	....	10
M. H. Stevenson not out	....	53
B 3, l-b 3	....	6

Four wkts., dec. 594

T. U. Wells, O. J. Wait, J. J. Warr, P. A. Kelland and H. W. Denman did not bat.

Bowling: Johnson 15–1–55–0; Jones 17–4–77–0; Valentine 32–3–97–0; Ramadhin 20–2–86–0; Williams 12–0–62–2; Worrell 12–0–45–0; Goddard 32–2–128–2; Stollmeyer 5–1–38–0.

WEST INDIES

R. J. Christiani lbw b Warr	....	111
J. B. Stollmeyer c Doggart b Kelland	....	83
F. M. Worrell b Wait	....	160
E. D. Weekes not out	....	304
K. B. Trestrail not out	....	56
B 3, l-b 8, w 2, n-b 3	....	16

Three wkts. 730

J. D. Goddard, C. B. Williams, P. E. Jones, H. H. Johnson, S. Ramadhin and A. L. Valentine did not bat.

Bowling: Warr 35–3–121–1; Wait 28–3–127–1; Kelland 33–0–105–1; Doggart 25–2–123–0; Rimell 36–1–128–0; Stevenson 12–1–69–0; Wells 3–0–28–0; May 2–0–13–0.

Umpires: F. S. Lee and H. Palmer

May 1950 – Two extremes of cricket, just a fortnight apart

by a friend. In those pre-motorway days and in a small car the journey took five hours and David had time to think about the last time he had been north of the Trent when he had what he hoped was a never to be repeated experience, that of being out twice in a day.

Alas, something even worse lay ahead. There were some strange pitches at Old Trafford at the time. Next day, the ball turned from the start, a circumstance for which Sussex were not equipped and Lancashire beat them in a day, one of only five times this has happened in first-class cricket since the war. I felt sorry for David, but if you are of the stuff of which bishops are made you doubtless shake off adversity more easily than others, and he batted so well and so consistently from then on that he played in the last Test match of that summer against West Indies.

Hubert Doggart played in the first two Tests of 1950, David Sheppard in the last, so I began 1951 not without hope that if I made enough

TEST TRIAL, Bradford

England won by an innings and 89 runs

THE REST

D. J. Kenyon c Evans b Laker	7	–	lbw b Hollies	9
D. S. Sheppard lbw b Bailey	4	–	b Laker	3
G. H. G. Doggart c Bailey b Laker	2	–	st Evans b Hollies	12
P. B. H. May c Hutton b Laker	0	–	b Laker	2
D. B. Carr c Bailey b Laker	0	–	st Evans b Hollies	2
E. A. Bedser lbw b Laker	3	–	c Evans b Hollies	30
R. T. Spooner b Laker	0	–	c Yardley b Bedser	22
R. O. Jenkins not out	0	–	c Bedser b Hollies	3
R. Berry b Laker	0	–	c Yardley b Bedser	16
F. S. Trueman st Evans b Bedser	1	–	not out	0
L. Jackson c and b Laker	5	–	st Evans b Hollies	1
B 3, l-b 1, w 1	5		B 4, l-b 6, n-b 3	13
	27			**113**

Bowling: *First Innings* – Bailey 6–4–3–1; Bedser 9–3–12–1; Laker 14–12–2–8; Hollies 7–5–5–0. *Second Innings* – Bailey 5–2–6–0; Bedser 9–2–22–2; Laker 18–4–44–2; Hollies 22.4–13–28–6.

ENGLAND

L. Hutton b Trueman	85
R. T. Simpson st Spooner b Berry	26
W. J. Edrich lbw b Jenkins	46
J. D. Robertson c Sheppard b Berry	0
J. G. Dewes c Doggart b Berry	34
N. W. D. Yardley c Trueman b Jenkins	13
T. E. Bailey c Spooner b Berry	7
T. G. Evans run out	1
J. C. Laker not out	6
A. V. Bedser c Jackson b Jenkins	5
W. E. Hollies st Spooner b Berry	4
L-b 1, n-b 1	2
	229

Bowling: Jackson 12–3–38–0; Bedser 13–0–60–0; Jenkins 10–0–38–3; Berry 32–10–73–5; Trueman 9–3–18–1.

Umpires: W. H. Ashdown and H. Elliott

runs I too might be given a chance. There was, however, not quite the same opportunity, for Denis Compton, who had missed most of the previous season through his knee injury, would obviously be back in the England side.

Things went pretty well during the Cambridge season and I suppose what clinched my selection for the fourth Test at Leeds was an innings of 119 not out for the Gentlemen. If you were a batsman trying to establish yourself you stood a better chance of doing so on the Gentlemen's side because the Players' bowling was always much stronger and to that extent the runs meant more. So I was fortunate in my timing and perhaps, too, in the fact that Reg Simpson, who had played some splendid innings for England that year, including the one in Melbourne which was largely responsible for England's winning the final Test in Australia, had not been at his best for the last few weeks.

I have said that my selection did not exactly come out of the blue but

every one must feel enormous surprise and excitement as he actually
hears his name read out on the radio in an England team for the first
time. We were playing Middlesex at Lord's and I had gone home to
Reading after the first day's play. After tea on the Sunday I switched on
the radio to hear the team for Headingley against South Africa on the
following Thursday and out it came: 'P. B. H. May'. Next day I played
rather well and so went into the Test match with two recent 100s behind
me since a disappointing University match.

I have sometimes been asked how I came to be picked for England
after only a handful of matches in the county championship. The only
reply I have is that I had made the runs. I have followed the same
principle as chairman of selectors. What we are asking players is 'You
make us pick you.'

If you stay involved with cricket after you have stopped playing, you
soon learn that modern players are not greatly interested in how you
lived and played thirty years ago. On technical matters they may show
a genuine interest. I have been asked, for example, about the weight of
my bat which was 2 lb 4 oz. Stuart Surridge used to give me two bats
at the start of a season. At the end of it, although I would often protest,
he took them off to his museum. I never cease to be surprised that
batsmen can cut with the bats of up to 3lb 4oz which are used today
by Ian Botham and others less strong than he is.

On the other hand, I envy the modern players the lovely lightness of
the rest of their equipment, especially on the feet. We still wore the
heavy boots which by the end of a day seemed to weigh a ton.

The players of today are not, I think, interested in our off-the-field
life and I go easy on the difference between how they live and how we
lived. It was so different then. We would go back to our hotel, sit in the
lounge and talk about the day's play. We usually travelled by train and
there was plenty of time for talking. Nowadays I see the England players
arrive for Test matches at Headingly in their Saabs and Audis and
Jaguars and I think back to my own arrival there for my first Test. It
was, in fact, the first time that I had ever been to Headingley. Alec and
I went up by train, took a taxi to Headingley and Alec helped me to carry
my bag into the ground. We stayed at the Queen's Hotel, something I
have a special reason for remembering as Virginia was staying there
with her father. It was the first time we met.

Two other members of that side, who sadly died recently within a
few months of each other, were playing in their first Test – Frank
Lowson, a good, correct player who was to open with Len, as he did
with success for Yorkshire, and the Yorkshire wicketkeeper, the amateur
Don Brennan. Don was thirty-three and the last two Tests of that 1951
series were the only ones in which he played. He retired from first-class

cricket two years later but he retained a keen interest in Yorkshire cricket and remained an active committee member until the upsets of the 1980s.

We were lucky in our captain, Freddie Brown, who under that tough exterior hid great kindliness. Little did I think then that before the 1950s were out we would be captain and manager in South Africa and then in Australia, but I soon came to know him and respect him. Freddie had been injured and had not been captain of the Gentlemen the week before. In fact, we had changed captains on the morning of the match at Lord's, Norman Yardley thoughtfully handing over to Nigel Howard, who was to captain the MCC side in India and Pakistan that winter.

Dudley Nourse won the toss and on a very easy-paced pitch Eric Rowan, a dour, efficient batsman but a lively, often controversial character, batted through the first day making 160 out of South Africa's 282 for 3. For most of the day we were a bowler short as Trevor Bailey had strained his back. Clive van Ryneveld, whom Cambridge had removed for nought in the previous year's University match, made 83. Next day Rowan went on to make 236 and South Africa 583, the nimble-footed McLean launching a powerful attack on our two spinners, Tattersall and Hilton, who between them bowled more than 120 overs.

My recollections of fielding in my first Test match are coloured by Alec Bedser's reaction to the support that he received from the close catchers. Compton dropped two catches off him, one standing bolt upright at leg slip. 'I'll have to catch the b——s myself,' Alec said in a high state of exasperation to those within range. On the second morning when we eventually got Eric Rowan out it was through a marvellous catch by Alec who took off to his right in the gully. He was delighted. 'I told you I'd have to catch 'em myself,' he said.

The pitch remained slow and true and there was no reason why we should not make a big score too, but accidents can happen after more than ten hours in the field and Len Hutton and Frank Lowson did very well to come through the last ninety minutes safely. Due to bat number three, I was especially grateful.

Next morning they took their opening stand to 99 before Athol Rowan, a very high-class off-spinner and a charming man, beat Lowson in the air. So the great moment had arrived and there I was coming in on a strange ground packed to the doors. As far as I can remember, my appearance out of the old pavilion was not the signal for any great show of enthusiasm. At Headingley young southerners and especially young amateurs from Oxford or Cambridge had to prove themselves before they were greeted with any cordiality – and quite right too. As Raymond Robertson-Glasgow wrote: 'Above all other spectators, those of York-shire tend to believe only what they see.'

I knew that it was a very good pitch, that the innings had been given a good start and that, coming in when I did, I had a great opportunity. The only thing which bothered me was the light. On an open ground without sightscreens the shirtsleeved crowd sitting in brilliant sunshine somehow created an unusual glare.

There was one ball left of Athol Rowan's over and I completely lost sight of it in the mottled background of the crowd at the top end. On these occasions you just have time to feel a sickening moment of horror and then you have to take action. 'Keep coming forward' had been so instilled in me by George Geary from my earliest days at Charterhouse that I was a staunch supporter of the old axiom 'When in doubt, push out'. I pushed.

On this very reliable pitch I had no reason to worry about the bounce if I played forward correctly. All I needed was to gauge the right line. I suppose that subconsciously I chose the line which I thought that a good off-spinner should be bowling and eventually, after what seemed an age, I felt the ball hit the bat. Not much of the bat, admittedly, for the ball had turned enough to find the inside edge. But any one who has watched cricket at Headingley will know that a ball edged fine at the football end runs away at a great pace down the hill. There was no stopping this one and my Test career had started with 4 runs off the first ball.

Between overs Len Hutton walked a few steps up the pitch and looked me up and down. 'Are you all right?' he asked.

'Yes, thank you,' I said. We never spoke again during our partnership. I did not expect it. I was happy just to be left to concentrate on my innings.

I felt suitably humble afterwards that I had escaped the fate of those many players, including my partner on this occasion, who had made nought in their first Test innings. Somehow I was immensely encouraged. I had been spared and was determined not to waste the golden opportunity of batting on a pitch full of runs against bowlers who were not likely to bowl any better as a hot day progressed. In fact, the South African bowlers stuck it out well. Cuan McCarthy, very fast through the air, and Geoff Chubb gave little away. Not many liberties could be taken with Athol Rowan, who eventually took 5 wickets. The supremely accurate slow left-arm Tufty Mann bowled 61 overs for 96 runs, figures which make me feel guilty until I remember how well he bowled.

Before the remaining Test of that tour Tufty, a charming man whose war had included an adventurous period as an escaped prisoner-of-war in Italy, was taken ill. A year to the day after the Headingley Test he died, to the great sadness of every one who knew him.

Len and I put on 129 together before he was bowled by Rowan for 100. My next partner was Denis Compton who came in and made 25 sparkling runs in a few minutes before he was lbw sweeping at Rowan.

ENGLAND v. SOUTH AFRICA, Headingley
(Fourth Test, 1951)

Match Drawn

SOUTH AFRICA

E. A. B. Rowan c Bedser b Brown	236	– not out	60
*J. H. B. Waite lbw b Bedser	13	– not out	25
C. B. van Ryneveld c and b Hilton	83		
†A. D. Nourse lbw b Brown	13		
J. E. Cheetham b Bedser	7		
R. A. McLean run out	67		
P. N. F. Mansell c Tattersall b Hilton	90		
A. M. B. Rowan b Brown	9		
N. B. F. Mann b Tattersall	2		
G. W. A. Chubb c Lowson b Hilton	11		
C. N. McCarthy not out	0		
B 1, l-b 6	7	L-b 2	2

1/40 2/238 3/267 4/286 5/392 6/480   538   (No wkt.)   87
7/498 8/505 9/538

Bowling: *First Innings* – Bedser 58–14–113–2; Bailey 17–4–48–0; Brown
38–10–107–3; Tattersall 60–23–83–1; Hilton 61.3–18–176–3; Compton
1–0–4–0. *Second Innings* – Bedser 4–1–5–0; Bailey 1–0–8–0; Brown 11–2–26–0;
Tattersall 16–9–13–0; Hilton 10–5–17–0; Compton 7–1–16–0.

ENGLAND

L. Hutton b van Ryneveld	100
F. A. Lowson c Mansell b A. Rowan	58
P. B. H. May b A. Rowan	138
D. C. S. Compton lbw b A. Rowan	25
W. Watson b Chubb	32
T. E. Bailey b Mann	95
†F. R. Brown c E. Rowan b A. Rowan	2
A. V. Bedser b Mann	8
*D. V. Brennan b Mann	16
R. Tattersall c E. Rowan b A. Rowan	4
M. J. Hilton not out	9
B 10, l-b 7, n-b 1	18

1/99 2/228 3/266 4/345 5/387 6/391   505
7/400 8/432 9/435

Bowling: McCarthy 41–10–81–0; Chubb 43–12–99–1; A. Rowan 68–17–174–5;
Mann 60.5–23–96–3; Mansell 4–0–11–0; van Ryneveld 8–0–26–1.

Umpires: H. Elliott and D. Davies

The first Test for a 21-year-old undergraduate

It is often forgotten that at this time, out of reaction, perhaps, to his
marvellous feats in the late 1940s, Denis was no longer everybody's idol.
He was constantly struggling against the impositions put on him by his
chronic knee injury and, although he was as good as ever on his day,
he had off days. The cavalier successful is everyone's favourite. The
cavalier when he fails is an easy target and on this occasion I remember
that Denis was criticized for taking things too lightly.

I batted on for the rest of the day, finishing 110 not out. It was never
easy against the defensive fields which were used almost throughout the

match but I recall few bad moments. I do, however, remember the din when I drove Athol Rowan straight for 4 to reach 100. It was apparently an exceptionally warm ovation by Headingley standards and I was very touched that it had been accorded not to an old friend but to a young stranger of twenty-one. I felt accepted. I was eventually bowled for 138 by Rowan on the Monday morning. Trevor Bailey ensured that we finished with over 500 and a match which was anyhow going to be a draw was mercifully cut short when rain washed out the last day.

After that innings at Headingley I received a telegram from Gubby Allen. At that time he used to come up to Cambridge every year to play for the Free Foresters against the University. In the previous year he had seen me get out rather unnecessarily to a careless shot. As I passed him he said, 'That was the most unconscious stroke I have ever seen.'

He spoke from strength, for on the two occasions on which I played against him at Fenners he made 9 and 81, 103 and 55 – this in his late forties. I accepted the criticism but I was extremely annoyed. I did not think that it was as bad as all that. In spite of my schooling under George Geary I tended in my early days at Cambridge to do what came naturally, perhaps not always treating the bowling on its merits. Since then my matches for Surrey had taught me not necessarily to cut out strokes but to discipline myself to play them more judiciously. So I felt that I had in some way been rewarded when I received the telegram from Gubby at Leeds which read: 'Charge of unconsciousness unconditionally withdrawn.'

Yet, but for a subconscious reaction to my first ball, I might not have had the chance to have played the innings at all. When you are thrown into a vital innings it really is immensely important to get off the mark. I used to say three things to myself. 'Grit your teeth, do your best, but enjoy it.' I say the same to my daughters when they are riding in an event.

South Africa had won the first Test of the series at Trent Bridge. With the weather on our side we had won the next two at Lord's and Old Trafford. Thus, after the draw at Headingley, the series was still to be decided at the Oval and it would have meant a lot to the South Africans to have squared it. They had come with a number of young and largely unknown players such as McGlew, McLean, Waite, Mansell and Endean who had not previously played in a Test match. They were under two very experienced players in Dudley Nourse and Eric Rowan, captain and vice-captain, but the side had received a severe setback early in the tour when Dudley broke his left thumb. Although he made 208 under handicap at Trent Bridge, he was never at his best afterwards and the younger players had to play a bigger part than had probably been anticipated. The hopes put in them were, of course, completely justified when they went to Australia eighteen months later and shared a series 2-all with an Australian side which had been widely expected to slaughter them.

England, for their part, were just beginning to recover from a postwar dearth of bowlers, a period in which Alec Bedser had been in a class of his own. Thus the stage was set for a good match at the Oval, although when one side is leading 2–1 and needs only a draw to win the series the omens are not propitious. This was an exception. The pitch gave a little help to bowlers of all types throughout and that meant an offensive approach from both sides.

Bedser, Statham, Tattersall, Laker and Freddie Brown bowled South Africa out for 202 on the first day and, after Frank Lowson had been caught at the wicket on the leg side off Michael Melle, I found myself batting with Len with an hour left. We batted comfortably enough until the last over when Len played back to Athol Rowan and was lbw.

This left the match evenly balanced, but when we resumed next morning after a short delay for rain I found the going much harder. The remarkable Geoff Chubb, aged forty, who had only played his first Test matches that summer, began a long accurate spell at his brisk medium pace which lasted well into the afternoon. On this pitch every ball needed careful watching. After half an hour he somehow altered his run and bowled me one which was well up and came back like an off break. I suppose one might say that it upset my poise. Anyhow it bowled me and but for an innings of great skill by Denis Compton, who was last out at tea, we should not have approached their score. As it was, they led us by 8 runs.

We dropped some catches early in South Africa's second innings but Bedser and Laker were always in control and after lunch on the Saturday, the third day, we needed 163 to win. My recollection is that, although we thought that we ought to score the runs, we recognized that we needed to bat pretty well against Chubb and Athol Rowan. However, the pitch had dried and was slower and I sat watching with my pads on with growing relief as Hutton and Lowson made 53 without much trouble.

At that point there occurred a historic incident. A ball from Rowan turned and lifted to Len's glove, ran up his arm and conceivably could have fallen on the stumps. Len, unthinkingly, flicked at the ball with his bat and missed it but in so doing he obstructed the wicketkeeper, Russell Endean, who was moving round the wicket on the leg side to take the catch. Endean appealed and, to the obvious approval of Frank Chester at square leg, Dai Davies gave Len out 'obstructing the field'. It was, I am sure, a perfectly fair decision in the spirit of the laws, even if Len's action had been purely involuntary.

It was an extraordinary incident in many ways. Russell Endean, in the absence of John Waite, was playing in his first Test match. What a thing to happen on such an occasion to one who was in any case not a regular wicketkeeper! Yet five years later in a Test match against England at Newlands, a South African batsman suffered another very rare dismissal – 'handled the ball' – and it was Endean. These are the only occasions when I have seen a batsman out in either way.

Another remarkable feature of the 1951 affair was that it should happen to one of the world's most famous batsmen at an important stage in a Test match. There was, as one would expect, a great hubbub going on as I walked to the wicket. I suppose that my concentration may not have been what it should have been coming in in a Test match against a spinner of Athol Rowan's class. Anyhow, I pushed forward to my first ball, it turned more than I expected and I was caught at forward short leg.

Meanwhile there was a nice state of confusion in the dressing room. As Len came in, every one rushed up to ask him what had happened. Nobody saw me out and I was almost back in the pavilion when some one looked out of the window and shouted, 'Another wicket's fallen.' Denis Compton eventually dashed out and presented as composed an appearance as he could but he was almost certainly the only person on the ground who did not know that he was on a peculiar type of hat trick, one which would have been earned by the bowler but not accredited to him.

Before long, Lowson and Compton were out and we were 90 for 4. We had Jim Laker batting at number seven and Derek Shackleton at number eight, both higher than they batted for their counties, and the result was very much in doubt. But Freddie Brown started to attack Rowan, and after one piece of luck when he might have been caught at deep square leg and one or two near misses, he settled the match with a rousing piece of bold hitting.

That was the end of my first taste of Test cricket. I think that it must have been accepted that I was not available for the winter's tour of India and Pakistan, for I do not remember having to turn it down. I wanted to take my finals in the following summer and could not afford the time away from work. I had also been elected captain of football at Cambridge for that winter.

In 1952 I played in all four Tests against India, the first in the last week of the Cambridge term when I had just finished my finals. After a slow start to the season at Fenners I had a spell of about eleven days when, on some superb pitches, almost everything went right. Beginning with

100 in the second innings against Essex, I made two more against Yorkshire and Lancashire and 92 against the Indians, so I was greatly looking forward to resuming Test cricket. But after the Indians had come the examiners and I only had time for a match against the Army before the First Test. It was not a first-class match and was shortened by rain but I made 90-odd and went up to Headingley with a confidence boosted by memories of batting there in the previous year.

There had been much speculation about the England captaincy during the previous month. David Sheppard, our captain at Cambridge that year, had been frequently mentioned as one candidate, but the selectors – Norman Yardley, Bob Wyatt, Freddie Brown and Les Ames – preferred the experience of Len Hutton. I suppose that this was what I expected, although at that stage I never thought much about the captaincy. The game and my own performance were my main concerns. No one else, of course, had Len's experience of the game apart from Denis Compton, who had been vice-captain to Freddie Brown in Australia, and Denis's knee made him an uncertain starter.

The doubts about the wisdom of appointing Len as the first England professional captain of modern times were founded partly on his limited experience of captaincy – Norman Yardley was the Yorkshire captain – and partly on fears that the burden of captaincy might be too much for one of relatively frail physique already carrying a heavy responsibility as an opening batsman. There may have been something in this, for within three years Len, although enjoying the captaincy from the outset, had had enough and, at thirty-nine, was in semi-retirement. But not before he had had a highly successful reign.

From the start Len proved to be a shrewd captain in the field. People say that he was defensive but nearly all captains are defensive in some degree unless they are leading sides which are so far superior to their opponents that they can take risks without fear of running into trouble. Len led by example. He was very shy and found difficulty in dealing with people. For example, he found it hard to bring himself to tell a player that he was being dropped. But we respected and admired him. I learned an enormous amount from him, as I did from Stuart Surridge when I was playing for Surrey.

At Headingley we won a match chiefly remembered for the start of India's second innings when they lost 3 wickets to Trueman and 1 to Bedser before they scored a run. It was a memorable sight, a scoreboard reading 0 for 4.

Their first innings depended almost entirely on their captain Hazare and the twenty-year-old Manjrekar who between them made threequarters of a total of 293. The innings finished abruptly on the second morning after overnight rain. Those were the days of uncovered pitches and England's innings in its early stages was a struggle against the tall off-spinner Ghulam Ahmed, for many years since then the secretary of the Indian Board. I myself played over a ball from the leg-spinner Shinde, a readier source of runs, so I thought, than Ghulam, who bowled 63 overs in the innings for 100 runs and 5 wickets. He tired towards the end and a revival started by Tom Graveney and carried on by Allan Watkins, Godfrey Evans and Roly Jenkins earned us a small lead.

This was not certain to be enough if India batted respectably and the pitch deteriorated in the last innings. However, Fred Trueman's extra pace made an awkward pitch look a really nasty one. Alec Bedser, upwind as usual, was almost as baffling to the batsmen and in fourteen balls the match was more or less decided. Hazare again batted stoutly, this time with Phadkar in support, but we needed only 125. We lost 3 wickets in making them, including mine, and although Len for once had been unsuccessful with the bat, he had started his captaincy with a good win.

The Second Test at Lord's fell during the Cambridge tour. I played in the first match of the tour, which by a stroke of luck was at Hove where we always seemed to play on ideal batting pitches. David Sheppard and I made 100s and I could scarcely have had a pleasanter and more encouraging preparation for the Lord's Test.

Although we won at Lord's by 8 wickets, it was Mankad's match. Vinoo Mankad was not a member of the Indian touring party as he was contracted to a club in the Lancashire League. After their defeat at Headingley the Indian management approached Haslingden for his release and he played in the three remaining Tests, beginning at Lord's with that extraordinary performance – two innings of 72 and 184 and in between them the bowling figures of 73 – 24 – 196 – 5. I was one of the 5, caught at the wicket on the leg side after a stand of 158 with Len Hutton.

Mankad was a left-arm spinner with a lovely loose action, although he was not, in my recollection, a great spinner of the ball. I have one particularly clear memory of him as a batsman.

After half an hour's play Len brought on Roly Jenkins – a challenging move on the first morning if ever there was one. I was a wide and deepish mid-on and had a perfect view of Mankad driving Roly's fourth ball for a huge 6 well up the free seats at the nursery end. 'This fellow's not a bad player' went through my head and over the next few days everything that happened made this seem a conservative estimate. I should have liked to have seen more of him than I did.

Just for once the Saturday's play was blessed by the sort of cricket that one always hopes the big crowd will see on the Saturday of a Lord's Test. We had finished the second day 50 runs ahead with 5 wickets left.

One of these was Godfrey Evans's and he started the Saturday off by nearly making 100 before lunch. His batting usually had that touch of impudence which always captures a crowd and he was in his element that morning. He and Tom Graveney put on 159 in just over the two hours and Jenkins, Laker and Trueman carried on at the same pace.

With no bowlers much above medium pace and with Mankad and Ghulam Ahmed toiling away hour after hour off a run-up of a few paces, India raced through their overs. Our whole innings of 537 occupied 207 overs but lasted only nine and threequarter hours, which means that the bowlers averaged more than 21 overs an hour. Nowadays we have to legislate to persuade them to bowl around 16 in Test matches. Without legislation some drop to 12 or 13.

India's contribution to that day's entertainment was not confined to their over rate. In spite of having bowled 31 overs since the start of play Mankad opened the second innings at a quarter to four and was in even more boisterous form than in the first innings. The final product of the day's cricket was 382 runs for the loss of 7 wickets.

Mankad was more powerfully built than most Indians and he hit the ball immensely hard on the Monday morning when he took his third-wicket stand with Hazare up to 211, of which Hazare made 49. Mankad batted only four and a half hours for his 184.

This must have made it even more difficult to understand the hard work that we made of scoring 77 to win in the last innings. The runs took us 50 overs and extended the match into the fifth day. Mankad inevitably opened the bowling and he and Ghulam were not easy to play on a pitch beginning to take spin quite awkwardly. Len batted throughout, I batted with him for all but a few overs, and I see that *Wisden* records that we gave a 'pathetic display'. But we won by 8 wickets!

There was a gap of three and half weeks before the next Test at Old Trafford and during this period Denis Compton, dissatisfied with his form, asked the selectors not to consider him for the next Test. Such was Denis's eminence that this caused a huge sensation. I had not thought that he was especially out of form but he was certainly out of luck.

He played instead for Middlesex against Surrey at Lord's and when I returned to the Oval I was given a colourful account of how the Surrey bowlers had trapped him there. He hooked a short ball from Loader downwards off the middle of the bat. Eric Bedser, a deepish backward short leg, took evasive action but the ball hit him on the top of the foot and lobbed gently up to the wicketkeeper standing back 20 yards away. Even Denis saw some humour in it and the most aggrieved party was

Eric who was put out of action for ten days by a toe which seemed to grow ever bigger.

At Old Trafford Denis was replaced in the England team by Jack Ikin. David Sheppard came in for Reg Simpson and did well with Len to give us a start in unpleasant weather. Rain interrupted the first two days' play. Batting was never easy and we struggled on into the third day when Godfrey Evans played another lively innings. Given a little luck, the unconventional can in some conditions be more effective than the orthodox, and Godfrey's 71 proved the final demoralizing factor for the Indians.

It was not their weather, and although the damp pitch had hitherto been no more than mildly unpredictable Fred Trueman's pace once again had the batsmen fending off the lifting ball, a manoeuvre for which they were ill equipped both because of their lack of height and their lack of experience on pitches with a lot of bounce. They were bowled out for 58, Trueman 8 for 31. I must have seen Tony Lock take hundreds of catches over those years but I remember in particular an incredible one which he took very close at short leg from Mankad off Bedser at the start of that innings. It was his first Test and this was the first time he touched the ball. He had an extraordinary method of catching in that he put his right hand behind and under the ball and clamped his left hand on top. And he always watched the bat, which I could never bring myself to do. I watched the ball.

India followed on and after Fred had taken the first wicket Bedser and Lock soon finished the match off. India were bowled out twice in less than a day's play, indeed in only 59 overs.

In the last Test at the Oval they were again out for under 100 but the weather was so awful that only one innings a side was completed. The first day was the only one uninterrupted and on it David Sheppard rounded off his year as captain of Cambridge by making 119 in a Test match.

The series had been a reminder of the huge difference between the game as played on the Indian subcontinent and as played on the fresher, damper pitches of many English summers, even now when pitches are covered. A visiting side without good fast bowlers is nearly always going to be hard-pressed to survive in England. The astonishing thing about India's Prudential World Cup victory in 1983 was that both at Old Trafford and Lord's where they played their most important matches they found pitches which made their medium pace and spin more effective than the fast bowling of their opponents. They still had to take the chance which this created for them and the fact that they did so was something for which Kapil Dev and his side deserve the greatest credit.

Even though the opposition had crumbled in 1952 in conditions foreign to them, there was good reason to believe that English cricket was on the way up. For years since the war Alec Bedser had been our only bowler of world class. With a suddenness which always encourages me to think that it might happen again, perhaps in the 1980s, a steady flow, almost a gush, of good bowlers was appearing.

Alec was still going strong, Jim Laker was reaching the peak of his powers, Trueman was becoming a formidable fast bowler. Lock in his first two Tests had been required to bowl only 15 overs but had taken 4 wickets in them. As one looked around, one saw other bowlers who promised to be equally successful.

Statham and Tattersall had not been called on in that summer's series. Nor had Wardle, though he took 177 wickets in the season. Illness had struck down Bob Appleyard, who had taken 200 wickets in his first full season in 1951. He played only in Yorkshire's first match of 1952 but it was hoped that he might be fit for the following season. I had been much impressed with Peter Loader both in the nets at the Oval and in the one match I had played with him for Surrey against the Indians.

So the 1952 season finished with genuine hope that we had the bowlers who in 1953 would play their part in recovering the Ashes. Although we did not know it, there was one other who was to play the biggest part of all in holding the Ashes in Australia two and a half years later.

If asked at the end of 1952 what I recalled of the young fast bowler who had bowled me at Lord's in an inter-services match in 1949, I should not have remembered him as very fast, if I remembered him at all. And since then I had not set eyes on Frank Tyson, who had not yet come into county cricket.

4
1953 – The Ashes Come Back

I remember very clearly how keenly I looked forward to the 1953 season during the previous winter. I started work in the City, played football on Saturdays and thought about the coming series against Australia.

Nowadays I would almost certainly have been expected to have a net once a week during the winter but in those days indoor nets were not as fashionable. I still looked on games as seasonal and did not have a bat in my hand throughout the winter. To some extent, of course, this may be a good thing in that one has a break and comes back refreshed. But at the time it merely increased my fervent anticipation of the excitements to come.

The South Africans' visit to Australia that winter had deepened the impression that Australia could be beaten and the Ashes recovered. It was only five years since Don Bradman's tremendous side had proved invincible in England but we had won the last Test of 1950–51 in Australia and I was not one of those who shrugged that off as a relaxation by the Australians after they had won the first four. We had so nearly won the first two Tests as well.

The Don had retired and so had Sid Barnes who had been almost as successful in 1948. The great bowlers, Lindwall and Miller, were now in their thirties. Amazingly, too, the buoyant young South African side led by Jack Cheetham had somehow managed to win two Tests and share the series. It was one of the great upsets of Test history, for the pretour publicity had mostly concerned the poverty of South Africa's cricket and even suggestions that the tour should be cancelled as they would not provide adequate opposition.

This was not entirely wild and exaggerated comment. The Australian Board, who had lost money over the previous year's visit by a much vaunted West Indies team, went on record as fearing an absence of public interest in as weak a side as the South Africans were widely expected to prove.

To their great credit, the South African Board promptly said that they were prepared to lose £10,000 on a tour which would be of educational value to a young side and a help to their cricket in the future. In the event, they finished up with the best result of any visiting side to Australia since the 'bodyline' tour of twenty years before and with a profit of £3000.

I tried to work out how it had been done and what lessons we might learn from it. To those who had seen them at close hand in 1951 it was not exactly a surprise that McGlew, McLean, Endean and others had come on so well. Hugh Tayfield's 30 wickets in the series were a surprise, for he had not done a lot when flown over as a support for Athol Rowan during the 1951 tour, and off-spinners were not at the time considered a good bet in Australian conditions. But Tayfield had looked to have the makings of a high-class off-spinner and I was told by the South Africans that he was a much better bowler at home than he looked in England.

The main reasons for the South Africans' success, however, seemed to be brilliant fielding, the product of many hours of practice, an ebullient team spirit and single-minded determination. Any side which could win a final Test which their opponents had begun by making 520 had an extra share of guts.

I could not honestly see England reproducing the South African virtues. We lacked the youth and agility to reach such a high standard of fielding. We would not have the advantages of the touring side which can build up a team spirit unattainable by a home side. Moreover, although the South Africans had made a lot of runs, these had largely been off the supporting bowlers. Miller and Lindwall had still taken their wickets at a fairly low cost. The conclusion, therefore, seemed to be that Australia were most likely to be beaten in England if Lindwall and Miller were contained – 'mastered' would have been too arrogant a word – and if our bowlers proved too much on English pitches for some of the younger Australian batsmen. These included the seventeen-year-old Ian Craig who had just made 50 odd in each innings of his first Test. But there remained Arthur Morris, Lindsay Hassett, Neil Harvey and Keith Miller, all players of the highest class with many runs behind them in England.

Not many things in life live up to really high expectations and it was probably inevitable that the start of the 1953 season was for me a swift disillusionment.

Of all places, I started my first full season for Surrey at Cambridge. A long innings on a perfect Fenners pitch should have set me off on the right note and I made 50 in the next match against MCC at Lord's. But the following match, before we started our championship programme, was against the Australians at the Oval and there I had my first experience of Australian competitiveness, entirely fair but very, very hard.

The Australians had already played three county matches, scoring more than 500 against Worcestershire and beating Leicestershire and Yorkshire by an innings. 'Hutton b Lindwall 0' at Bradford had an ominous look about it and did not suggest any deterioration in the great bowler's powers.

We played them on a pitch which gave the bowlers a lot of help. We lasted a day and a half and were also beaten by an innings, May contributing 0 and 1.

The match began on a grey, murky Oval morning, perfect for bowling. It was obvious by a certain tautness and expectancy in the field as I walked to the wicket in the first innings with the score 4 for 2 that, as a newcomer to Test cricket since they last played against England, the Australians viewed me as a young man to be put firmly in his place from the start. I suppose that I should have regarded it as a compliment that I should receive such treatment, but as Ray Lindwall bowled me a bewildering over I saw little cause to feel flattered. He bowled me five late away-swingers which had me groping, followed by an in-swinger which went through everything.

He was a master of control. In 1956 MCC were experimenting with a slightly smaller ball which a committee, after numerous meetings, had decided was worth a trial. When a ball was produced according to the proposed specifications, Ray Lindwall happened to be at Lord's and he was asked to try it out at the nets. It swung all over the place and would have been uncontrollable by most bowlers. Ray returned it to the committee with a broad smile and said that if they brought it in he would play for another ten years.

On that morning at the Oval in early May no two balls seemed quite the same. I must have looked a novice. I survived the over – a mistake, somebody told me! – and improved to the extent that I did touch one soon afterwards and was caught at the wicket. In the second innings I improved still further by avoiding being out to Lindwall and being bowled by Ron Archer at the other end. In these conditions Archer was almost as formidable. He was a fine cricketer, only nineteen then, and very unlucky to have his career cut short a few years later by injury.

The Australians' performance in beating us by an innings was made to look even better five days later when Surrey, in their first championship match of the season, beat Warwickshire in a day. Alec Bedser took 12 for 35 and Jim Laker, who was not needed in the first innings but opened the bowling in the second, 5 for 29. Only once before, in 1857, had a match at the Oval finished in a day.

I was not present on this occasion as I was playing for MCC at Lord's against the Australians. The MCC captain was Freddie Brown, by now chairman of selectors. No play was possible on the Saturday – the day, incidentally, when a few miles away Surrey were completing their match at the Oval – and our first innings roughly followed the pattern of Surrey's suffering a week before. In Lindwall's first five overs he removed Reg Simpson, David Sheppard and Denis Compton, and although I batted for an hour before I was lbw to the leg-spinner Doug Ring, I cannot have exuded much confidence. In the second innings I was lbw to Lindwall.

Ray Lindwall at this time may have been a shade slower than five years before but it mattered little. He had the knack, which Lillee was to acquire later, of being able to conserve his energy with a lovely easy action and, without any obvious extra effort, to produce suddenly a ball which was a yard faster than anything before. Whereas in 1948 the slower ball had been the variation, now the faster one was the extra subtlety. I have already mentioned his control. His accuracy was extraordinary.

The weather was not a great help perhaps, but with the odd exception I did not play well in the next few weeks either for Surrey or in a Test trial at Edgbaston. However, by a stroke of luck, we won the toss at the Oval on the day before the team for the First Test was chosen and I made 136 against a Northamptonshire attack in which the chairman of selectors bowled 34 overs. I was, in fact, eventually caught and bowled Brown. In case this sounds as if I gave my wicket away in a timely piece of sycophancy, I should add that Freddie, although prewar a leg-spinner of almost medium pace, had turned himself in his forties into a fine bowler of above medium pace who moved the ball a lot. Immensely strong, he could bowl for most of the day and could still turn to leg-spin if needed.

Anyhow I was chosen for the First Test, a frustrating affair at Trent Bridge in which almost no play was possible on the last two days after England had bowled Australia out twice. I have always bitterly regretted the dismal Nottingham weather, not so much because it probably robbed us of a Test victory but because it would have been a victory which would have stood as a sort of memorial to Alec Bedser's prowess. None of the other formidable bowlers in the match, even Lindwall, was as consistently awkward to play and Alec's 14 wickets for 99 must have been a matchwinning feat in any other circumstances.

Alec's great strength was that he not only used the new ball and the second new ball superbly but did the donkeywork in between. This was especially valuable here, for we had gone in with only four bowlers – two fast-medium, Bedser and Bailey, two spinners, Tattersall and Wardle.

The first day's play was relatively uneventful. A gloomy light and occasional rain took away at least an hour and half's play, and Australia, painstakingly but with some good careful batting by Hassett and Morris against Bedser at his best, made 157 for 3. Alec took all 3 wickets (for 26 in 25 overs).

Hassett *v*. Bedser was a rich spectacle for the connoisseur. Elegance is not a word one associates with a batsman small in stature but somehow Lindsay Hassett had it. He was a beautiful cutter but is remembered also for his balanced driving, his timing and his gracefulness in all he did.

What endeared him so much to many of his English opponents was his sense of humour; I always remember a story told about him on the second day of this Trent Bridge Test when he was eventually bowled, for 115, by a ball from Bedser to which no batsman would have had the answer.

'What happened, skipper?' they asked him in the dressing room. He appeared to give the matter serious thought.

'Well, it looked like Alec's normal in-swinger,' he said, 'and I shaped to play it as such. Then, late in flight, it swung rather more and I followed it. Then, after pitching, it changed course like a fast leg break and hit the top of the off stump. But it still shaved the edge of the bat as it passed. I reckon I can't be such a bad player after all.' And he went off smiling to his bath.

By this time Bedser and Bailey with the new ball had changed the whole course of the innings in a few minutes. I remember Godfrey Evans diving yards down the leg side to catch Richie Benaud off Bailey. The last 6 wickets fell for 6 runs and of the 244 scored from the bat, Hassett, Morris and Miller had scored all but 7.

But if Bedser could do it, what about Lindwall? The answer was that with the score at 17 he had Don Kenyon, Reg Simpson and Denis Compton out in eight balls. The Australians were holding some marvellous catches and two more by Richie Benaud removed Tom Graveney, when he had put on 59 with Len Hutton, and then Len himself.

By the time Len was out to Alan Davidson I had come in at number six. It would be wrong to say that I was at ease, for the light was miserable and I was having to sort out the intricacies of Jack Hill, whom I had not played previously. He was not rated a great bowler, indeed he only ever played in three Test matches, but he was unusual at first meeting. He was one of those spinners who run up suggesting that they will turn the leg break a lot. In fact, nothing much happened. He bowled the googly, but mostly the top-spinner which, because it bounced more than most, was awkward until you were used to it. If the leg break happened to turn, that was a bonus for him.

Charlie Oakes used to bowl similarly for Sussex in those days and it was always interesting watching new batsmen, however carefully warned, playing for a leg break which seldom came.

It was about six o'clock that evening at Trent Bridge and there had already been an appeal against the light turned down when Hill started another over to me from the pavilion end. I suspect that my undoing was the rare leg break which turned just enough. It certainly bounced more than most and I was caught at the wicket.

The score was 92 for 6 and I was no sooner back in the dressing room than the others followed me in. The umpires had decided that the light was too bad. I very rarely admitted to myself that I might have been unlucky to be out but this may have been an exception, especially as it had far-reaching results.

Although Alec Bedser had them out for 123 when Australia batted again with a lead of over 100, it rained and rained and rained for the next two days. We started after tea on the last day but it was too late. We finished 100-odd short with 9 wickets standing.

I did not have a second innings, and when the team for the next Test was announced the following weekend I was not in it. It was the only time that I was ever dropped. I was disappointed but not very surprised. I was not in the greatest form and later, although not then, I looked on it as a blessing in disguise.

The weather in the week after the First Test had been no help to a batsman needing to restore his confidence. Surrey had a rain-interrupted match against Essex at the Oval and a disastrous visit to Derby where we were beaten by an innings inside two days. Any lingering doubts which the selectors may have had must have been dispelled on the Sunday morning when they read 'May b Jackson o'.

The selectors were not in an easy position and I have no doubt that as chairman of selectors similarly placed now I would have dropped P. B. H. May. We needed a fifth bowler for Lord's, so Brian Statham, the one left out at Trent Bridge, was brought in in place of a batsman, myself. Willie Watson replaced Reg Simpson, a rather inspired selection, as it turned out. Willie had been well out of form for Yorkshire and had only twice recently made runs. But once was at Lord's against Middlesex and the other occasion was against the Australians.

The third change in the side was a far more historic one, brave and successful. There was a shortage of all-rounders at the time and a leg-spinner was always considered desirable at Lord's. The chairman, Freddie Brown, under heavy pressure from his colleagues, Bob Wyatt, Les Ames and Norman Yardley, picked himself. There has been, I might add, absolutely no chance of the chairman of selectors in the 1980s doing the same.

Freddie contributed 50 runs, more than 50 overs and 4 wickets to

England's effort in the Lord's Test, the first of the three in Coronation Year which I missed. At the start of the last day England, with only 7 wickets left, were considered certain to lose on a wearing pitch, but after Denis Compton had halted the decline of the previous evening, Willie Watson and Trevor Bailey saved the match with a long and dogged partnership which lasted until time was running out. Freddie sat with his pads on for hours, superstitiously refusing to move. Any sustenance required had to be brought to him.

At Old Trafford the weather made a draw certain in the third Test and the drama in the match was reserved for the last two hours when Australia went in to play out time after tea on the last day. Whether they would have found Wardle, Laker and the turning ball as impossible to play if more had depended on it will never be known but they finished with the startling score of 35 for 8.

In those days the last train from Manchester to London used to leave at about 5.15 and I was told that those members of the press who had left early for assignments down south next day, assuming a nice, quiet draw, had a nasty shock when they reached Euston.

Viewed in the light of what happened at Old Trafford in damp and not dissimilar conditions three years later, this period of play was far more significant than any one thought at the time.

Between showers at Headingley Australia were always on top. When they started their last innings they needed 177 to win in just under two hours. Trevor Bailey bowled his controversial spell outside the leg stump to a strong leg-side field and they fell 30 runs short with 6 wickets standing. It was not the most glorious way in which to earn a draw but it meant that the series was still level with the final Test at the Oval to come.

Clearly England's performance at Headingley had been disappointing. There was speculation in the press about changes in the batting and a call for a better balanced side. Except when Freddie Brown had come in for the Lord's Test, only four bowlers had been played. Reg Simpson had been short of runs – not that any of the batsmen had been prolific – and Willie Watson had done little since Lord's.

I suppose that I was hopeful that I would be brought back, though I was not having a particularly consistent season. However, I had a good bank holiday match against Nottinghamshire and, on the day before the team for the final Test was chosen, played probably my best innings of the summer so far – 159 at Lord's against Middlesex who at that time were ahead of us in the championship.

On the Sunday I heard that Simpson and Watson had been dropped. I was back for what was to be the first of fifty-two successive Test matches spread over six years. Fred Trueman, who had not previously played in the series, was also picked. The bowling – Bedser, Trueman, Bailey, Laker and Lock – looked balanced and just about right for the Oval as it was then.

The match was due to be played over six days and started on a Saturday. There was no question of having three days off to prepare for the Test as Surrey had a vital match against Leicestershire who that week had suddenly emerged as our closest rivals. The Australians had a day off but only because they polished off Essex in two days. I shudder to think of the hullaballoo which such a programme would arouse nowadays.

As Alec Bedser, Jim Laker and I drove down from Loughborough on the Friday evening after a day in the field, we turned on the radio and heard the Australian team announced. We listened in silence and at the end said in one voice, 'They're not playing a spinner.'

We stopped and went into a village pub near Sandy in Bedfordshire for a drink while we digested the news. We had a good idea that the Oval pitch would take spin fairly soon, certainly long before the end of a six-day match. Although that Australian team had no finger spinners of the type likely to succeed in England, we had thought them certain to include Richie Benaud. Instead they played Bill Johnston who had had knee problems throughout the tour but was fit again now.

I do not remember anything like the tenseness of that Test match. Len Hutton lost the toss, as he had done in the other four Tests, and we were all the more grateful that we had five bowlers. In fact, the wickets on that first day were spread among all five of them and Fred Trueman, who took 4, bowled especially well. One of his wickets was the vital one of Neil Harvey. He mis-hooked and I can still remember the agony of watching while Len Hutton ran back from short leg and took a very good catch.

The pitch, freshened perhaps by light showers, was not without life and by mid-afternoon we had seven out for 160. But Davidson and Lindwall were still there and a spirited piece of hitting by Ray Lindwall after tea took the score up to 275.

Len's opening partner was Bill Edrich, whose fearlessness and imperturbability greatly appealed to Len. Len did not like nervous partners. On this occasion he must have been especially glad to have Bill with him, for they had what could have been a very difficult twenty minutes ahead. In fact, the light failed after two overs but not before Len had an unusual escape, in fact two unusual escapes to the same ball.

A very fast short one from Lindwall lifted to the handle of the bat and flew towards the packed slips. But first it knocked off Len's cap and this had the effect of making it drop just short of the slips. The cap could have fallen on the stumps but that too just missed.

On Monday morning Bill Edrich played well for a time and the score was 37 before I went in to join Len. It was hard going. The Australians bowled and fielded superbly, Lindwall was at you all the time and you had the feeling that every run was an achievement. We batted well into the afternoon and added 100 before I was out.

From the dressing room I noted with interest that even Denis Compton did not find it easy, and after Len was out the innings began to fall away. In those days the new ball could be taken after 65 overs but the bowlers were so much on top that Lindsay Hassett delayed taking it for threequarters of an hour. He was about to take it when Denis was caught by the wicketkeeper down the leg side off Lindwall. With the new ball Lindwall then had Tom Graveney well caught at first slip by Keith Miller. This made it 170 for 5.

Godfrey Evans on his day could be an infuriating batsman to bowl to with a new ball and a close-set field. On this occasion the ball was soon flashing through and over the field and, with Trevor Bailey reliable in defence as ever, a revival was well under way when Godfrey slipped and was run out.

Yet that evening, at 235 for 7, we were within range and the match was evenly balanced, perhaps tilted a shade in our favour if spin became an important factor in the second innings as seemed increasingly likely. Graeme Hole, an occasional off-spinner, had been given a few overs, and although he was not a great spinner of the ball, enough happened to suggest that we might hold the key to the rest of the match in Laker and Lock.

Next morning Bailey and the later batsmen carried on the good work until lunch and we gained a lead of 31 runs. Trevor and Alec Bedser added 44 for the last wicket amid great enthusiasm and in the context of that match it certainly was a priceless contribution. The fact that during the morning the Australians were forced more onto the defensive than before suggested that the pitch was losing some of its value to the fast bowlers.

This was Len Hutton's interpretation and it was soon reinforced as Morris and Hassett made one of those busy starts to an innings which suggest that the batsmen are determined to make the most of the fast bowling while it lasts and before spin casts a blight over them.

It lasted only five overs before Len had Bedser and Trueman off and Laker and Lock on. The results were immediate. Hassett played back to the last ball of Laker's first over which straightened to have him lbw.

The spinners passed quickly through the more experienced batting. Graeme Hole played a few aggressive strokes, but when he was out Harvey, Miller and Morris soon followed.

The Australia response to this was typical of their reaction to adversity.

ENGLAND v AUSTRALIA, Kennington Oval
(Fifth Test 1953)

England won by 8 wickets

AUSTRALIA

†A. L. Hassett c Evans, b Bedser	53	– lbw b Laker	10
A. R. Morris lbw b Bedser	16	– lbw b Lock	26
K. R. Miller lbw b Bailey	1	– c Trueman, b Laker	0
R. N. Harvey c Hutton, b Trueman	36	– b Lock	1
G. B. Hole c Evans, b Trueman	37	– lbw b Laker	17
J. H. de Courcy c Evans, b Trueman	5	– run out	4
R. G. Archer c & b Bedser	10	– c Edrich, b Lock	49
A. K. Davidson c Edrich, b Laker	22	– b Lock	21
R. R. Lindwall c Evans, b Trueman	62	– c Compton, b Laker	12
*G. R. Langley c Edrich, b Lock	18	– c Trueman, b Lock	2
W. A. Johnston not out	9	– not out	6
B 4, n-b 2	6	B 11, l-b 3	14

1/38 2/41 3/107 4/107 5/118 6/160   275   1/23 2/59 3/60 4/61 5/61 6/8562
7/160 8/207 9/245 10/275   7/135 8/140 9/144 10/162

Bowling: *First Innings* – Bedser 29–3–88–3; Trueman 24.3–3–86–4; Bailey 14–3–42–1; Lock 9–2–19–1; Laker 5–0–34–1. *Second Innings* – Bedser 11–2–24–0; Trueman 2–1–4–0; Lock 21–9–45–5; Laker 16.5–2–75–4.

ENGLAND

†L. Hutton b Johnston	82	– run out	17
W. J. Edrich lbw b Lindwall	21	– not out	55
P. B. H. May c Archer, b Johnston	39	– c Davidson, b Miller	37
D. C. S. Compton c Langley, b Lindwall	16	– not out	22
T. W. Graveney c Miller, b Lindwall	4	–	
T. E. Bailey b Archer	64	–	
*T. G. Evans run out	28	–	
J. C. Laker c Langley, b Miller	1	–	
G. A. R. Lock c Davidson, b Lindwall	4	–	
F. S. Trueman b Johnston	10	–	
A. V. Bedser not out	22	–	
B 9, l-b 5, w 1	15	L-b 1	1

1/37 2/137 3/154 4/167 5/170 6/210   306   1/24 2/88   (2 wkts.) 132
7/225 8/237 9/262 10/306

Bowling: *First Innings* – Lindwall 32–7–70–4; Miller 34–12–65–1; Johnston 45–16–94–3; Davidson 10–1–26–0; Archer 10.3–2–25–1; Hole 11–6–11–0. *Second Innings* – Lindwall 21–5–46–0; Miller 11–3–24–1; Johnston 29–14–52–0; Archer 1–1–0–0; Hassett 1–0–4–0; Morris 0.5–0–5–0.

Umpires: D. Davies and F. S. Lee

How the Ashes were won back

They attacked – and they still had players such as Archer, de Courcy, Davidson and Lindwall who might have made things difficult for us if they had won the initiative back. Remember that we had long been in an era of Australian supremacy. We were not used to being in a winning position and Laker and Lock did not have the reputations then which they were to earn later. Indeed, Jim Laker had been one of those bowlers off whom Australia had made 404 for 3 on the last day at Headingley in 1948.

The counterattack very nearly came off. We had a slice of luck when a brilliant piece of fielding by Trevor Bailey ran out de Courcy, but by tea Archer and Davidson had put Australia 100 ahead and were going depressingly well.

However, after tea the spinners soon broke through again. Alec Bedser came on twice to keep an end tight and the innings was finished off for 162.

This meant that we needed only 132 to win. I have often wondered what would have happened if we had had to make 180 or 200. I believe that it had been over fifty years since England made 200 or more to win a Test match in England. We would certainly have known that it was not an inaccessible target technically on that pitch against a side without specialist spin, but the enormity of the prize and the great length of time since we had last won a series against Australia might have had an oppressive effect. I was twenty-three and could not remember our holding the Ashes.

As it was, we lost Len Hutton in the fifty minutes we had to bat on the third evening through one of those elementary misjudgements which even the greatest players can make. He and Bill Edrich had made 24 together very soundly when de Courcy fumbled Len's stroke to square leg. Len went for a second run and did not make it. 'Never run for a misfield,' they tell you when you are in your cricketing cradle.

Poor Len looked in a daze of disappointment as I passed him on my way out with a quarter of an hour left. I have no recollection of being offered a night watchman but I would have refused one. It seemed important to stop the Australian bowlers from capitalizing on their stroke of luck. Bill and I did so and the innings was a great experience to have had.

I was always a little nervous on a big occasion but the atmosphere throughout England's last innings was to me unique. Winning seemed to mean so much to so many people. I can never remember an English crowd in such a state of excitement. I was greatly comforted by the sight of Bill Edrich at the other end. He was not the player then that he had been in the immediate postwar years but there was an indestructible quality about him which inspired confidence. In fact, in his later years, I always thought of him as a relatively better player in a crisis or on a bad pitch than when it was easy going. If somebody was bowling short to him and hitting him round the head and chest, he seemed in his element.

The Oval in those days, with less seating around the banking and with thousands sitting on the grass, accommodated about 30,000 and it was crammed full next morning when Bill and I resumed, needing another 94. The tenseness and excitement seemed, if anything, even greater than the evening before.

Again every run had to be fought for. Lindwall bowled magnificently for the first hour and a quarter with scarcely a ball which did not have to be played, although by now the pitch had little to offer him. Bill Johnston in his slower style bowled throughout the morning from the Vauxhall end and he too scarcely bowled a bad ball. The Australians fielded with immense hostility and with not a suggestion that they might have given up hope.

Gradually we drew nearer the magic figure of 132. I hoped that we were sailing into easier waters but at 88 Keith Miller, bowling off breaks, had me caught by one of the finer short legs. Bill Edrich told me later that he had not thought I was out and I did momentarily wonder if it had been a bump ball.

I was disappointed not to be in at the finish but there seemed something appropriate about victory being clinched by the old heroes, Edrich and Compton, who had given so much pleasure and done so much for England in the years since we last held the Ashes.

As for myself, I was thrilled to have been given the chance of sharing in the historic victory. I was delighted, too, to know that, with the blessing of benevolent employers, I would be going in the second half of the coming winter to West Indies on my first tour.

5
Escape in West Indies

Looking back from a distance of thirty years, I can see that MCC's tour of West Indies in 1953–54 almost certainly marked the start of a new and more demanding era in international cricket.

Previously England's strongest teams had only gone to Australia, although the 1948–49 team to South Africa must have been just about the best except for Bill Edrich. Elsewhere there had nearly always been leading players who were not available either because it was considered that they needed a rest or because they were amateurs and could not spare the time. Denis Compton's cricket career had been so interrupted by the war and by football with the Arsenal that in 1953, sixteen years after he first played Test cricket, he had been on only three tours, two to Australia and one to South Africa. The very length of tours, especially those involving a long sea journey, meant that some players could not or would not make themselves available.

Tours to West Indies before the war had by all accounts been highly enjoyable, partly social events, the sides being often well stocked with amateurs. The first Test series there in 1929–30 was played by one of two MCC teams touring that winter. The Hon. F. S. G. Calthorpe captained that team, whilst Harold Gilligan, destined thirty years later to become my father-in-law, captained a side which played the first Test series in New Zealand.

Even in 1947–48 when MCC made their first postwar tour of the Caribbean, their team was a long way from the best that England could select. It was realized, of course, that West Indies had formidable new batsmen, among them the three Ws who had been making huge scores during the war and thereafter. But English cricket, mainly for the reasons already given, did not have all its best players available. Bedser, Compton, Edrich, Washbrook and Wright did not go. Hutton only went out later when called for in an emergency. There was no obvious captain available and Gubby Allen, aged forty-five, took on the job.

All this had to change after West Indies had won their first victory in England in 1950 by a convincing 3–1 margin. The strongest side possible had to go to West Indies in 1953. The days of the missionary work and of Caribbean semi-holidays were over. It was recognized that this was going to be a difficult series to win.

There was really only one player not available, Alec Bedser, who had bowled a huge number of overs since the war – over 1250 in the 1953 season alone – and was now thirty-five. Surrey felt that he badly needed a rest and would not be able to give of his best if he went. He and the selectors realized that if he did go he would be of doubtful use a year later in Australia where he had always bowled so well. Otherwise the side chosen was generally considered our best, although, as I have said, I personally regretted that a place was not found for Robin Marlar.

The new seriousness with which England approached the tour was one difference from the past. The other was the emergence of a cricket tour as making political and diplomatic demands well beyond those encountered hitherto.

The 'bodyline' tour of 1932–33 had, of course, penetrated government corridors in two countries but the issue then had been the way in which cricket was played. Now influences outside cricket were at work, nationalism and local political issues among them. A cricket tour required diplomatic ability with which few cricketers were equipped. Good manners were no longer enough.

I was amazed, for example, to hear in some islands that MCC were considered to have slighted West Indies by sending a team under a professional captain. I was embarrassed to hear European residents impressing on members of the MCC team the vital importance of beating West Indies. As I understood it, they feared their own position if England lost. It is one of the saddest things about modern international cricket that you cannot often be beaten without being 'humiliated'.

The inter-island rivalries also helped to confuse the situation for visiting cricketers, who had thoughts simply of playing cricket with the added attraction of spending a winter bathing in warm Caribbean waters.

The start of the tour in mid-December was a great improvement on that of the last tour when MCC had been thrown into a match with Barbados within three days of a voyage on a small ship doing its best against the Atlantic in midwinter. This time we flew to Bermuda and spent eleven days there. It was the first time that an MCC team had left by air.

This was a great experience for me. I had been on a Butterflies tour to Germany. I had been vice-captain of the Cambridge soccer team in Greece. I had been to Switzerland with Pegasus. But that was the extent of my overseas travel, and the flight to Bermuda and the stay there were something entirely new.

Nowadays it is still considered that a side coming from an English midwinter needs a minimum of three weeks to be anywhere near ready for its first Test. In Australia in the old days the First Test did not take place until about two and a half months after the team had left England and by that time it had played first-class cricket from Perth to Brisbane.

This time we had just over a month's preparation before the First Test and the eleven days in Bermuda should have been an ideal period for practice including, as it did, two three-day matches in Hamilton against the Island. Perhaps it was a little unreal. We played on matting laid on concrete and the ball bounced so much that it had to be of a very full length to hit the stumps. However, when we went on to Jamaica after Christmas we seemed to have profited from it. We became the first MCC side to beat Jamaica and did so by an innings. Nor were Jamaica all that weak. Four of their side played at some time or other in the subsequent Test series.

I was the only batsman apart from Godfrey Evans who did not take the chance of batting practice offered by the splendid pitch at Sabina Park in Kingston, but in the second rain-interrupted match at Melbourne Park, which was drawn, I made 100. It was not the greatest innings ever played but it was valuable practice.

In this match I had my first real look at the legendary George Headley – 'King George', as they called him. He was forty-four but had been brought back to Jamaica from England by public subscription for the MCC visit. In the second innings he showed the famous defensive technique which had probably not been severely tested during his years in the League. His long innings earned him a place in the First Test but his return, alas, was the product of sentiment rather than reason and was a little sad. Yet it was a sign of the respect in which he was held, and of the way in which the game was still played, that when he came in to bat in the Test match the field withdrew at Len's instruction and Brian Statham gave him one to get him off the mark.

This start in Jamaica, following the recovery of the Ashes a few months before, and the impression that our standards were rising, especially in bowling, sent us into the First Test with some confidence. The impact made by Worrell, Weekes and Walcott, the three Ws, in 1950 and by Ramadhin and Valentine in partnership was too recent to be forgotten but in those days no other first-class cricket was played in the Caribbean during an MCC visit and most of the best West Indians had no recent form to commend them. Frank Worrell, for one, was out through injury.

Our confidence was soon ebbing. We played four fast bowlers and Lock. No Laker. The bowlers took 2 wickets on the first day, 5 more on the second and it was the third morning before we batted against a score of over 400. Test matches in West Indies then were of six days, each of five hours' play.

Willie Watson was soon bowled by an in-swinger from Gerry Gomez and there was a deafening noise when Len Hutton played on to Valentine, a Jamaican. The noise abated very little during my partnership with Denis Compton. I thought that we were playing rather well but Denis, down the pitch to Valentine, was lbw and I forced a shorter, faster ball from Ramadhin off the back foot to midwicket. My 31 was top score. Though Trevor Bailey's defence was as impenetrable as ever, he had made only 28 when the innings ended on the fourth morning.

West Indies led by nearly 250 runs but Jeff Stollmeyer decided to bat again, partly, I imagine, because the shooter was occurring more frequently and partly because Ramadhin's spinning finger was giving some trouble.

We had dropped catches towards the end of the West Indies first innings. We had batted without distinction. But we had quite a successful morning and afternoon on that fourth day. Just before tea West Indies in their second innings were 119 for 6. It was no great help to us in the context of the match, for they were nearly 400 ahead on a pitch always capable of producing the unexpected, and after tea we lost control again. Lock had been no-balled for throwing his faster ball just after he had delivered a shaft of lightning which ended George Headley's distinguished Test career, and this deprived him of a variation which he was wont to use with much effect.

We did not drop as many catches as in the first innings but the wicketkeeper, McWatt, who had been lucky then, played much better now in support of Everton Weekes who batted brilliantly. They were still together, Weekes 90 not out, when Jeff Stollmeyer declared.

He had left his bowlers nine and a half hours in which to bowl us out. Not many would have bothered to add that we needed 457 to win in that time, but when at the end of the fifth day we were 227 for 2, it was just conceivable that on this small ground with a fast outfield we might still make history.

I realized that evening the passions and confused loyalties of West Indian cricket. Jeff Stollmeyer's decision not to enforce the follow-on had been widely criticized in Jamaica. He had been booed both going to and from the wicket. He came from Trinidad, nearly 1000 miles away, and could not expect much sympathy in Jamaica if West Indies failed to win. There were also alarming stories that Perry Burke, one of the umpires, had been threatened and his family accosted because on the second day he had given the Jamaican, Holt, out lbw when 94.

The cracks in the pitch which caused the occasional ball to squat had widened without doing much more damage and Len Hutton and Willie Watson had begun our second innings with a handsome partnership of 130. I went in when Len was lbw pushing forward to Gerry Gomez and surprised myself two overs later by driving Gerry straight for 6 as my second scoring stroke. I found that I was not quite at the pitch of the ball and, encouraged by the closeness of the straight boundary at Sabina Park, went through with the stroke.

Willie reached a most spirited 100 and we had sailed past 200 when, with only a few minutes left, he fell to an unlikely bowler, Jeff Stollmeyer. Jeff bowled high-flighted leg breaks and googlies as if to amuse himself and could undermine the concentration of the most talented and the most obdurate. His other two victims in the series were Compton, when 93, and Bailey. It was the googly which accounted for the left-handed Watson that evening in Kingston. As he aimed to play it quietly on the on side, it turned and lobbed back to the bowler off the front edge.

Thus ended one of Willie Watson's finest innings. William the Silent, I used to call him. He seldom had much to say but was a great thinker about the game and, as befitted one of the last to play both cricket and football for England, a beautiful mover on his feet.

For about eighty minutes next day Tom Graveney and I moved on towards the target but increasingly slowly once West Indies went on the defensive, which they did with some thoroughness. Esmond Kentish, who three years later appeared at Oxford as a thirty-nine-year-old under-graduate, bowled on and outside my leg stump with seven on the on side. Gomez favoured the off side and a dense off-side field. The England batsmen were being repaid for the tactics which Trevor Bailey and other bowlers used in that era before on-side restrictions became law.

With a feeling that we were getting nowhere and that something had to be done, I began to attempt strokes which I would not otherwise have played. Soon after lunch I glanced a wide ball too fine and the wicketkeeper caught it.

A score of 277 for 3 still seemed to hold possibilities but in fact we staged a spectacular collapse. Six wickets fell to Kentish and Ramadhin for 1 run, and although Trevor Bailey survived the mayhem as usual, the match was over an hour after lunch and we had lost by 140 runs.

The Second Test in Barbados was no improvement. This time Frank Worrell played but Everton Weekes was unfit. It made no difference. Our performance was still inglorious.

We made an encouraging start after Len had lost the toss for the seventh Test in a row. Presumably through not hearing in the hubbub what the other was calling, both Holt and Stollmeyer arrived at the same end and Stollmeyer was run out for nought. Two balls later Frank Worrell played on to Statham. Our bowlers found Clyde Walcott the most difficult West Indian batsman to bowl to because he had such power, and here he played a remarkable innings of 220 out of a total of 383.

On the second evening Willie Watson and I were both out cheaply to

Ramadhin. I drove him straight to cover point. The only virtue of this was that it spared me from direct responsibility – we had, of course, a sort of collective guilt – for what happened next day when in five hours we scored only 128 runs, losing 7 wickets in the process. On the other hand, my early departure may have contributed to the prevailing apprehension. Ramadhin in the day was allowed to bowl 41 overs for 37 runs and 2 wickets. Valentine was treated with almost the same caution. There was no excuse. We just became bogged down.

Again Jeff Stollmeyer did not enforce the follow-on, although early on the fourth morning our innings finished 201 behind. It was still a good pitch, in fact it looked a beauty, and Laker and Lock had little effect. The only wicket which we took on that depressing day was when, for the second time in the match, Holt and Stollmeyer found themselves in fatal proximity, this time in the middle of the pitch. Stollmeyer was again the one who had to go.

Holt went on attacking our spinners with some marvellous strokes and finished the day with 166. At that time he looked such a high-class player that it was amazing that he never played against England again after that series and indeed scored only one more Test 100, in India five years later. The explanation may have been that he was already thirty and at his peak whilst other younger players were on their way up.

As in Jamaica, West Indies declared early on the fifth day and, as in Jamaica, England made a start to the last innings which was in refreshing contrast with our first effort.

This time Willie Watson was caught at the wicket in the first over and I had one or two pieces of luck both against the tall fast Frank King with the new ball and when Ramadhin came on. But, having survived, I was determined not to be dominated by Ramadhin and Valentine and things began to go rather well. The spinners were taken off and, with Len active at the other end, the score moved up past 100 before, overambitiously, I tried to force Gomez square and was well caught by Walcott to his right at slip.

Len went on into the evening. Denis Compton, from an uneasy start, began to play some of his most brilliant strokes and it began to look as if we would again start the last day with an outside chance of bringing off an improbable win, though this time we needed 495. However, Len was caught at square leg off Ramadhin from a stroke not normally in his repertoire, the sweep, and at 214 for 3 that night there was still a long way to go.

It was soon evident next morning that England had only a draw for which to play, as rain delayed the start for fifty minutes and indeed returned later. But at lunch Compton and Graveney were still there with three and a half hours left.

After lunch, however, Denis was lbw to Stollmeyer for 93 when well down the pitch. I was not sure that the bowler appealed. Though Tom Graveney, tall and elegant, went on serenely, the others raised only 9 runs between them and we lost by 181 runs.

If ever there was a time for rethinking, this was it. We had been soundly beaten twice and had played some poor cricket. But we could not be as bad as we looked. West Indies had a greater depth of batting but we surely had the edge in fast bowling if our bowlers ever found a pitch to give them any help. Yet we were two down and three to play – and of those three remaining Tests, one was in Georgetown, British Guiana, which could provide one of the best batting pitches in the world, and another was on the jute matting of Queen's Park in Trinidad, on which a draw was considered almost inevitable.

There was certainly a chance that the weather might affect the conditions in Georgetown, but as we flew just off the coast of Venezuela to British Guiana the odds against our saving the series must have been colossal.

In Georgetown we beat British Guiana by an innings without doing anything to raise hopes dramatically. Moreover, there was a difference of opinion between one of the umpires and Fred Trueman in the colony match, which did not help, and an objection laid by Len Hutton to those umpires who were due to stand in the Test match. In those days umpires did not travel about. Each island or colony provided the umpires for the Test which it staged. In this case the British Guiana Board agreed to replace the two.

The colony match produced rather conflicting evidence. On the first morning Len Hutton, Denis Compton and I were all out to the new ball which moved about briefly. We thus missed the opportunity of batting on a superb pitch. Willie Watson and Tom Graveney took their chance and made over 200 each, putting on 402 for the fourth wicket.

Satisfactory as this was, it suggested that the best West Indian batsmen would find conditions greatly to their taste in the Test match. It was significant that Bob Christiani, British Guiana's only batsman approaching Test class, made 75 and 82 with ease. On the strength of these innings he played in the Test.

Georgetown, at the mouth of the Demerara River, is subjected to tropical deluges, and as the ground is below sea level the pitch, normally flawless, can sometimes be very different. I am sure that most people considered that we needed a lot of timely help from nature if we were to bowl West Indies out twice on it. On the other hand, Godfrey Evans, with whom I shared a room at the Tower Hotel, was always confident when we discussed the match, which was only occasionally. Our waking hours did not often coincide.

At last Len won the toss but we made only 153 for 2 on the first day. The ball was not coming onto the bat and perhaps that weighed more than it should on a side short of confidence after recent failures. Storms the day before had left the outfield slow. But although Len batted through the day for 84 and Denis Compton played soundly with him later in the day, it was not a very healthy output from 106 overs.

My own contribution was meagre. I was still trying to work the pitch out when I thought that I detected a friendly long hop from Denis Atkinson. I hooked, missed and was lbw.

The second day's play was an improvement as Len played very well to make 169. Denis Compton shared in a third-wicket stand of 150 with him, the later batsmen nearly all did their stuff and on the third morning we finished with a total of 435.

One of the penalties of fielding for a long time – and West Indies had fielded for 221 overs – is that it can take its toll in injuries. Holt had pulled a muscle and Jeff Stollmeyer took Frank Worrell in with him. In fifty minutes before lunch both of them and, to our special delight, Walcott were out in a marvellous piece of bowling by Statham. Having begun with a wide, he had Worrell caught at the wicket next ball. In his third over he moved a ball away from Stollmeyer to have him caught at the wicket and in his next, as Walcott tried to drive, he bowled him off the inside edge. Such can be the rewards for bowling a full length.

The joy of having West Indies on the run was swiftly damped. It began to rain during lunch and there was no more play that day. We resumed on the fourth morning not quite knowing what was in store. It turned out to be an eventful day in various ways.

Weekes and the local hero Christiani made a steady start but Christiani was out before lunch to a fine diving catch by Willie Watson at midwicket off a firmly hit on drive. Christiani waited for the umpire's decision, which in the light of later events may have been unwise.

Gomez stayed while Everton Weekes confidently approached 100 and West Indies seemed to be easing out of trouble. Then Gomez played on to Statham and suddenly they were collapsing again. Tony Lock unexpectedly turned a ball to bowl Weekes and then took a left-handed return catch from Atkinson which seemed to come off the middle of the bat. West Indies were then 139 for 7.

At this point things began to go wrong. We had given the left-handed McWatt a lot of lives in Jamaica and he had made only a few runs here when Denis Compton dropped him at second slip off Statham. Subsequently Denis held some very good close catches but generally at this stage in his career he was not allowed in the slips in Test matches if it could be avoided. Here he was deputizing for Bailey who had broken a finger. If held, that catch would have made it 141 for 8 with just Ramadhin and Valentine to come. As it was, McWatt shared in a stand with Holt which added 99 before it had an ending which has filled one of the grimmer pages of cricket history. Realizing that they might be looking for a second run to bring up the 100 partnership, I raced in, picked up and threw in to Godfrey Evans as fast as I ever did in my life. McWatt was yards out. He kept on running and Ramadhin replaced him.

Ramadhin was about to take guard when scuffling broke out in a stand behind square leg and dozens of bottles were hurled towards the square leg umpire who had given McWatt out. McWatt, of course, was from British Guiana. The bottle-throwing spread, the noise increased and the game was stopped.

To the young reader of today accustomed to seeing violence in sporting arenas on television, this may not seem very remarkable. But its impact at the time was immense. Riots on cricket grounds were unknown in modern times. It seemed a calamity that such a thing should happen in a Test match and a variety of reasons were put forward – drink, disruption for political ends and dissatisfaction with umpiring decisions which was all the greater in an excitable part of the world where they love to bet on cricket, for example on a 100 partnership.

Mounted police moved in on the scene of the disorder and after a discussion with officials Len decided that we should stay on the field, which turned out to be one of the most popular things we did on the tour. Our immediate reward was the wicket of Ramadhin, bowled in the last over by Laker.

I am quite sure that the betting on the 100 stand was at the heart of the trouble and that two previous incidents had stirred the crowd up. The first was the decision against Christiani. The second was the bowling of Weekes by Lock. A bail fell forward and a section of the crowd decided that Godfrey Evans had kicked it off.

What with this riot and the eighth-wicket resistance of Holt and McWatt, the fourth day had been a disappointment. But the follow-on in those days was enforceable with only a 150-run lead and early on the fifth morning they started their second innings 184 runs behind. After a Sunday's rest, all was quiet.

Holt, who had been 48 not out at the end of the first innings, went in first this time, still with his runner, and he and Stollmeyer made 79 in a way that did not hold out much hope for our chances of winning. But Compton, at leg slip to Laker, held a brilliant low catch from Stollmeyer and from then on batsmen came and went with gratifying frequency.

The catches stuck. Trevor Bailey, bowling despite the broken finger on his right hand, took 2 wickets. And the fifth day ended with the three Ws all gone, Gomez and Atkinson batting and West Indies, with six out, only 21 ahead. Since Statham's spell the West Indian batsmen had looked rather less than the all-conquering giants of the past month. For our part, we were doubtless encouraged by success to bowl and field better.

By lunch on the last day Wardle and Statham had finished the innings off. Here and in the final Test Wardle was to prove very useful with the chinaman and googly which he had not long been bowling.

We needed only 73 to win and Len, having been on the field almost throughout the match, sent in the youthful Graveney and May. I had not previously opened in first-class cricket but it seemed a good time to do so and for the first two overs while we made 18 runs I enjoyed it. I then ran into a shooter from Denis Atkinson and it was left to Willie Watson to make the remaining runs with Tom Graveney.

The crowd seemed to take it well. We took it even better and left Georgetown with real hope that the tide had turned.

My brief appearance as an opening batsman had not been without significance, for the tour selectors were thinking of returning Watson to his normal place farther down the order and were in search of another opener. Thus in the match against Trinidad at Port of Spain I went in first with Ken Suttle. The experiment of lowering Willie Watson in the order worked all right. He made 141. But, batting at number three, he still had to face the second ball of the innings. The first, a swinging yorker, had been too much for me.

The selectors had a better idea in the second innings when they sent in Trevor Bailey, who made 90. Denis Compton made 90 not out and we won by 7 wickets. We had thus beaten all four colony sides – Jamaica, Barbados, British Guiana and Trinidad – and we were the first side to beat Trinidad on their jute matting since M C C in 1930.

It was a good game on the mat. If you saw the ball spinning, you knew it would turn. Ian Peebles used to say that cricket on the mat was the best game of all.

This win did not alter the general view that a draw was the almost inevitable outcome of the Test match. The bounce of the matting was so wonderfully consistent that once players of the class of the three Ws established themselves they were almost permanent fixtures. In fact, in West Indies' score of 681 for 8 the three of them made nearly 500 runs.

We were still very much aware of the need to control emotions on the field but in conditions such as those in Trinidad, where a batsman wrongly given not out may go for another day without offering a chance, some players are sorely tried to remain impassive. Just before lunch on the first day there occurred the sort of incident which a fielding side accepts philosophically if confidence in the umpiring exists but which otherwise may strain self-control to the limits.

Holt had not previously played Denis Compton with much confidence. He did not seem to be able to pick the googly and Len brought on Denis for his benefit. In fact, Denis promptly took a good return catch when Stollmeyer tried to drive him. By the time that Everton Weekes had come in and taken a single, it was certain that this would be the last over before lunch. For the last ball Denis gave Holt a rather enticing half-volley. Holt played at it, it was the googly, and he edged it up to be comfortably caught by Tom Graveney at slip about waist high.

This seemed to be a highly satisfactory conclusion to the morning's play but to our surprise Holt, after starting to move off, stopped and looked at Ellis Achong, the umpire.

'Come on, give him out, Ellis', said Denis. 'He's waiting.' To his amazement Achong said it was not out. It had been a bump ball. Denis said something to the effect that bump balls must be different in Trinidad from anywhere else and went in to lunch. These exchanges had been no more than often take place without exciting notice but unfortunately at the other end Graveney, who had seen the ball right off the bat, threw it down in frustration and disbelief.

This action, which Tom, not normally demonstrative, undoubtedly regretted, was recalled for many years afterwards as evidence of unsporting behaviour and I have still heard it referred to as such in an age when, alas, countless more robust and offensive gestures are being made. The best thing about it was that it was a reminder of the need for irreproachable conduct on the field.

The size of the West Indies score was no surprise. The big disappointment was that Brian Statham, who was being kept for Test matches, pulled a muscle in the ribs on the first morning badly enough to finish him for the tour.

When we went in, needing 532 to avoid the follow-on, the main danger seemed to be a poor start as a result of weariness induced by two and a half days in the field. The opening stand of 73 by Hutton and Bailey put the worst fears at rest before Len, fending off a short ball from King, was caught at short leg and I went in. For the rest of that evening our main problems came from the little Trinidadian leg-spinner, Ferguson, who had the reputation of being able to turn the ball a lot off the mat.

We were held up for forty-five minutes next morning for, to me, unique reasons. Frank King's studs had apparently gone through the mat and roughened the mixture of sand and clay underneath. This was repaired but was still wet when the mat was due to be relaid and we had to wait. Without adding a run, Trevor produced the forward defensive stroke which he played with such relish and regularity but this time Ferguson turned the leg break enough to have him caught at slip.

Denis Compton came in and played very well from the start. It would be misleading to categorize him as a brilliant player of spin because he played all types of bowling equally well but I remember being fascinated that morning by the masterly way in which he handled Ferguson. If given further encouragement after his early success, Ferguson might have changed the picture.

Thus began a stand between Denis and myself which lasted until after tea adding 166. We made 134 of these between lunch and tea. I always had the happiest relationship with Denis and I remember how unselfish he was on this occasion, letting me have all the bowling he could when he saw things going well for me. For those who are nowadays led to believe that his running between wickets presented a permanent hazard for his partners, I should say that here we had a most harmonious understanding.

I had passed 100 by tea but was out for 135. Having hit King through the covers once, I tried again and was caught at cover point.

I was upset about getting out, for there were so many runs to be made on that pitch. I was even more upset when as a result West Indies rather took control for the rest of the day. King became very fast and lively and Willie Watson had a difficult time before he was miraculously caught by Denis Atkinson at square leg when hooking Walcott. Compton played very responsibly and, although we still needed 200 to avoid the follow-on, the runs were eventually scored after the weekend. Denis made 133, Tom Graveney 92 and late on the fifth evening our last pair of Trueman and Statham put us out of danger and made the last day's play relaxed and of little importance.

Before the last Test in Jamaica six days later we had a two-day match in Montego Bay, which was largely washed out by rain, and a lot of problems with injuries. Statham was clearly not to be considered. Laker, who had been hit in the eye in Trinidad, was still not a thing of beauty. Evans, ill in Trinidad where Dick Spooner had kept well in his place, now had a chipped finger, and Willie Watson needed stitches over the eye after being hit on the wet pitch in Montego Bay. In the end, all except Statham were fit – just.

West Indies had Alf Valentine unfit and replaced him with a seventeen-year-old boy, Garfield Sobers, who had batted quite well against us in Barbados and had bowled a lot of overs of orthodox left-arm spin.

In the First Test in Jamaica we had clearly erred in leaving out Jim Laker and in relying on four fast bowlers and Lock. The general opinion now was that it would again be a good toss to win and that the ball might turn a little later. Thus Laker and Wardle replaced Statham and Moss from that first side. This meant that Trevor Bailey would open the bowling as well as the batting but, as he took the new ball on the first morning when West Indies batted after winning the toss, he can have had no idea that he was, as it were, in the first minutes of his finest hour.

If one looks at the scores and sees that West Indies were bowled out for 139, Bailey 7 for 34, the assumption is that the pitch had an early greenness and perhaps the ball swung more than usual. This would be a considerable exaggeration. It was a good pitch. Luck certainly played a part in that a lot of catches went to hand but the main factor was a superb, supremely accurate piece of bowling that used everything in the way of movement offered by atmosphere and pitch. Trevor was, of course, a highly intelligent and thoughtful bowler.

Bailey was well supported by Fred Trueman who had not had a great tour in various ways. I thought that a lot of the publicity given to his behaviour was a bit unfair. He was a young man with an extrovert character, probably not strong on manners or etiquette, but he was too readily given the label of bad boy.

Trevor's fifth ball had Holt beautifully caught by Lock at short leg. He had Everton Weekes in trouble before, in his third over, he brought a ball back to bowl him off the inside edge. Two overs later he had Stollmeyer caught at the wicket, and when Frank Worrell turned a lifting ball from Trueman to short leg the scoreboard showed an unbelievable 13 for 4.

There we stuck for a time. Walcott and Atkinson were still there at lunch and it was well into the afternoon before Trevor had Atkinson lbw and Gerry Gomez caught at third slip. The score was only 75 for 6 but Clyde Walcott was such an imposing batsman in those days that we were always afraid that he might recover the initiative and turn the match. By a great piece of luck, however, he misjudged a shortish ball from Lock and gave a catch to an isolated mid-on.

At this point, 110 for 7, Gary Sobers came in to play his first Test innings, in which he was undefeated. He was soon interrupted by a drizzle which came down from the hills and led to an extended tea interval, but when play started again Bailey and Trueman, despite a wet ball, took the last 3 wickets in half an hour.

This left us with half an hour's batting but no West Indian bowler was going to spoil Trevor's day and he and Len Hutton came through it safely.

They did equally well next morning when King bowled very short, mostly to Bailey, on a pitch which had been under covers for much of the early morning because of light rain. In the afternoon, when we badly needed to raise the pace if we were to avoid losing the initiative, Trevor was caught at the wicket – cutting in Sobers's first spell in Test cricket. The score was still only 43 when I came in and was grateful to receive first ball a half-volley which went nicely through the covers.

Sobers was then an orthodox left-arm slow bowler who had the action and the control to become a high-class performer, so we thought. My own problems, however, were mainly with King, who was hard to score off because he bowled so short and fast, and with Walcott, who always had to be watched carefully for his variations of medium pace.

I drove Sobers straight for 6 and was becoming rather pleased with the speed with which we were approaching West Indies' score with only one wicket down. Moreover, I had temporarily removed Walcott from the attack when he damaged a finger trying to stop a well-middled drive and had to retire for repairs.

At this point Ramadhin bowled me a wide one. I drove it very hard through the covers – or so I thought – but Bruce Pairaudeau, fielding for Walcott, dived and brought off a wonderful catch. This was heart-breaking because I was playing well and felt that I was taking some of the pressure off Len.

Much the same happened to Denis Compton. He came in full of strokes and was going very well when King, with the new ball, bowled him a short one. It bounced very high but as Denis moved inside and under it, he lost his balance and fell, bumping his head on the hard pitch. In falling, he flicked a bail off with his pad and was out hit wicket.

I have mentioned the burden on Len. It was already a heavy one, and when Watson and Graveney were both out that evening after Denis, Len was entitled to think that the salvation of the tour rested on him alone. We were only 55 runs ahead, had lost 5 wickets, had to bat last on a pitch which might be increasingly helpful to the West Indian spinners. None of our later batsmen was completely useless but we had some ugly collapses to our name in the series and Len must have wondered what support would be forthcoming this time. He himself had reached 93 at the end of that second day.

In fact, the later batsmen, especially Evans and Wardle, did him proud. There was one difference that was a help to them and to Len. They did not have to evade bumpers from King, for he had strained a muscle in the thigh on the previous evening and did not bowl again in the innings. But the heat and humidity were intense – we were now into April – and it was a great physical as well as technical achievement for Len to bat through until after tea.

Godfrey Evans defended doggedly through the morning but after lunch both he and Len raised the pace and Wardle raised it even higher with one of those whirling left-hander's innings which by conventional and other means defeats the best-set fields. Len was out immediately after tea, caught at the wicket for 205, but he had ensured a lead of over 250.

When he came in to a great ovation at tea, drained from his long hours of concentration in the heat, he scarcely noticed one member offering even heartier congratulations than the others. He pushed his way through the crowd, acknowledging the general applause but still far too absorbed in his innings for the identity of individuals to sink in. It was only later that he found himself accused of having ignored and insulted Mr Alexander Bustamante, the Chief Minister of Jamaica.

This always seemed to be a particularly unfair charge unless it is part of a captain's job to be prepared for diplomatic exchanges at all times. It was probably one of the reasons why, within fourteen months of this innings, Len had given up the captaincy and retired from Test cricket.

We took no wicket in the last half-hour that night and only 4 wickets next day, the fourth day. But they were good ones, three of them taken by Trueman who had his best bowl of the tour. He might well have had Walcott, too, but soon after he came in I lost a high hook in the sun at long leg. As it was, Walcott was 50 not out that night and went on confidently next day.

Gomez was fifth out in the morning but Atkinson made an active partner for Walcott and lasted until the arrears of 275 were almost cleared off. Wardle, a deepish extra cover, held a marvellous catch from McWatt but still Walcott went on, past 100 by now and troubled only by a wrist injury. The pitch was lasting well and this was only the fifth day, so we had no real cause for worry, but there are always fears that a victory which means so much may somehow be snatched away and we breathed a sigh of relief when Clyde Walcott did not quite get to the pitch of a ball from Laker and was caught at slip.

We had to work hard to take the last 2 wickets that Saturday afternoon, for the young Sobers played comfortably at one end and Ramadhin and King held out for long periods at the other. Eventually Lock, through a catch by Compton at leg slip, earned the distinction, as it proved, of being the first bowler to take Sobers's wicket in Test cricket and the innings ended.

By now, however, a problem had arisen with the clock. We had to make 72 and only about seventy minutes remained for play that day. The great fear, of course, was that we might be deprived of victory by a tropical storm on Monday. But who wanted to come back on Monday morning to make the few runs still needed in anticlimax and an empty ground?

I was selected with Tom Graveney to go out and finish the match in haste. We had an early mishap when Tom was well and truly yorked by King, but Willie Watson and I sailed into the attack. We finished the job with ten minutes to spare.

As we ploughed back towards Avonmouth I had plenty of time to reflect on the good and bad things of what had in many ways been an imperfect tour. I rather think that relief and the satisfaction gleaned from fighting back were the predominant emotions.

6
To Australia – with Success

It was inevitable that the series against Pakistan in 1954 would be widely considered as a trial for the coming winter in Australia. Pakistan were making their first visit to England, and although they had players of the class of Fazal, Hanif and Imtiaz it was hard to believe that they would be a strong enough side to master English conditions.

In fact, the conditions were often English at their worst. It was teatime on the fourth day before the First Test at Lord's could start. The weather was better for the Second Test at Trent Bridge in which Denis Compton made his 278 but we won a one-sided contest by an innings.

At this time in his career Denis had neither the taste nor the physical fitness for a long innings when it was not needed and after he reached 100 he ran through his full repertoire of brilliant strokes without caring whether he was out or not.

He had, in fact, other matters on his mind besides adding to an already large England score. As he left the dressing room after lunch he asked me to keep him informed of the progress of Jaroslav Drobny in that afternoon's Wimbledon final in which Denis had a financial interest. When Drobny won a set, I went onto the balcony and between overs gave Denis the thumbs-up sign. The strokes proliferated. I was interested to read in the next day's papers that Compton had accelerated in response to a signal from the dressing room.

It rained again at Old Trafford at the wrong time for Pakistan and they had followed on a huge number of runs behind when the last two days' play was washed out.

Thus by the time that the Fourth and last Test was played at the Oval, the apparent inability of Pakistan to give England a game in English conditions had deepened the impression that the series was above all preparation for Australia.

During the fortnight between the last two Tests the team for Australia was chosen. It was not an easy one to pick and there were some notable omissions in Laker, Lock and Trueman. Yet it was to prove an inspired piece of selection in that two of the new players chosen, Tyson and Cowdrey, were to play major parts in the winter's series.

Unfortunately the selectors were so absorbed in picking the touring team that they forgot almost to the end that they also had to pick a team for the Oval Test. As they were making off to catch their trains, therefore, it was hurriedly decided to include in the twelve, for experience, the three members of the touring party, Tyson, Loader and Cowdrey, who had not previously played in a Test match. Colin Cowdrey, in fact, became twelfth man.

This would probably have worked perfectly satisfactorily on most pitches. Not at the Oval. It meant that Alec Bedser was left out on the ground where he had bowled so well for so long. So was Trevor Bailey, who usually bowled well at the Oval and whose absence left the side with Godfrey Evans at number six and a long tail behind him. Laker, Lock and Trueman, who had bowled Australia out at the Oval a year before, were not in, as they were not in the touring party.

To the sense of unreality which this created was added the fact that Len Hutton had been kept out of the two previous Tests by injury. David Sheppard had been captain. On his return Len's thoughts not surprisingly were more on the coming tour than on a series in which he had had little part – less than a day and half's play – and which in any case seemed to be more or less wrapped up.

Thus the approach to the final Test of 1954 was unlike any I knew before or after, the very opposite to that of 1953. It was, as it proved, dangerously relaxed. I can remember the bemused look on Colin Cowdrey's face as he experienced for the first time the (quite untypical) dressing room atmosphere of a Test match.

Nothing occurred on the first day to suggest that England were in for a nasty shock. Rain delayed the start until after lunch and Pakistan, in fearful trouble against Statham, Tyson and Loader, were soon 51 for 7. The last 2 wickets added 56 but the Pakistan total of 133 seemed a meagre one.

Next day a cloudburst swamped the ground, and when we batted on the third day the going was transformed. The ball lifted from a length and Fazal and Mahmood Hussain bowled us out for 130. Not all the catches were held but Denis Compton, who played with great skill to make 53, and I were the only batsmen to exceed 20.

The pitch was drying out when Pakistan batted again and it was here that we missed the expertise and local knowledge of Laker, Lock and Bedser. Wardle bowled well enough in his orthodox method and took 7 wickets but Pakistan should not have been allowed to reach 164, especially after being 82 for 8.

Even then, midway through the fourth day, the extent of our task against a bowler of Fazal's class was not fully appreciated and we started with some idea of finishing the match that evening. We would have needed 168 at about a run a minute.

I remember playing a lot of strokes and making a quick 50 before I was caught off Fazal at mid-off. I was very disappointed in my stroke. With so few batsmen to come it was irresponsible.

We then needed 59 to win from 7 wickets but only half an hour remained that night and I was greatly surprised to be passed as I came in by Godfrey Evans, promoted, so it seemed, to finish it off that evening. Of course, the worst happened. Godfrey, Tom Graveney and then Denis Compton, who had again been playing well, were all out in the last half-hour and there was no recovery next day against Fazal and a Pakistan side uplifted by exceeding their wildest hopes. Fazal was a marvellous bowler in these conditions and, moving the ball in the air and a lot off the pitch at a brisk medium pace, he took 12 wickets in the match. Pakistan won by 24 runs. Good luck to them – but it should never have happened.

When the team for Australia had been announced, I had not heard that I had been appointed vice-captain to Len Hutton. Somebody congratulated me on it that night but I had to wait for confirmation until I saw next morning's papers.

I was genuinely surprised. I was only twenty-four, and although I had played in all or part of five series I looked on myself as one of the junior members of the side. I had imagined that Trevor Bailey was being groomed as Len's successor but it may be that, as a thirty-year-old bowler in an era of several other good bowlers, his expectancy of life in Test cricket, despite his batting, was not considered all that great. No one, of course, foresaw that this would be Len's last series.

We sailed on the *Orsova* in mid-September. I found the three-week voyage immensely interesting with its stops at Gibraltar, Naples, where Len and the other Yorkshiremen visited Hedley Verity's grave, Port Said, Aden and Colombo. The ship was slightly behind time and we fitted in only four hours' cricket in Colombo. On the whole, I believe that sailing to Australia, when it could be done in three weeks, was a good thing. It gave players a rest after a strenuous season and it helped them to get to know each other. Only in the third week from Colombo to Fremantle did I become impatient to start the cricket.

I had always heard that Perth, after the first hour, provided the best and often the fastest pitches in the world. It was not hard to acclimatize in those conditions but one always had to be prepared for the greater bounce. For example, the long hop from the leg-spinner would bounce rather more than expected and would hit the bat high up with undesirable results. But the light was much brighter than in England and we found that we threw the ball farther in the clear air.

I took over the captaincy of an M C C side abroad for the first time halfway through the first first-class match against Western Australia. Statham, Bailey and Loader had bowled them out cheaply on a greenish pitch after which Len set the tone for our batting with one of his most cultured innings. Unfortunately he had to retire when 145 with a pulled muscle and I was left to direct operations in the second innings when Western Australia offered rather more resistance, especially in a fourth-wicket stand between Meuleman and Carmody. This was broken by Jim McConnon.

Nowadays we have become accustomed to off-spinners doing pretty well in Australia but I had it on no less an authority than Ian Peebles, that great student of spin bowling, that McConnon was the first slow off-break bowler whom England had sent to Australia this century. Bob Appleyard, who was also in the side, was of brisker pace and not solely an off-spinner. He could take the new ball if necessary, and with his high action achieved more bounce than most.

For Peter Loader, his wickets in this match must have a special significance, for they were the first taken in a city which he was to make his home when he retired from cricket.

We beat Western Australia, who had not lost to M C C since 1929, and in the other match in Perth we beat a Combined XI (Western Australia reinforced by Harvey, Hole and Ian Johnson) by an innings. I won the toss and, as Len had done in the first match, put them in. It was not such an obvious decision as in the first match, for there was less damp in the pitch, but our bowlers had them out for 86. I had double cause to be pleased as I made 100, savouring for the first time the delights of getting in on a good Australian pitch.

When we left Perth, there was still a month to go before the First Test in Brisbane. It was a month in which things went encouragingly for us, though we beat only South Australia and that narrowly. That was the match in which Denis Compton, delayed in England by treatment on his knee and delayed again by a most agonizing emergency landing in Karachi, elected to play on the morning after arriving in Adelaide. He was not only short of sleep but of cricket equipment, for his cricket gear had been stolen from his car just before he left London. We won the toss and Denis made 113; the next highest score was Len's 37. He tired at the end of his innings but otherwise played with a mid-season serenity which anyone would have envied.

The bowling was reinforced in Melbourne by Alec Bedser, who had had a painful attack of shingles in Perth. The bowlers generally were working themselves into form, although New South Wales, a strong side, took nearly 400 off them in Sydney. Most of the batsmen made runs and Colin Cowdrey scored 100 in each innings on his first appearance on the Sydney cricket ground.

When it came to picking the team for the First Test, I would like to be able to record the thinking behind the decisions of the tour selection committee but, to the best of my recollection, we did not have one. I certainly do not remember sitting down at a table in deep discussion. I imagine that Len picked the teams after consulting those of us whom he thought might help.

The issues here were fairly straightforward. We had made plenty of runs but not many had come from number seven onwards. Len decided therefore to play six batsmen. Tom Graveney had had influenza and Vic Wilson had been out of form. This left us with Hutton, Simpson, Edrich, May, Compton and Cowdrey. Having added Bailey and Evans, Len had to settle on three bowlers, one for certain being Statham.

The choice of the other two was from Bedser, Tyson, Appleyard and Wardle, for McConnon was unfit and Loader had recently been less successful than the others. It was an acutely difficult choice because we had come to look on Alec Bedser as an essential member of any England side, one of the world's great bowlers. It was only eighteen months since he had taken 14 Australian wickets for 99 at Trent Bridge. Yet he was short of bowling – for once – and there was a well-founded doubt as to whether he had fully recovered from his shingles. He wanted to play – he always did – and in the end it was decided that he should. For the other bowler the choice was Tyson, for he was the fastest and we had just played Queensland at the Gabba on a fast pitch.

I must say that I was uneasy about omitting Appleyard, for whom I always had a high regard, especially as Denis Compton, our possible fifth bowler, had only bowled one over in public on the tour so far. Anyhow, once we had decided on six batsmen, we had little option in view of how the previous pitch had played.

The choice of four fast bowlers meant that we needed to bowl first. In the previous match Queensland had put us in and Lindwall and Archer had had us 18 for 3. Len won the toss and we duly put them in but it is extraordinary how the gods who regulate these matters frown on you, and no doubt rightly, when you have the temerity to go into a six-day match with only four bowlers.

First, those gods attended to the pitch which, although not dissimilar in appearance from its lively neighbour, proved very mild. Then, when the Australian innings was already making smooth progress, they prompted Denis Compton to run into the boundary fence, breaking a finger in his bowling hand. So departed not only a leading batsman but our possible fifth bowler and our only spinner. Before the match we had suffered another unwelcome blow when Godfrey Evans was laid low with a chill. His absence not only lengthened the tail but brought in a wicketkeeper, Keith Andrew, who had only once kept to Bedser before. The Bedser — Evans combination had over the years been one of England's great strengths.

The rest is history and not very palatable history for the English reader. Australia declared on reaching 600 and bowled us out twice to win by an innings and 154 runs. To rub it in, they took 8 wickets with the spin of Ian Johnson and Richie Benaud.

There were consolations in defeat. Trevor Bailey, 88 in the first innings, had fought it out stoutly, as had Bill Edrich in the second innings. Colin Cowdrey had played particularly well to make 40 in his first Test innings. The big disappointment had been the ineffectiveness of the bowlers, especially of Frank Tyson. One for 160 — what a prelude to a triumphant, indeed historic personal performance!

We had two and a half weeks in which to work it all out. The cricket in this period was pleasant but not greatly informative — a two-day match 500 miles up the Queensland coast at Rockhampton (Appleyard 9 wickets), a one-day match against the Prime Minister's XI in Canberra (May 101) and a drawn match against Victoria (May 105 not out, Cowdrey 79 and 54).

I was pleased about my runs and we were all delighted with the quality of Colin's batting, but the most significant event was Frank Tyson's 6 for 68 in Victoria's first innings, especially as his victims included the first four in the batting order, three of them bowled.

Very properly for a schoolmaster, Frank was not short of grey matter and was now experimenting with a much shortened run of under 20 yards. In a modern television or radio documentary the conversion from his previous long run, one of the decisive moves in Test cricket of that period, as it proved, would probably be dramatically depicted as the result of much brilliant thinking and long hours of practice. But a lot of history is made gradually and casually, not in one clear-cut moment of inspiration.

As I recall it, all that happened was that Frank expressed himself fed up with rushing in 40-odd yards in the heat, mentioned it to Len and one or two of the other bowlers, and tried bowling off a shorter run in the nets.

Here he had a problem, for nobody fancied batting against him in a net. He was so wild and so fast. He was incapable of bowling slowly. However, he practised a little, developed a shorter run which began with a sort of stutter, and found it some improvement. I only wish that fast bowlers of today would try it and that coaches at all levels would encourage them to try it. The immediate results of Frank's change were an increase in accuracy and only a slight decrease in pace, for although barely 6 feet, he was powerfully built around the chest and shoulders.

The problems of selection before the second Test in Sydney were clearer and in one respect more distasteful. Tom Graveney had been playing well and replaced Reg Simpson, another very good-looking player, who had seemed out of form against Victoria. Denis Compton was unfit but was not replaced by another batsman. Five had to be enough. Godfrey Evans was fit again. Of the bowlers, Statham and Tyson were certainties, as was Bailey, who was to open with Len Hutton. Obviously at Sydney we had to play two spinners, Appleyard and Wardle. Thus although Alec Bedser was included in the twelve, he was left out on the morning of the match.

This was one of those occasions when Len's shyness was a great handicap to him. He should have taken Alec aside, explained the decision, which was a rational one, and told him how sorry we all were that one who had done so much for England had to be left out. In fact, Alec had to look at the list to find his name was not there and was bitterly hurt.

The morning was humid and overcast, the pitch was not short of grass, but when Arthur Morris, a delightful man who had taken over the captaincy for that match from the injured Ian Johnson, put us in, we were not entirely apprehensive. We were not sure that the pitch would last. The immediate future, however, was likely to be fraught with difficulty against bowlers of the class of Lindwall, Archer, Davidson and Johnston. A leg injury prevented Miller from playing.

Nothing much happened until, after bowling three overs, Lindwall switched to the pavilion end, which gave him a wind from cover point. He at once produced an in-swinging yorker to bowl Bailey. I made a few runs off the right part of the bat and then glanced Archer to backward short leg. We were 19 for 2 and they had us out that evening for 154.

It was reasonable to suppose that the new ball would still swing, so Trevor Bailey was given it instead of Tyson and in the last over of the day had Morris caught at leg slip.

This was encouraging but the next morning's clear, fresh weather was not. Favell, always full of strokes and Burke, usually the opposite, set off at a depressingly brisk pace until both were caught at second slip off Bailey. By then the score had reached 100 but, although we did not know it, the first impact of Frank Tyson on the series was about to be felt.

He suddenly found a new rhythm in his shortened run-up and with it an extra yard of pace which the batsmen clearly did not appreciate. Harvey was caught off the splice, Hole was bowled by something near a full pitch and Australia were out with a lead of only 74. It was not a lot if the pitch began to deteriorate later on.

However, on the Monday morning the Australian lead was soon looking pretty useful, for just before lunch we were 55 for 3. I had gone in when Trevor Bailey was caught at the wicket off Archer and for a time Len Hutton and I played comfortably, Len indeed rather dashingly. But Bill Johnston had him caught in the gully off an untypical shot and three balls later had Tom Graveney caught at the wicket.

Apparently, as I had walked to the wicket, one knowledgeable observer had given his opinion that I was playing my last innings in Test cricket. He was told by some illustrious neighbours that he was being ridiculous and I am grateful to say that I did not let them down.

Some people always took longer than others to accept that an amateur from one of the universities could play at the top level and I did not look on this innings as marking a turning point in my career. I did make a profound statement to Colin Cowdrey as we walked out after lunch. 'If I had the chance to play the innings of my life,' I said to him, 'I would like to do it this afternoon.' But that was prompted by the thought that we were threatened with going two down in the series and would never be in greater need of runs.

Some say that Colin never played better than at the age of twenty-one and he made a splendid partner throughout that afternoon until inside the last half-hour of the day. I do not remember a mistake by either of us until Colin, temporarily bogged down by Richie Benaud, mis-hit a googly which probably turned less than he expected.

This was one of the occasions when I was delighted to see the small determined figure of W. J. Edrich advancing belligerently from the pavilion and we were both there at the end of the day, May 98 not out.

This very finely balanced match which meant so much to us took another nasty turn next morning when Bill and I had increased the lead to 148 with 6 wickets standing, a reasonably hopeful position. It was a dreary morning and I had no sooner made the 2 runs needed for the 100 than a drizzle stopped us. When we returned, Arthur Morris waited for the outfield to dry and then unleashed Lindwall with the new ball. He promptly bowled me with an in-swinging yorker. I was very cross with myself for getting out when we were moving towards a winning position.

Frank Tyson had once or twice batted promisingly on the tour but he must have been surprised to find himself at number seven for England. He soon ducked into a fast bumper from Lindwall and was hit on the back of the head. I can remember my own dismay as the escorting party helped the wounded warrior into the dressing room. To make matters

AUSTRALIA v. ENGLAND, Sydney
(Second Test, 1954–55)

England won by 38 runs

ENGLAND

†L. Hutton c Davidson b Johnston	30	–	c Benaud b Johnston		28
T. E. Bailey b Lindwall	0	–	c Langley b Archer		6
P. B. H. May c Johnston b Archer	5	–	b Lindwall		104
T. W. Graveney c Favell b Johnston	21	–	c Langley b Johnston		0
M. C. Cowdrey c Langley b Davidson	23	–	c Archer b Benaud		54
W. J. Edrich c Benaud b Archer	10	–	b Archer		29
F. H. Tyson b Lindwall	0	–	b Lindwall		9
*T. G. Evans c Langley b Archer	3	–	c Lindwall b Archer		4
J. H. Wardle c Burke b Johnston	35	–	lbw b Lindwall		8
R. Appleyard c Hole b Davidson	8	–	not out		19
J. B. Statham not out	14	–	c Langley b Johnston		25
L-b 5	5		L-b 6, n-b 4		10

1/14 2/19 3/58 4/63 5/84 6/85   154   1/18 2/55 3/55 4/171 5/222 296
7/88 8/99 9/111   6/232 7/239 8/249 9/250

Bowling: *First Innings* – Lindwall 17–3–47–2; Archer 12–7–12–3; Davidson 12–3–34–2; Johnston 13–3–56–3. *Second Innings* – Lindwall 31–10–69–3; Archer 22–9–53–3; Davidson 13–2–52–0; Johnston 19.3–2–70–3; Benaud 19–3–42–1.

AUSTRALIA

†A. R. Morris c Hutton b Bailey	12	–	lbw b Statham		10
L. Favell c Graveney b Bailey	26	–	c Edrich b Tyson		16
J. Burke c Graveney b Bailey	44	–	b Tyson		14
R. N. Harvey c Cowdrey b Tyson	12	–	not out		92
G. B. Hole b Tyson	12	–	b Tyson		0
R. Benaud lbw b Statham	20	–	c Tyson b Appleyard		15
R. G. Archer c Hutton b Tyson	49	–	b Tyson		8
A. K. Davidson b Statham	20	–	c Evans b Statham		0
R. R. Lindwall c Evans b Tyson	19	–	b Tyson		1
*G. R. Langley b Bailey	5	–	b Statham		6
W. A. Johnston not out	0	–	c Evans b Tyson		12
B 5, l-b 2, n-b 2	9		L-b 7, n-b 3		10

1/18 2/65 3/100 4/105 5/122 6/141   228   1/27 2/34 3/77 4/77 5/106 184
7/193 8/213 9/224   6/122 7/127 8/136 9/145

Bowling: *First Innings* – Statham 18–1–83–2; Bailey 17.4–3–59–4; Tyson 13–2–45–4; Appleyard 7–1–32–0. *Second Innings* – Statham 19–6–45–3; Bailey 6–0–21–0; Tyson 18.4–1–85–6; Appleyard 6–1–12–1; Wardle 4–2–11–0.

Umpires: M. J. McInnes and R. Wright

The tide turns. My first hundred against Australia and Frank Tyson's first destruction of the Australian batting

worse, Bill Edrich was out before lunch in a maddening way, trying to remove the bat but touching the ball onto the stumps off the under edge.

There was no immediate improvement after lunch except that Tyson proved to be splendidly resilient and went out to bat again when Godfrey Evans was out. He did nothing to stem the collapse, but the last-wicket partnership of Appleyard and Statham added 46 runs and greatly complicated Australia's task. They now needed 223.

By that evening they had made 72 for 2, which left the match still open. Statham and Tyson had taken a wicket apiece but from soon after tea Jimmy Burke and Neil Harvey had dug in. Harvey's first innings and the start to his second had raised some hope that he was finding Tyson too fast for him but next day he played beautifully. Fortunately his partners from the start were in trouble against Tyson who, of course, owed much to Statham's pace and accuracy at the other end.

I wish that some modern bowlers of all countries could have seen Frank Tyson as he bowled in that series. There was no hint of intimidation. I remember only the occasional short ball. He bowled very, very fast and he pitched the ball up.

His first wicket on the last day in Sydney was typical of quite a few. His pace was such that the full pitch could be past the batsman before he knew it and Burke was bowled by what one might at least call a very full yorker. Five wickets were down by lunch and a renewed onslaught by Tyson and Statham took 4 more soon afterwards. With Australia still needing 78 we were on the brink of victory with only Bill Johnston to remove.

Harvey then began to attack in earnest. He was one of the very best batsmen I played against, like a ballet dancer on his feet to the slower bowlers, and, of course, a magnificent fielder first in the covers, later at slip.

Len was forced onto the defensive and a widespread field did not exactly show off our fielding at its best. There were not many agile athletes among us. Bill Johnston, whose batting was normally a source of amusement, kept out the relatively few balls which he had to face and made a few runs off Tyson with a sort of one-handed wave. He played him with a fine disdain as if he did not merit the use of two hands. They made half the 78 needed and, with the fast bowlers running out of steam and Harvey playing brilliantly, things were beginning to look serious when Johnston flicked at Tyson once again and Godfrey Evans took the catch down the leg side. I was at long leg and saw it off the bat. It was a glorious moment. The relief and joy of it come surging back as I think of it now.

Tyson had taken 10 wickets in the match, Statham 5. They had beaten so many batsmen by their sheer pace through the air that there seemed no reason why they should not also be effective on slower pitches, but we spent Christmas in a state of uncertainty as well as hope. The memory of our heavy defeat in Brisbane made it still a little hard to believe that we were level in the series.

We played a three-day match in Newcastle against New South Wales which established that Denis Compton was fit again. I captained the operation and, batting at number six, made my fourth 100 in successive matches. It was a good pitch, there were good players in the opposition and I realize now, even if I did not then, how lucky I was to have an attack of Bedser, Loader, Wardle and Appleyard to launch at them. The minor matches on a tour can be discouraging and frustrating with a half-strength attack. We won this one by 9 wickets.

So on New Year's Eve we started the Third Test with qualified optimism and with Denis Compton back. Bill Edrich was opening again with Len. After an unproductive start to the tour, Bill had batted well in both Tests.

The first day was an undoubted let down, being too much like the first day in Sydney for English tastes. First, Len had to take the decision to leave out Alec Bedser again, a particular blow to Alec, who had always bowled so well on the Melbourne Cricket Ground. The reasoning was simply that Len thought, rightly as it proved, that the pitch was drier than it looked with its covering of rolled grass cuttings and that we needed two spinners. The differences from Sydney were that this time Len chose to bat and that Keith Miller was back in the Australian side.

We knew that the pitch might be lively early on but I certainly was not prepared for the ball from Lindwall which lifted steeply from a good length and lobbed up off the glove and handle into the gully. It was my twenty-fifth birthday and I did not think much of this as a present.

Some batsmen can walk away after making nought with head up, making it look like a triumph. Keith Miller's demeanour almost invariably suggested that the bowler had made a grave mistake. I like to think that I used to look no more than ordinarily disconsolate but on this occasion I was halfway back on the long walk to the Melbourne pavilion when a surge of depression overcame me. What a birthday, I thought. My head dropped and I glared miserably at the ground. When I looked up, I had missed the pavilion gate by 10 yards. Loud cheers from the huge crowd.

Miller had already had Bill Edrich caught at short leg and he then surprised Len Hutton with an out-swinger which had him caught at first slip. The score became 41 for 4 when he produced a ball to Denis Compton which, like mine, kicked off a full length with similar results, except that this time it sent Denis back to hospital with what happily turned out to be only a badly bruised thumb.

Keith Miller's bowling had its great moments such as this because it fell into no particular pattern. It was unpredictable, especially in its variations of pace. He did not always bowl off the same mark but rather when the mood took him. He was immensely strong and supple as well.

Colin Cowdrey had come in when I was out and he proceeded to play an innings which was as valuable and technically excellent as any in the long career to come. He played fast bowling wonderfully well even then, and was, of course, summoned to Australia to confront rampant fast bowlers no less than twenty years later.

Trevor Bailey was an ideal supporting partner, Godfrey Evans played better than for some time and Colin reached a memorable first Test 100 before he was out for 102 in anticlimax, playing no stroke to an off break from Johnson which turned sharply. It was a remarkable innings to have played out of a total of 191.

The next day our doubts about the pitch were handsomely justified. The ball began to go through at varying heights; when it keeps low for bowlers of the pace of Tyson and Statham, the batsmen have problems.

It is sometimes forgotten how useful Bob Appleyard was on that tour in support of Tyson and Statham. He was an unusual type of medium-paced off-spinner, immensely accurate, so accurate that when he did occasionally offer the loose ball, batsmen frequently misjudged it in their excitement. He told me of Emmott Robinson's words to him: 'Concentrate on five good balls an over and the sixth mustn't be a bad 'un!' On this occasion he came on when the fast bowlers were halted after lunch and bowled Harvey, who had seemed the main danger.

Bob was a determined competitor off the field as well as on, for he had to contend with a long illness at the peak of his cricketing career. It was no surprise that he later made a success in the business world.

The spinners also removed Benaud and Archer. Statham bowled Lindwall and with an hour to go on that Saturday evening Australia were 151 for 8. There we stuck against two Victorians, Maddocks and Johnson, who had nearly reached our score by the close of play.

The events of that weekend have gone down in cricket history as one of its great unsolved mysteries. It had been a baking weekend with a hot dry wind blowing off the interior of the continent. Yet when we looked at the pitch on the Monday morning it had become so damp that spikemarks could be seen on it.

It was impossible to believe that in that weather the pitch would have sweated to that extent. One theory was that an underground spring had suddenly started flowing out! No official explanations were ever forthcoming that I heard. Inquiries were held and the Melbourne Cricket Club announced later in the match that the pitch had definitely not been watered. The local newspapers said it had. It was widely assumed that the new curator, not knowing much about the cracks which were wont to form on this particular ground, had become alarmed, had tried to treat them and had overdone it. Both sides accepted the situation and the match proceeded.

Happily, it made little difference and if anyone suffered it was not us. Admittedly the pitch played rather more easily on the Monday morning and by the time Statham had taken the last 2 wickets, Australia had a first-innings lead of 40. But we batted in better conditions in the second innings than they did.

Hutton and Edrich had cleared off the arrears when I went in in mid-afternoon against Bill Johnston, who was bowling in his slower vein as a left-arm spinner. The fear of the ball which kept low was always there but at this stage the ball was coming nicely onto the bat and I found driving held no problems. Len Hutton, not in great form at this time, was out and Colin Cowdrey was scarcely recognizable as the majestic player of the first innings, being well and truly tied down by Benaud. But Compton, despite his damaged thumb, stuck it out to the end of the day when we led by 119 with 7 wickets standing.

Our tail at that time was of unpredictable length – on paper not worth many runs on recent form but capable on a good day of something far better. We usually had to prepare for the worst.

Next morning I was soon out for 91, bowled pushing forward to a ball from Johnston which turned. Denis followed, but Trevor Bailey, at his most defiant and least productive, stuck it out to the end while Evans and especially Wardle made more robust contributions at the other end.

So far the shape of the match had been remarkably similar to that of the previous one in Sydney. This time Australia needed 240 and on the fourth evening were placed, much as at Sydney, at 75 for 2.

The difference came next day. On the evidence of Appleyard's four overs on the previous evening there was speculation in the press that he would be the key bowler. In fact, Len opened with Tyson and Statham, the ball from time to time kept low, and by lunch Australia were out for 111, Tyson 7 for 27. He was too fast for them. This time the margin was 128 runs. I fielded in the slips in that match and Frank's pace was such that I would not have backed myself to hang on to anything snicked at me.

Highly elated though we were by finding ourselves 2-1 up in the series with two to play, we had plenty to stop us from becoming complacent. Amongst other things the management had to settle the disposition of forces over the next fortnight.

The management, I should say, was almost entirely Geoffrey Howard, except in strictly cricketing matters. Helpful and unruffled he made the whole thing work. He had no assistant manager, no accountant, although he did have George Duckworth as baggage master and wise counsellor. Len was wrapped up in the cricket and was not by nature a gregarious soul. I was the link between him and the other players. Many of them were ten years older than I was, but to a man they were friendly, cooperative and a great help to the young vice-captain.

With eighteen players in the party – Vic Wilson had been added when doubts arose about the Compton knee – there were even trickier problems than usual in keeping all in some sort of practice. On the other hand, Len badly needed a rest. The strain of two tightly fought Tests must have been considerable and by his standards he had not been batting well. It was therefore decided to split the interval between the Third and Fourth Tests into two parts. Len would play in the two matches in Tasmania which I took off. I would take over for a two-day country match at Mount Gambier and the following match against South Australia in Adelaide.

I thought that I had the better of the deal. The practice then was to play a Combined XI in one of the two matches in Tasmania. Several Test players were brought over from the mainland, which often meant that our bowlers found themselves toiling against batsmen of whom they had seen quite enough already. On this occasion we had bowlers of the calibre of Bedser and Loader fresh and with Bailey they gave a respectable account of themselves in a drawn match against seven Tasmanians plus Favell, Harvey, Benaud and Davidson.

When I took command in Mount Gambier we found that an air of carnival prevailed, for while we were there the town became a city by charter. We watched the ceremonies from our hotel balcony, congratulated the attractive girl pipers, autographed the bass drum and toasted the new city. It had achieved this landmark with its 10,000th inhabitant and all 10,000 of them seemed to be at the station to see us off to Adelaide. I am afraid that players of today miss a lot in their hectic rush about Australia from one big city to another playing one-day matches.

We won by an innings both in Mount Gambier and Adelaide. Against South Australia I batted number seven and shared in a stand of over 200 with Denis Compton, who made 184. He had played in all four matches between the Tests, had made runs in all of them and seemed right back to form.

We expected a very good pitch at the Adelaide Oval and when we lost the toss and failed to take a wicket on the first morning of the Fourth Test the prospects of clinching the series there seemed bleak. Arthur Morris was still not in his form of a few years back but we knew that his new partner, Colin McDonald, was difficult to dislodge, and the heat was such that the fast bowlers had to be used in short bursts. The bounce in any case was consistent and comfortable.

After lunch Tyson made one bounce to have Morris caught off the glove and, most conveniently, Australia began to make heavy weather against the spinners. I was stationed at forward short leg and caught McDonald there off Appleyard. When Tyson came on again, Burke also gave me a catch there.

Next day I took a third catch at forward short leg off Appleyard, this from Benaud, and by way of variation caught Archer off Tyson at third slip. This number of opportunities concentrates the mind wonderfully on close fielding. By now a cool breeze made fielding easier and when, soon after lunch on the second day, Australia were 229 for 8 we thought that the bowlers had done a tremendous job. We reckoned without a ninth-wicket stand of 92 between Maddocks and Johnson and the eventual total of 323 was more than we had come to expect.

We passed Australia's score by 18 runs, mainly through Hutton, Cowdrey and Compton, although with one exception the batsmen all made runs. I was the exception. Richie Benaud bowled me two leg breaks which turned and bounced. I avoided the first but not the second and was brilliantly caught by Ron Archer at slip.

During much of its course our innings had promised a bigger lead than 18, especially as Ian Johnson and Ron Archer, suffering from injuries, had scarcely bowled in the second half of the innings. Thus we did not exactly have victory in our sights when Australia's second innings began after tea on the fourth day. By the end of it, we had taken 3 wickets, those of Morris, Burke and Harvey, but all had fallen to rather ill-judged strokes against Appleyard.

Again one read in next morning's newspapers that Appleyard held the key to the match. Again Len started with his fast bowlers and again Statham and Tyson raced through the Australian batting taking 3 wickets each. Soon after lunch they were out, as at Sydney, for 111, and we needed only 94 to win the series on a pitch showing no more than normal fifth-day wear.

The climax to the series was not as tense and drawnout as that at the Oval eighteen months before, although there were similarities and a painful start to our innings. Lindwall had been kept out of the match by injury but there was still Miller and, in a typically inspired opening spell, he yorked Edrich and had Hutton and Cowdrey caught in the slips.

We were 18 for 3 and it was as Colin was out that Len made his famous remark. 'The so-and-sos have done us,' he said.

It was often very hard to tell when Len was being serious and I doubt if he genuinely thought that we were in trouble. I was not, in fact, present myself. I was batting. The humour of the remark lay in the fact that it was made in front of Denis Compton, still one of the world's great batsmen and sitting there adjusting his pads preparing to go in.

'Steady on, Len,' he said. 'There's still me.'

Until Miller ran out of steam Denis and I had to work very hard but we raised the score to 49 before I was out in the last over before tea, a little unluckily, I thought. I drove Bill Johnston hard and wide of extra cover but Keith Miller dived and caught the ball as he rolled over.

On the left is P.B.H. May, aged eight, in his first year in the Marlborough House XI. If I had been told then that I would one day be vice-captain to Len Hutton, who in that same year, 1938, made his 364 against Australia, I would have been greatly surprised

Under the eyes of two famous Surrey players who became successful coaches, Andrew Sandham (left) and Alf Gover

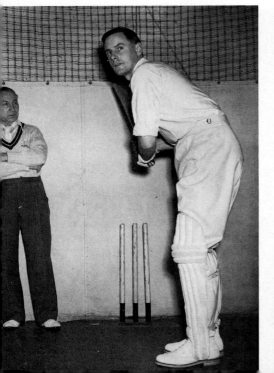

With George Geary again at a Test Match

The Old Carthusians, winners of the Arthur Dunn Cup in 1951. My brother John is on the left of the back row. (Note the future cabinet minister further along the row.) Back row, from left: John May, Tony Williams, Michael Rimell, Graham Clarke, Jim Prior, Tim Savill. Front row: myself, Malory Hollis, Peter Bennett, John Tanner, John Larking

August 1953. The England team which won back the Ashes at the Oval. Back row, from left: Trevor Bailey, myself, Tom Graveney, Jim Laker, Tony Lock, John Wardle (twelfth man), Fred Trueman. Front row: Bill Edrich, Alec Bedser, Len Hutton, Denis Compton, Godfrey Evans

The same team and others who took part in the series reunited in Sheffield nearly thirty years later. Back row, from left: Trevor Bailey, Brian Statham, myself, Tom Graveney, Jim Laker, Reg Simpson, Don Kenyon, Roy Tattersall, John Wardle, Fred Trueman. Middle: Bill Edrich and Godfrey Evans. Front: Alec Bedser, Len Hutton, Denis Compton. Missing: Freddie Brown, Willie Watson, living in South Africa, and Tony Lock, living in Australia

Grenada. What a ground on which to start a tour! We played the first match there in 1960 and had also played in these exotic surroundings in 1954

Cottesloe Beach, Perth, at the start of the 1954-55 tour with Frank Tyson, who little knew the fame and success which lay ahead of him

Trent Bridge 1955. Leading England out for the first time followed by Bailey, Evans, Graveney, Wardle, Kenyon, Appleyard, Barrington (his first Test), Statham and an invisible Tyson and Compton

With Freddie Brown during the Oval Test of 1956 when we met to discuss plans for our coming tour of South Africa as captain and manager

Four previous England captains apparently hanging on my words in Durban during the 1956-57 tour of South Africa: *(from left)* Col. Ronnie Stanyforth, Freddie Brown, Walter Hammond and Arthur Gilligan

A late cut off Ramadhin at Edgbaston played in ignorance of the fact that it brought us level with the 388 of Ponsford and Bradman at Leeds in 1934, the previous Test highest for the fourth wicket

ABOVE LEFT: Edgbaston 1957. Reaching 100, a relatively early landmark

ABOVE RIGHT: Looking rather pleased with ourselves on the fourth evening after batting together since twenty minutes after the start. Cowdrey 78, May 193, the stand so far worth 265

At the declaration

Nº3	TOTAL		Nº7
285	583		29
WICKETS			4
LAST PLAYER		1	54
7	BOWLERS		6
75	FIELDER		SUB
LAST WKT. FELL		5	24

Presented to the Queen during her welcome but, as far as the cricket was concerned, ill-fated visit to Guildford in 1957

BELOW LEFT: Talking it over with Arthur McIntyre during a match against Notts in 1958

BELOW RIGHT: Stuart Surridge, a painting by Frank E. Beresford which hangs in the Oval pavilion

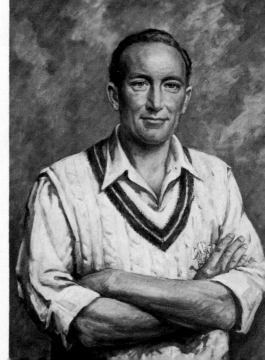

During his roll he lost it but was of the opinion that he had held it long enough, so I departed.

However, Denis was at his very best, Trevor Bailey until near the end provided the support one came to expect from him and we won by 5 wickets. Australia had suffered more than their share of injuries before and during the match but still took some beating. We were, I think, entitled to be absolutely delighted with our success and I doubt if I was the only one who appreciated what it meant to Len to have come to Australia and to have beaten the 'old enemy' in their own country.

Before the last Test we played Victoria in a rain-ruined match and lost narrowly to New South Wales after the scores had been level on first innings. I suppose that some sort of relaxation was inevitable.

The final Test in Sydney was turned into anticlimax by appalling weather. It should have started on Friday. It eventually started after lunch on Tuesday, which left only two and a half days' play. The Test matches in this series were of six days, although as yet none had run into a sixth day.

Ian Johnson put us in but the pitch was of little use to the bowlers. Tom Graveney, opening with Len, played a sparkling innings of 111, Compton, Bailey and I made runs and we declared at tea on what should have been the fifth day. On the last day Australia made an unexpectedly poor job of playing Wardle's chinaman and googly and, having followed on 150 behind, were 118 for 6 when the match ended.

We thus left Australia feeling thoroughly worthy winners, and fairly swept through our four matches in New Zealand on pitches affected by a very wet spell. Only one innings total exceeded 250. Only three individual scores of over 50 were made against us, the sternest opposition coming from Gordon Leggat, later to become chairman of the New Zealand Cricket Council and much missed when he died in his middle forties. He battled away for Canterbury against us for over four hours before running himself out going for his 100th run.

We finished the long tour at the end of March with a piece of history in the Second Test. New Zealand began their second innings only 46 behind on a lovely afternoon but on a pitch of varying bounce which took spin. Wardle removed Bert Sutcliffe, then easily New Zealand's best player. Tyson, Statham and Appleyard did the rest and New Zealand were out for 26, still the lowest total in Test cricket. Bob Appleyard recalls with the Yorkshireman's blend of humour and indignation that when he had taken 4 for 7 he was taken off so that the fast bowlers could finish the innings off. Those were the days!

We flew home in high spirits, leaving behind Len Hutton who, seeking to relax, chose to return by sea. I certainly had not the slightest idea that with the rout of New Zealand in Auckland he had come to the end of a great Test career which had begun before the war when he was already a good enough player to make 364 against Australia and when I myself was not yet promoted to long trousers.

7
Captain of England

Early in the 1955 season, which was to produce one of the best Test series of all, Len Hutton was appointed captain for all five Tests. This was an unusual compliment in those days but a natural follow-up to his triumph in Australia. Thus for the first month I enjoyed myself playing in a highly successful Surrey side without any idea of what lay ahead of me. When I dropped out for the First Test in early June our record was played ten, won ten.

I had been in fair form without making a huge number of runs. Much more to the point, as it proved, had been Len Hutton's season. Only recently returned by sea from Australia, he did not play in Yorkshire's early matches but in the middle of May came in against Somerset and made 66 in the second innings. I doubt if the cold damp weather at Headingley did him much good, for when he captained MCC against South Africa at Lord's in the following days an attack of lumbago forced him to retire.

He tried again a week later in the Roses match at Old Trafford but was apparently in no sort of form. He went down to Hove and made 54 and o before coming to the Oval for a match over the weekend during which the team for the First Test was picked.

There was a huge crowd on the Saturday, for Yorkshire were already emerging as our main challengers that season, but the pitch was wet and Appleyard next to unplayable. We were bowled out cheaply and Len then made o again, caught at the wicket off Loader. He said nothing to me about his health.

That evening, to my great surprise, Gubby Allen, the new chairman of selectors, rang me up and said that Len had withdrawn because of his lumbago. He invited me to captain England in the First Test, starting at Trent Bridge on the following Thursday. Gubby says that he also made it a condition that I stepped up the over rate, but I do not remember that! I accepted anyhow. I was surprised and flattered but it had still not sunk in that it could be other than a temporary appointment.

On the Sunday I attended my first meeting of selectors, according to the custom, probably unique to England, I think, of coopting the captain. We met, Gubby, Les Ames, Brian Sellers, Wilfred Wooller and myself, at the Bath Club, then at the bottom of St James's Street. After the winter's tour the main bulk of the team was obvious.

On the Monday morning at the Oval I commiserated with Len and said that I hoped that he would soon be fit again. He was as reserved as ever and did not elaborate on his health and future. I certainly still had no idea that, at thirty-eight, his Test career was over. Poor chap, he made only 1 run in the second innings of the match, which we won by 41 runs, before he was bowled by Loader. When we played Yorkshire at Headingley a fortnight later he was out twice to Alec Bedser for almost nothing, and although he worked his way back into form and fitness to the extent that he made 194 against Nottinghamshire in late June, his season was ended by ill health soon afterwards. That proved to be the end of his first-class career.

Len's retirement was to me a melancholy event because it seemed so abrupt and premature. Yet I had realized that he was no longer enjoying his cricket, and when we were batting together I often used to marvel at his remarkable ability with a left arm so much shorter than the right, the legacy of a wartime accident.

I set off for Trent Bridge with the knowledge that I had no easy introduction to the captaincy. The South Africans had not had much luck with the weather but, when given a chance, as when they beat MCC at Lord's, had shown the makings of a good young side shrewdly captained by Jack Cheetham. He was one of the first captains to put a great emphasis on fitness and fielding, admittedly always easier to do with a team of young players brought up in the open air than with relatively middle-aged Englishmen.

As well as Len, Colin Cowdrey had to be replaced in the England side. Since returning from Australia Colin had been in and out of the RAF. Turned down because of a foot condition, he did not resume first-class cricket until mid-June but then did so with such a flood of runs that it swept him into the side for the Third Test.

Otherwise we had picked for Trent Bridge the team which finished the series in Australia with Don Kenyon and the young and promising Ken Barrington replacing Hutton and Cowdrey. We named eleven with Arthur Milton as twelfth man, but when he had to withdraw through injury we brought in Tony Lock. By then there had been a lot of rain and we thought seriously of playing Lock instead of Tyson but eventually stuck to our original plan. As Tyson took 6 for 28 in the second innings, we could congratulate ourselves on our decision.

I can remember very well going out to toss for two reasons. One was that it looked a good if soft pitch and the weather forecast was none too promising, a big consideration in those days of uncovered pitches. I fervently hoped that we could bat first. As I was on trial I naturally welcomed all the luck that was going. The other reason was that the coin rolled off down the pitch and took an inordinately long time to tip over after Jack Cheetham had called heads. We pursued it and, mercifully, it was a tail.

Apart from Ken Barrington, all the batsmen made runs and I was 81 not out at the end of the day. I was soon out next day and our 334 was hard work for various reasons – the accuracy of the bowling, especially of Goddard and Tayfield operating to defensive fields, the brilliance of the fielding and the slowness of the outfield.

South Africa soon ran into trouble against Tyson and Statham and though it took us five hours to dig out Jackie McGlew, his only support came from Jack Cheetham. McGlew's batting was not for the connoisseur unless it was for the connoisseur of sheer guts and application. In these qualities he took a lot of beating. He batted for nine and a quarter hours in this match.

My first, not very difficult, major decision was whether to enforce the follow-on when South Africa narrowly failed to avoid it. As we were nearing the end of the third day and the bowlers had the weekend to recover, I enforced. I would not have been able to face Stuart Surridge when I got back to the Oval if I had done otherwise. He was a staunch believer in keeping the opposition down.

In fact, we did not take a wicket that evening and time became even more pressing when heavy rain over the weekend delayed the start on Monday. It was still some time before we broke the opening stand of McGlew and another very determined batsman in Trevor Goddard. It was only the agility of Statham at mid wicket and his throw from there that did it then.

By now the pitch was beginning to do a bit for the faster bowlers from the pavilion end. I kept Tyson and Bailey going from that end, the ball occasionally lifted awkwardly and the match was over that evening. Tyson was much too fast for them and finished it off by taking 5 wickets for 5 runs.

Frank had then taken 52 wickets in nine Test matches and had only just passed his twenty-fifth birthday. As I drove back to London, I remember thinking that if he could do it on such a slow pitch, there must be a great future ahead for him and any side for which he played.

Yet that proved to be just about the climax of his short career. He was only fit to play in one more Test that year and in only the last of 1956. Plagued by injuries, he lost the extra yard of pace and some of his accuracy. He was never again the matchwinner of those few months. He played in only eight more Tests spread over four years and took only another 24 wickets.

After that first Test, which proved to be the least eventful of the series,

I was appointed captain for the series. At Lord's we had to replace not only Tyson but Appleyard, who was also unfit. We had a ready-made deputy for Tyson in Fred Trueman and instead of Appleyard we played Fred Titmus in his first Test match. He had first played for Middlesex six years before but was still only twenty-two and had already taken nearly 50 wickets at Lord's that season.

If this haul of wickets for an off-spinner suggests that Lord's was producing turning pitches in dry weather in 1955, it deceives. The clarion call had gone out for faster pitches and MCC had set the example at Lord's by leaving a lot of grass on heavily rolled pitches. They were some of the fastest on which I ever played but, alas, there were snags. A really fast pitch requires a true surface, otherwise it becomes dangerous, and Lord's could not always guarantee a really flat pitch. One or two Gentlemen and Players matches around that time left a trail of bruised and broken fingers behind them. Moreover, on a first morning while a little damp was left in the lush grass the fast bowlers could be devastating.

In a year or two MCC had to take off some grass and slow the pitches down but I remember looking at the square on the first morning of the Second Test of 1955 and being in some doubt as to which was the pitch on which we were to play.

Nowadays, with pitches covered, the captain who won the toss in such a situation would put the opposition in with no hesitation and with a sigh of relief. In those days, one had to think of the weather over the next five days. On this occasion rain was forecast over the weekend. I knew, too, that as the pitch lost a little pace, it would become a good one and we were more likely to profit from that in the second innings if we batted first. So I batted.

I can still see the first ball which Peter Heine bowled to Don Kenyon, a good consistent opener for Worcestershire whose few chances in Test cricket were against formidable opposition. Don pushed sedately forward to a good length ball which kicked and, as the saying goes, almost parted his hair.

Heine, a big powerful young man standing over 6 feet 4 inches, was playing in his first Test match. He and the rather wirier Neil Adcock were to prove a formidable combination of fast bowlers over the next two years. On that first morning he bowled me a ball which stood straight up and he did the same to Denis Compton, though Denis by then had made 20, which was 20 more than I had mustered. With Trevor Goddard's accuracy in support, Heine hammered away, nobody looked like staying long and by mid-afternoon we were out for 133.

I was not at that stage unduly worried, for the pitch did not seem to be losing its fire yet and it was certain that Statham and Trueman would not be much fun to play. This seemed to be confirmed when Statham with his first ball of the innings had McGlew caught at the wicket and Trueman removed Goddard in the same way, also for nought. After their long resistance at Trent Bridge, disposing of these two so swiftly seemed too good to be true.

It was. After tea the pitch eased a little and the South African batsmen started a revival which did them much credit even if we helped by dropping catches. The highlight was a spectacular innings by Roy McLean which continued through the second morning until he was bowled by Statham for 142 just before lunch. What a player he was on his day! Strong, quick-footed, with lightning reflexes and superb timing.

Roy scored at such a pace that although South Africa gained a first-innings lead of 171, it was still only mid-afternoon on the second day when their innings ended. We then lost Don Kenyon playing no stroke to Trevor Goddard.

Trevor Goddard, left-arm medium pace over the wicket to a largely on-side field, was in those days generally regarded as a defensive bowler. Certainly he was one of those bowlers whose methods led to the legislation which brought in the on-side limitations. But he was young then, and although he was already very accurate and could swing the ball a lot, he was still short of the confidence which comes to a bowler who has learned his craft to the full. It was no surprise to me years later, long after I had retired, to hear Billy Griffith, then secretary of M C C, say that, in a Test match against Australia in Johannesburg which he had just watched, Trevor Goddard had given the best exhibition of swing bowling that Billy had ever seen. I did not see Goddard in his later years – South Africa won in England in 1965 without him – but he must have been far from defensive then.

By the end of that second day Tom Graveney and I had both reached 50 and I went on with Denis Compton next day to make a particularly satisfying 112. It was always a thrill to make runs on the Saturday of the Lord's Test and batting on this pitch, which was still much faster than most, was an exhilarating experience. We were playing a little below the centre of the square and there were no spectators on the grass on the Tavern side. The ball would go off the bat like a bullet and I can remember cutting Heine and seeing it rebounding quite a way back towards me off the fence.

Denis and I had added nearly 100 in quick time when I slipped and trod on my wicket. I cannot remember doing it on any other occasion.

After Denis, nearly everybody made a few runs but five were out to the off spin of Tayfield, a master of flight and variation. He was not renowned as a great spinner of the ball but he did spin it; he bowled from very close to the stumps and, when it turned, it seemed to turn unexpectedly and a lot.

South Africa went in half an hour before the end of play on the Saturday evening needing 183 to win. I was hopeful that Statham and Trueman, not needing to spare themselves, would take a wicket or two. In fact, Statham removed both McGlew and Goddard, which was an immense help to us. Jackie McGlew received only three balls in the match and his 'pair' was an isolated and incongruous failure, for in the rest of the series he was just about the hardest man on both sides to dislodge and, despite the 'pair', averaged over 50.

My delight at the taking of these 2 wickets was lessened by a nasty accident off the last ball of the day. Trueman and Statham, both very fast, had given the batsmen an uncomfortable time and as his last ball Fred Trueman bowled a short one which lifted sharply to hit Jack Cheetham on the left elbow. He was in such pain that we at once suspected a bad injury. In fact, he had chipped a bone, took no further part in the match and was out for a month, missing the next two Tests.

So far the match had been played in lovely weather but Monday was a murky day with the light only just good enough. It was to give us a big advantage.

I soon had to accept that South Africa had some good players left and that only Statham looked likely to upset them. Even he took only 1 wicket in the first hour.

'George' Statham, with his wiry, not very strong-looking physique, was always a bowler whom a captain liked, if possible, to use in fairly short bursts, but I had few runs to spare and gave him a longer opening spell than usual. I had Trevor Bailey in reserve but on this pitch the extra bounce which Statham obtained made him more penetrating than the others.

After an hour I was just considering resting him when the light faded still further and we went off until well into the afternoon. He thus had two hours with his feet up and he started again refreshed while the batsmen were correspondingly unsettled. McLean, Waite, Endean and the left-handed Keith all fell to him in a wonderfully sustained piece of bowling. This clinched the match beyond all doubt, but he had taken the first 7 wickets, was well on top and wanted to go on. So I let him. And, given another rest by the tea interval, he bowled throughout the innings of 111, 29 successive overs. Wardle took the last 2 wickets and we won by 71 runs.

I contemplated the rest of the series with rather less confidence than a 2-0 lead might suggest. The Second Test had been a close-run thing. It had been an exasperating match for the South Africans. They had been in a winning position and they had lost not entirely through their own fault. The luck had gone against them. However, at Old Trafford a fortnight later they had another chance.

This was another memorable and exciting match. We made three changes, bringing in Cowdrey, Lock and Tyson for Barrington, Wardle and Trueman. On the day before the match Statham had to drop out and Alec Bedser came in for what was to be his last Test. I went out to toss with a new opposite number in Jackie McGlew. Jack Cheetham's place was taken by a tall dashing front-foot player, Paul Winslow, the sort of batsman whom one liked to see succeed but who took too much of a chance to be consistently successful.

I soon found myself in much the same position as at Lord's, apprehensive of the well-grassed pitch on the first day but forced to bat for fear of what the Manchester weather might have in store. This last fear proved totally unwarranted. We had five warm and glorious days.

Our innings of 284 really concerned one man, Denis Compton, who joined me at 22 for 2 and made 158. It would be wrong to say that he was having an Indian summer in 1955 because, despite his awful knee condition, he had through the years still batted many times with his own unique flair. In 1955, however, with the sun on his back, he played some remarkable innings. Six weeks before Old Trafford, Middlesex had been bowled out for 206 in the Whitsun match against Sussex at Lord's. John Warr was second top scorer with 13. Denis made 150.

At Old Trafford he alone gave our score some respectability but it was not enough on what was by the second day a superb batting pitch. As McGlew and Goddard put on 147 for the first wicket, I felt the full frustration of the captain who knows that his bowlers have no penetration and can only bowl tidily and wait for something to turn up.

In fact, we finished the day far better placed than had seemed likely. After Goddard was out to Tyson, McGlew retired with a damaged hand. Having bowled for hours at the opening pair without success, we then took 3 more good wickets, Mansell, Endean and McLean going to Tyson and Lock. At 199 for 4 we had emerged from a difficult day reasonably well.

But a much more difficult one lay ahead on the Saturday. The catches were not sticking and John Waite, who was missed in the slips early on, made 100. Waite was a very good player to find coming in at number seven and Winslow on his day was a particularly unkind number eight. This *was* his day. He drove with great power in an innings which must have been fine entertainment for the big Saturday crowd. He too made a 100, reaching it with a tremendous straight drive for 6 off Lock over the sightscreen and far beyond. Tony Lock's comments were unprintable. After that McGlew returned to add another 100 to the roll of honour before declaring at 521 for 8 on the fourth morning.

We were 237 behind with not much hope, still less when Kenyon and Graveney were soon out to Heine and Adcock. Denis Compton came in to join me with the score 2 for 2. I think he and I took the same view, which was to ignore the score and to enjoy the splendid batting conditions. Anyhow he played even better than in the first innings and made 71 while we added 124 in an hour and threequarters. He rated this as one of his very best innings. Colin Cowdrey followed in one of his more restrained moods after being dropped early on. But he stayed and we had almost cleared off the arrears when I was out for 117 near the end of the fourth day. I took a liberty with the gentle leg spin of Percy Mansell, a scholarly looking bespectacled figure who always seemed to have strayed into this stern arena from some Old Boys' festival. He was a useful all-round cricketer but, unfortunately for both him and me, this was his only wicket of the series.

On the last day nearly all the batsmen made a few runs, including Godfrey Evans who came in last with a broken finger in plaster and made 36 of the last 48 runs with Trevor Bailey. Trevor, as unmovable as ever when there was defeat in the offing, batted through the last three hours of the innings for 38 not out.

The last-wicket stand had turned South Africa's task from a simple one into one which could easily cause them some trouble, especially after they had spent a day and a half in the field. They needed 145 in 135 minutes.

It was still a splendid batting pitch and on the evidence of the first innings I had to rely on Bedser, Tyson and Lock to drive them behind the clock. Lock had bowled 64 overs in the first innings at under 2 runs an over.

Bedser and Tyson soon had them 23 for 2 but McGlew and McLean hit back with a most spirited attack. Roy McLean made a brilliant 50. When he was run out the score was 95 for 3, and we subsequently had them 135 for 7 and worried. But they batted a long way down and they won a wonderful match by 3 wickets with three minutes to spare.

The sun went on shining, the public appetite had been whetted by the manner of the South African victory and the interest at Headingley during the Fourth Test was such that the gates were closed at midday on the fourth day. And Headingley would then hold 36,000. It proved another remarkable match.

The South Africans must have been further heartened by having beaten Surrey, the county champions, in their only match between the Third and Fourth tests. At Headingley they played the same side as at Old Trafford but we had to make a lot of changes, bringing in Arthur McIntyre, Doug Insole, Peter Loader and John Wardle. Godfrey Evans's finger had not recovered. Cowdrey and Tyson had been injured in the

Gentlemen and Players match at Lord's. Appleyard was only just starting playing again after nearly a month off. Willie Watson, whom we picked on the Sunday to replace Don Kenyon, was injured next day playing for Yorkshire on another lively pitch at Lord's. I seemed to spend most of my time on the telephone to Gubby Allen in those days and after another conversation we called up Frank Lowson who had just made his first 100 of the season at Lord's.

This time I lost the toss, which seemed a pity at the time but not after we had South Africa 38 for 5. It did not happen at once, but when I switched Loader to the top end he promptly removed three of them, including McGlew and Goddard. Bailey bowled Mansell and Wardle ran out Waite.

They staged a partial recovery through McLean and Endean, who despite a recent loss of form was a well-equipped player to have coming in at number eight. But they were out for 171. Statham finished off the later batsmen. Bowling at the stumps as he did, he was always good at doing this.

The pitch had not given the fast bowlers much help and we were entitled to think that it would be easier going for us, especially after Neil Adcock had retired early in our innings with a broken bone in the foot. But we lost our opening pair, Bailey and Lowson, that night, and although Compton and I reached 117 for 3 next day, we capitulated for 191 to South Africa's three remaining bowlers – Heine, Goddard and Tayfield.

I remember being fascinated that Jackie McGlew could achieve all this with just two bowling changes between the start of play and tea. Heine's great strength was probably the deciding factor, for although the other two were fine bowlers with relaxed economical actions, Jackie had to bear in mind that Trevor Goddard would be opening the innings and he did not bowl him after lunch.

This paid off handsomely, for by that second evening the opening stand of McGlew and Goddard was still intact and was worth 107. Next day, sensing that they could win if they did nothing silly, they extended their lead very carefully and lost only 5 wickets. On the Monday they made absolutely certain as Russell Endean, with 116 not out, steered the score up to 500.

This left us with about eight and a half hours' batting. I sent in Graveney with Lowson this time instead of Bailey, a sort of dual-purpose move. Tom Graveney would keep us up with the clock if we made a good enough start to think about scoring 481 to win and Trevor Bailey would be in reserve to battle for a draw if that became necessary, as seemed far more likely.

In fact, we lost both opening batsmen that day and when Doug Insole and I resumed on the last morning we were still 366 short of victory. The events of that day were made all the more remarkable by the fact that South Africa were effectively now down to two bowlers, Goddard and Tayfield. The foothold at the top end had given trouble since the first day, first damaging Adcock's foot, then restricting my use of Statham. Now Heine, attempting a trial run at the start of play, found it so dangerous that he did not bowl all day.

Jackie McGlew did not fire both his main guns at once but opened with Goddard and Mansell. Insole and I came safely through the first hour but Doug was then out to Goddard. Soon afterwards South Africa made their only bowling change of the day and in the last over before lunch I went back to Tayfield and was lbw for 97. The ball certainly turned an unexpected amount but this was one of the occasions when I bitterly reproached myself for getting out.

The ball was turning frequently by then and that was more or less the end. When South Africa won at tea by 224 runs, Trevor Goddard had bowled all day and he and Hugh Tayfield had shared the wickets equally.

South Africa had squared the series and without their captain. It was an effort much to be admired and I remember praying that neither the weather nor the players would make the final Test at the Oval an anticlimax.

The South Africans went on their way, beating three more counties before the last Test, but by then the weather had begun to break. Their bowlers, although now without Adcock, would have been relatively more effective on good hard pitches such as we had had in the north. We had more problems of selection to sort out. This time Dick Spooner of Warwickshire kept wicket. Tyson was fit again and taking wickets. We had asked Kent if Colin Cowdrey might open the innings for them as preparation for opening for England, and he had done so with fair success, but on the day before the match both he and Tyson were unfit.

We had gone in for one of those pieces of theory which are shrewd or silly according to whether they succeed or not. As a counter to Trevor Goddard's nagging accuracy around the leg stump, we had decided to bring in two left-handers, Ikin and Close, for Graveney and Bailey, plus Willie Watson who had been an original choice for Headingley. So, with Spooner and Statham, we now had five left-handers. In the first innings they mustered 78 runs between them, in the second 18!

As originally chosen, the only survivors from Headingley would have been May, Compton, Statham and Lock, but when Cowdrey and Tyson dropped out we restored Graveney and Bailey.

We did have the wisdom to bring in Jim Laker who had not played in a Test that summer. He had not had one of his best seasons but, a fortnight before, had taken 6 for 5 on a dry turning pitch at the Oval against Nottinghamshire. As England had won there with Laker and Lock in 1953 and lost there without them in 1954, I for one was in no doubt about which spinners we should play this time.

The match started on a Saturday. The South Africans had been playing at Leicester the day before and Close had to come from Scarborough. I had been more fortunate as Surrey had beaten Somerset in Weston-super-Mare early on the second day.

I knew the recent record of sides batting last at the Oval, which was not encouraging, so I was glad to win the toss. I also knew how the ball would swing on a grey August morning such as this. So I was prepared for a testing day's play. In fact, it only lasted until half an hour after lunch when rain set in with our score 70 for 3. I was actually first out, for Jack Ikin retired feeling sick after being hit in the stomach by Heine.

The fast bowlers moved the ball a lot and Eddie Fuller, a lively substitute for Adcock, had me caught at second slip. Close was well caught in the slips in the last over before lunch, and although Ikin resumed his innings after lunch he went to another splendid catch just before rain set in. Jack Ikin, a gentle kindly Staffordshire man, made many runs for Lancashire in his time, and although this was his last Test, his subsequent contributions to English cricket, as assistant manager in Australia and as a coach, were considerable despite his indifferent health.

The rain lasted for a long time and although Sunday and Monday morning were fine the pitch was soft when our innings continued. Batting was a struggle and soon after lunch Goddard and Tayfield had us out for 151.

The ball went on turning and keeping different heights and South Africa had an even harder time against Laker and Lock. McGlew fought hard but of the others only Waite and Cheetham reached double figures. We led on first innings by 39 runs.

Next day the pitch eased a little, though it was never one on which the later batsmen were likely to make many runs. Thus when we were 30 for 2 the match was still finely balanced, especially as the Compton knee, which had been dormant that season, had started to swell again.

I promoted Tom Graveney ahead of Denis and he made 42 very well before Tayfield bowled him. Tayfield was the main danger and if South Africa had had a left-arm spinner to support him we would probably have lost. As it was, he had to try to do it all himself. Five for 60 in 53.4 overs shows how successful he was.

Early in my innings, which was to last five hours, there occurred one

ENGLAND v SOUTH AFRICA, The Oval
(Fifth Test, 1955)

England won by 92 runs

ENGLAND

J. T. Ikin c Waite b Heine		17	– c Goddard b Heine	0
D. B. Close c. Mansell b Goddard		32	– b Goddard	15
†P. B. H. May c Goddard b Fuller		3	– not out	89
D. C. S. Compton c Waite b Goddard		30	– c Waite b Fuller	30
W. Watson c Mansell b Tayfield		25	– b Fuller	3
T. W. Graveney c Fuller b Goddard		13	– b Tayfield	42
T. E. Bailey c Heine b Tayfield		0	– lbw b Tayfield	1
*R. T. Spooner b Tayfield		0	– b Tayfield	0
J. C. Laker c and b Goddard		2	– b Tayfield	12
G. A. R. Lock c McLean b Goddard		18	– lbw b Heine	1
J. B. Statham not out		4	– lbw b Tayfield	0
B 2, l-b 5		7	B 4, l-b 6, n-b 1	11

1/51 2/59 3/69 4/105 5/117 6/117   **151**   1/5 2/30 3/95 4/157 5/165   **204**
7/118 8/123 9/130   6/166 7/170 8/188 9/197

Bowling: *First Innings* – Heine 21–3–43–1; Goddard 22.4–9–31–5; Fuller 27–11–31–1; Tayfield 19–7–39–3. *Second Innings* – Heine 25–6–44–2; Goddard 19–10–29–1; Fuller 20–3–36–2; Tayfield 53.4–29–60–5; Mansell 6–0–24–0.

Umpires: D. Davies and T. J. Bartley

SOUTH AFRICA

†D. J. McGlew c Spooner b Staham		30	– lbw b Lock	19
T. L. Goddard lbw b Bailey		8	– c Graveney b Lock	20
H. J. Keith b Lock		5	– c May b Lock	0
W. R. Endean c Ikin b Lock		0	– lbw b Laker	0
R. A. McLean b Lock		1	– lbw b Laker	0
*J. H. B. Waite c Lock b Laker		28	– b Laker	60
J. E. Cheetham not out		12	– lbw b Laker	9
P. N. F. Mansell lbw b Laker		6	– c Watson b Lock	9
H. J. Tayfield b Statham		4	– not out	10
E. R. H. Fuller c Spooner b Lock		5	– run out	16
P. Heine run out		5	– c Graveney b Laker	7
L-b 7, n-b 1		8	L-b 1	1

1/22 2/29 3/31 4/33 5/77 6/77 7/86   **112**   1/28 2/28 3/29 4/33 5/59   **151**
8/91 9/98   6/88 7/118 8/118 9/144

Bowling: *First Innings* – Statham 15–3–31–2; Bailey 5–1–6–1; Lock 22–11–39–4; Laker 23–13–28–2. *Second Innings* – Statham 11–4–17–0; Bailey 6–1–15–0; Lock 33–14–62–4; Laker 37.4–18–56–5.

The deciding Test of a tremendous series. A match which South Africa, with only a little more luck, might have won

of those incidents which are remembered long after many others more spectacular are forgotten. I know that South Africans well placed to see will swear to their dying day that I should have been lbw to Tayfield when only 4. I was playing straight but the ball turned a lot and hit me on the back leg. The only explanation which I have heard for Tom Bartley's decision was that the ball turned so much that it might have missed the leg stump. My own thoughts at the time were that it must have been very close and I had been lucky.

What must have been particularly hard for the South Africans to bear was that next day Endean and McLean were both given out sweeping when they thought the front leg was far enough down the pitch to be safe. However ruefully these incidents were remembered in later years, Jack Cheetham and his team never said or did anything which would have detracted from the pleasure which a marvellous series had given to everyone.

Denis Compton came in after Tom Graveney was out and, although under an obvious handicap – our progress between the wickets was safe but prolonged – stayed for over two hours while we moved the score up to 157 for 3, a lead of 196. Once Denis was out, the innings subsided and I was left 89 not out. It was as hard an innings as I ever played, for although Tayfield needed the closest watching and never bowled a bad ball, Goddard and the fast bowlers could restrict batsmen on this pitch just by bowling a length.

Our innings just lasted into the fourth day, so that I was able to have the heavy roller on. Jack Cheetham refused a roller. South Africa needed 244.

We had no early success, but when Laker and Lock did break through 4 wickets fell in eighteen balls and South Africa were 33 for 4. McGlew was still there and John Waite, a fine player of spin, began to bat with what to me was entirely unwelcome skill and assurance. He made 60 but nobody else stayed with him for long and we won by 92 runs.

To a touring team living and playing together for months with one aim, victory means so much that I felt a lot of sympathy for the South Africans. They had come so near and contributed so much to our summer – in the county matches as well as in the Test matches. They had also shared in one piece of cricket history. It was the first time that not one match in a five-Test series in England had been drawn.

8
Australia Be-Lakered

I had been lucky that my first year of captaincy coincided with such an exciting series and that we had won it. But we had only just won and there was no cause for complacency as we faced up to retaining the Ashes in 1956.

Nowadays it is customary to look back on the 1950s as relatively golden years because England did not lose a series for eight years after 1950-51. We certainly had the bowlers, especially for damp English summers and unpredictable pitches. Some of our longest selection committee meetings owed their length to painful decisions which had to be made to leave out bowlers of proven Test class just because others might be more effective on the type of pitch expected or were thought to be fitter or in better form at the time.

There was no such abundance of Test-class batsmen and especially of opening batsmen. When the 1956 season began we were still considering the idea of persuading Colin Cowdrey to open. It seemed sensible because he was such an outstanding player of the moving ball and of fast bowling in general. I had talked to him about it and he had agreed willingly but without enthusiasm. He never liked it. Having fielded, usually at slip, a position requiring high concentration, he liked to sit down and get the feeling of batting before he went in.

Colin had had a chequered season in 1955, what with his passage into and out of the R A F, but there was no reason why he should not be back at his best. We hoped too for a last full season from Denis Compton, who wanted to finish his Test career on the tour of South Africa in the following winter. It was soon clear that we could not count on him. Denis had had his right kneecap removed in November and did not start to play for Middlesex until early July. By the time he could be judged fit for a five-day Test, there was only one Test left.

Australia, captained by Ian Johnson, were in transition and obviously vulnerable. Miller, Lindwall and Johnson himself were almost certainly just past their best and for once there did not seem to be the youthful talent about to bloom. On good hard pitches they might have settled down, both bowlers and batsmen. In one of the wetter English summers they were badly handicapped.

They made plenty of runs on good firm pitches but there were not many of those to be found that summer.

When they played Yorkshire in early May, Appleyard and Wardle bowled them out for 94. When they came to the Oval a week later, Surrey beat them by 10 wickets, the first time an Australian side had lost to a county for forty-four years.

I played a very minor role in this Surrey win, so I can say without immodesty that it was a thoroughly conclusive and well-deserved victory on a pitch which was dry but by no means bad, especially when Jim Laker took all 10 wickets on the first day. He bowled 46 successive overs in an innings of 259 and took 10 for 88, a feat sometimes overlooked in the light of what happened at Old Trafford two months later. I certainly always had in mind from then on that the Australians were vulnerable to good off spin. After Bernard Constable had made 100 and we had gained a first-innings lead of 88, Tony Lock, 7 for 49, was almost as deadly. The historic win was a nice bonus for Stuart Surridge in his last year of captaincy.

We had one new selector that year in Cyril Washbrook who replaced Brian Sellers. As I remember it, Cyril was fitter than most of the players we had to consider for the First Test. Tyson and Trueman were injured and we eventually decided to take fourteen to Trent Bridge. Of these, Statham and Wardle were left out on the morning of the match as not being fully fit. We finished up with an attack comprising Moss, Bailey, Laker, Lock and Appleyard.

The injuries to bowlers accrued during the match, Lindwall and Davidson retiring on the Australian side and Alan Moss, as a result of a rashly athletic piece of fielding in the covers, on our side. It did not matter, for the weather was such that the spin bowlers did most of the bowling on a pudding of a pitch when play was possible, which was not often.

We derived some satisfaction from that drawn match at Trent Bridge because our new opening partnership of Colin Cowdrey and Peter Richardson put on 53 and 151 in the two innings. They had only just become acquainted, as it were, in the first innings when there occurred the famous muddle still enjoyed in retrospect by those who were present or watching on television.

Cowdrey drove Miller wide of cover point and they set off with 3 runs in mind. But the ground had been slowed by the morning's rain and Davidson cut the ball off. His brilliant left-handed pick-up and throw on the turn to Gil Langley, the wicketkeeper, upset their plans and Colin, having started on the second run, sent Richardson back. Richardson, several yards up the pitch, slipped on the wet turf and fell, which left both of them far from home with the ball almost in Langley's gloves. As I saw Peter Richardson fall, I picked up my gloves and set off towards the first of the two flights of stairs which have to be negotiated without delay if you are to cross the incoming batsman on the field of play.

However, Cowdrey had decided to go on as the prostrate Richardson obviously could not recover in time. Langley, no doubt distracted by an abundance of shouting and by the sight of strange events out of the corner of his eye, fumbled momentarily. The impression in the dressing room was that he could still have run Cowdrey out, but exhortations from the other end prompted him to throw the ball there, which he did inaccurately. It was now Miller's turn to fumble the awkward throw and Richardson, having scrambled to his feet although without his bat, just got home before Keith dived and swept all three stumps down.

It made a welcome piece of light relief for the first morning of a Test match. Colin Cowdrey has always claimed that taking the second run was one of his best decisions, for he learned more Australian dialect in the next minute of recriminations than he would ordinarily have learned in a year.

Gubby Allen had said before the season started that what we needed was an opening batsman who would average 35. In fact, one had turned up who averaged 45. Peter Richardson had batted well on an MCC "A"-team tour to Pakistan during the winter, had made 100 for Worcestershire against the Australians in their first match and had been consistent since. He was enormously confident, an amusing character to have in the side and, as a left-hander, provided useful variety.

He was a great leg-puller. I suppose that one of his better known successes in this field was when he was batting at Dover and stopped the game, complaining of a 'booming' noise coming from the commentary box. The umpire who went to trace the alleged boom found that he was being directed to Jim Swanton in the middle of a B B C commentary.

When we gathered for the Second Test, Australia were without Lindwall and Davidson. We, however, were able to bring in Statham, Trueman and Wardle who, with Bailey and Laker, seemed to provide us with just about the right attack for Lord's. Yet they made almost no impact on the opening stand of McDonald and Burke — I say almost because I seemed to be peppered with half-chances near the wicket and it was one of those days when they were not sticking.

The rain of recent weeks had left a pitch on which the ball moved about throughout the match. Given that opening stand of 137, Australia never relinquished their hold. They batted better than we did and, more surprisingly, bowled better. Keith Miller, who took 5 wickets in each innings, was at his best. Ron Archer made a formidable partner for him and some spectacular catches were held. The one which those who saw it will not forget was in the gully by Richie Benaud off 'Slasher' Mackay. The ball was almost a half-volley to Colin Cowdrey, who hit it uppishly without much movement of the feet but timed it perfectly. I was at the other end and instinctively thought that it must be 4 runs. I was amazed to see Benaud, reeling back under the force of it, hang on to it head-high.

We held some good catches too. I remember Trevor Bailey diving full length at leg slip to catch Harvey off Trueman. But Australia led by over 100 on first innings and put the match beyond doubt on the fourth day with a remarkable piece of batting. While Mackay, that weird spidery figure at the crease, batted four and a half hours for 31, Richie Benaud sailed into our bowling. He was a tremendous hitter on his day, a beautifully clean striker of the ball to whom it was very hard to set a field, and he snatched back the initiative which briefly on the third evening we had gained for the first time in the match.

When I was batting with Colin Cowdrey in the second innings it seemed to me that the massive figure of Peter Burge at forward short leg was too close to him and might be distracting him. I asked Colin and then spoke to Ian Johnson who moved Burge slightly squarer out of Colin's vision. I think he was either on or leaning over the pitch. This is now forbidden under Law 41, so I suppose that I was ahead of my time. I made 50 in each innings but it was not a match on which England had anything to congratulate themselves. We were well beaten – by a below strength side who had not yet beaten a county.

Before the next meeting of selectors there were many informal telephone conversations. Gubby Allen had seen Alan Oakman of Sussex play well and, as he was also a prodigious close catcher very long of arm – he was about 6 ft 5 inches – Gubby was keen to bring him in. I had not seen him make runs but accepted that he was one of those batsmen who suddenly blossom when given the chance to open the innings. Since succeeding John Langridge that summer, he had been helping Don Smith to give the Sussex innings a vigorous start – and there had not been much vigour evident in England's batting recently.

The other change for which Gubby sought my support was one which went into the history books – no less than the choice of one of the selectors, Cyril Washbrook. This was the first of Gubby's three come-back coups – Washbrook, Sheppard, Compton, all marvellous successes. He was a great believer in class. A player who had done it before in Test cricket was more likely to do it now than one who, although making a lot of runs for his county, had not looked of the highest class. I admit that I thought recalling Cyril was retrograde but I was outvoted, and I was certainly impressed by the fact that Cyril himself wanted to have a go.

Cyril was forty-one then and had not played for England at home for six years. He had become something of a father figure, captaining Lancashire, no longer opening but batting around number four. I had not seen him bat that year and in fact he did not make 100 all season, so it was truly a selection of inspiration and imagination. Our main opposition was going to come from fast-medium bowling and I knew what a good player of that he was.

The selectors, already in bad odour for the defeat at Lord's, were roundly condemned for the recall of Washbrook, which was by most accounts a backward step and panicky.

Most of my previous experience at Headingley had been of good batting pitches. This one was dry but, after the rain of recent weeks, possibly not as solidly based as some. On the morning of the match we decided to play an extra batsman, Doug Insole, instead of Statham.

I won the toss and we batted. Just over an hour later we were 17 for 3 with Cowdrey, Oakman and Richardson all out to Archer. What would have happened then if Keith Miller had been available to bowl is anybody's guess, for he must have achieved the same bounce and movement as Ron Archer. But, although in the field, Keith was prevented from bowling by a knee injury.

As Richardson departed, I watched Cyril Washbrook come out to a great reception from the Yorkshire crowd. No Roses partiality on this occasion. I found myself encouraged by the air of disdain that he habitually wore. With head tilted slightly upwards and cap at a jaunty angle, he advanced as if unworried by the score and still less worried by what any upstart Australian bowlers could do to him.

I had never batted with Cyril before but knew him to be a fine runner between the wickets and, as we worked our way slowly out of the morning's difficulties and batted through the afternoon and into the evening, things began to go increasingly smoothly. Cyril had one piece of luck in his 40s when he slashed at Ian Johnson, and Keith Miller at cover point dropped a catch coming head-high, probably out of the crowd. Otherwise we batted steadily on and relief began to dawn, slowly but all the brighter as the occasional ball turned and seemed to confirm my suspicions that there would be something in the pitch for the spinners.

The score was past 200 when with five minutes left I was out in an unusual and unexpected way. Ian Johnson was not the sort of off-spinner to make the most of this pitch and I played him comfortably enough. I had just passed 100 when suddenly the ball seemed to slip from his hand and he bowled me a high full pitch. He stoutly maintained afterwards that he bowled it on purpose but it certainly looked accidental. It was that awkward height, around head-high, but I could have

ENGLAND v. AUSTRALIA at Headingley, Leeds
(Third Test, 1956)

England won by an innings and 42 runs

ENGLAND

M. C. Cowdrey c Maddocks b Archer	....	0
P. E. Richardson c Maddocks b Archer	....	5
A. S. M. Oakman b Archer		4
†P. B. H. May c Lindwall b Johnson	....	101
C. Washbrook lbw b Benaud	....	98
G. A. R. Lock c Miller b Benaud	....	21
D. J. Insole c Mackay b Benaud	....	5
T. E. Bailey not out	....	33
*T. G. Evans b Lindwall	....	40
J. C. Laker b Lindwall	....	5
F. S. Trueman c and b Lindwall	....	0
L-b 9, b 4	....	13

1/2 2/8 3/17 4/204 5/226 6/243   325
7/248 8/301 9/321 10/325

Bowling: Lindwall 33.4–11–67–3; Archer 50–24–68–3; Mackay 13–3–29–0; Benaud 42–9–89–3; Johnson 29–7–59–1.

AUSTRALIA

C. McDonald c Evans b Trueman	....	2	– b Trueman 6
J. W. Burke lbw b Lock	....	41	– b Laker 16
N. Harvey c Trueman b Lock	....	11	– c and b Lock 69
P. Burge lbw b Laker	....	2	– lbw b Laker 5
K. Mackay c Bailey b Laker	....	2	– b Laker 2
K. R. Miller b Laker	....	41	– c Trueman b Laker 26
R. G. Archer b Laker	....	4	– c Washbrook b Lock 1
R. Benaud c Oakman b Laker	....	30	– b Laker 1
*L. Maddocks c Trueman b Lock	....	0	– lbw b Lock 0
R. Lindwall not out	....	0	– not out 0
†I. W. Johnson c Richardson b Lock	....	0	– c Oakman b Laker 3
B 4, l-b 6	....	10	B 7, l-b 4 11

1/40 2/59 3/59 4/63 5/69 6/142   143   1/10 2/45 3/108 4/120   140
7/143 8/143 9/143 10/143   5/128 6/136 7/138 8/140
                                      9/140 10/140

Bowling; *First Innings* – Trueman 8–2–19–1; Bailey 7–2–15–0; Laker 29–10–58–5; Lock 27.1–11–41–4. *Second Innings* – Trueman 11–3–21–1; Bailey 7–2–13–0; Laker 41.3–21–55–6; Lock 40–23–40–3.

Umpires: J. S. Buller and D. Davies

The Third Test of 1956, begun with Australia one up

hit it anywhere. Prudently, so I thought, I pulled it downwards off the middle of the bat, but to my disgust Ray Lindwall, a sort of backward square leg, dived to his right and held a wonderful catch near the ground.

Poor Doug Insole, who had played in his first Test six years before and in only one since, had spent the day with his pads on pacing up and down the dressing room. He was not called on to go in at twenty-five past six, as we had in Tony Lock a mad keen night watchman who could not go in high enough in the order.

Cyril Washbrook came into the dressing room a few minutes later, 90 not out, having given a tremendous performance. Things could not have looked much blacker than when he joined me that morning – 17 for 3 and already one down in the series with three to go. I know that, to most people's thinking, selectors do not get much right but on this one occasion it was generously conceded that they had not done too badly.

'I'm very glad I listened to you about Cyril,' I said to Gubby when he came into the dressing room that evening. Gubby thought that it was an unusually generous remark but, as the main beneficiary of Cyril's innings, I could do no less than admit that I had been wrong.

Next morning, to the general disappointment, Cyril when 98 pulled at a faster ball from Benaud and was lbw. After that, the later batsmen, mostly rather painstakingly, set themselves to raise the score to a figure which would give our bowlers a sound backing.

How they did it I left to them. They were experienced cricketers, they knew what we were trying to do and normally I gave no instructions which might make them depart from their natural approach. Thus Godfrey Evans played in his usual breezy way, making 40 out of 53 with the inevitable Bailey at the other end. When Lindwall finished off the innings, we had reached 325.

The full significance of the extra runs added for the eighth wicket by Evans and Bailey became clear over the weekend. On the Friday Trueman, in his first over, had McDonald caught at the wicket and after tea Laker and Lock took 5 wickets, the ball turning just enough to undermine confidence. Bad light stopped play when Australia were 81 for 6. That night, however, it started to rain, Saturday's play was lost and it was not until nearly lunch time on Monday that play could resume. Having lost so much time, we badly needed to enforce the follow-on and Laker and Lock duly made this possible.

The rain may have bound the pitch to some extent, and although Australia again lost McDonald to Trueman early in the innings the batsmen knew better now what was required against the spinners. They had more than halved the first-innings arrears of 182 by the end of the fourth day and had only lost 1 more wicket.

Next day I gave Trueman a few overs at the start against Harvey and Miller, who had both played very well on the previous evening. After that I left it to Laker and Lock in the hope that as the pitch dried out the ball would turn more quickly. Sure enough, Laker made one turn and lift sharply to Miller's glove, and he was too much for most of the other batsmen. Those who escaped him fell to Lock, among them Neil Harvey who had made 69 with much skill when he gave a return catch.

Looking back on the hundreds of catches which I saw Tony Lock take near the wicket and off his own bowling, I can split them into two categories. There were those which he made look ridiculously easy and there were those, undeniably difficult, which were given full value by the amount of rolling which he did after diving to catch the ball. This brilliant return catch from Harvey was a rolling job.

The series was level at 1-all with two Tests to go and, for what was to prove a momentous match at Old Trafford, Gubby Allen pulled out his second surprise card in the shape of David Sheppard. David was not exactly a light of other days – he was only twenty-seven – but he was then a curate at St Mary's, Islington, and had only started to play for Sussex in his holidays the week before. In one of two isolated first-class matches earlier in the season he had made 97 against the Australians. So we picked him for Old Trafford.

Whenever I have to answer a question about my part in Laker's Match on the lines of 'What did you do in the Great War, Daddy?' I take full credit. 'I put him on,' I say. Yet it is a curious fact that, although he was to become the first and doubtless the last bowler to take 19 wickets in a first-class match, there were quite long periods when he was not bowling.

It is often not realized that although Australia were bowled out on the second afternoon in only 40 overs, Laker 9 for 37, the second innings, in which he took 10 for 53, began on Friday evening and did not end until half past five on Tuesday. Such was the weather over that wet weekend! We were working against time to finish the match and Jim Laker rounded off his extraordinary feat only through a temporary break in the rain.

Next day the unhappy Australians were due to play, of all counties, Surrey. The rain was back and I can remember looking at the tape machine in the basement of the Oval pavilion and seeing that not a ball had been bowled in any first-class match in the country. It really was an awful summer.

The Fourth Test of 1956 was probably unique in one other way not concerning Jim Laker, certainly in modern times. The England batting order began Cowdrey, Richardson, Sheppard, May, Bailey – five amateurs. The reader may draw what conclusions he likes, for it was brought about by a number of different factors. But the five of us produced a score of 309 for 3 on the first day, the Australians bowled well over 100 overs and the crowd had a great time.

The match began on a miserable grey morning and on a reddish closely shaved pitch. Richardson and Cowdrey were soon rattling along at a rare pace, 111 for no wicket at lunch. I had Trevor Bailey ready to go in if we had an early mishap, as I did not think it fair to expose David Sheppard to the new ball. I reckoned that while playing for the London Clergy in recent weeks he would not have met any one like

Lindwall, Miller and Archer. In fact, he went in at 174 when Colin Cowdrey, driving at Lindwall, was caught at the wicket. I joined him when Peter Richardson was out for a lively 104 and, having had a good look at the second new ball, we returned to the former brisk tempo. The fast bowlers could do little. The bounce for them was constant and there was no pace in the pitch. I can remember David hooking Archer for 6 with time to spare.

The only blot on the evening's play, my own dismissal, was not totally depressing, for I received a ball from Benaud which turned and lifted steeply to the shoulder of the bat, suggesting that we had already had the best of the pitch.

Next day David Sheppard went on to make 113. This was, of course, one of his first comebacks. He was still coming back – and making 100 in a Test match in Melbourne – six and a half years later, after I had retired.

The Australian innings began comfortably against Statham and Bailey. As soon as I brought on Laker and Lock, Burke and McDonald lived more dangerously. Then, just before tea, I switched them round. I was always a great believer in variety if one was not getting anywhere, whether it was changing ends or asking bowlers to try bowling round the wicket rather than over it.

On this occasion Laker turned a ball to have McDonald caught at backward short leg. Despite a knee injury early in the second innings which forced a temporary retirement, Colin McDonald was easily Australia's most effective batsman in the prevailing conditions, playing the turning ball extremely well and making nearly half the runs.

By tea on that second day Laker had bowled Neil Harvey. The really historic wicket, the one that got away from Jim, fell to the first ball after tea, although as Lock had Burke nicely caught by Cowdrey at slip the significance of it was beyond any one's imagination. Laker then took 7 for 8 in twenty-two balls.

By then he had a hoodoo on them. The batsmen seemed mesmerized by his accuracy and powers of spin. In the two innings they gave a lot of catches to Oakman and Lock, two backward short legs, although Jim hit the stumps five times and had three lbws.

I gave equal thought to helping Lock at the other end, but with singular lack of success. He beat the bat countless times and one always expected him to take a wicket but, after that one success, he never did. It was a cruel reminder of how many fewer ways there are of getting out to the ball leaving the bat. Once it has passed the outside edge, it is usually harmless. If it misses the inside edge, it can bowl you, have you lbw or even have you caught off pad and bat. Yet, less than three weeks before, Tony Lock had himself taken all 10 wickets against Kent

ENGLAND v AUSTRALIA, Old Trafford
(Fourth Test, 1956)

England won by an innings and 170 runs

ENGLAND

P. E. Richardson c Maddocks b Benaud	....	104
M. C. Cowdrey c Maddocks b Lindwall	....	80
Rev. D. S. Sheppard b Archer	....	113
†P. B. H. May c Archer b Benaud	....	43
T. E. Bailey b Johnson	....	20
C. Washbrook lbw b Johnson	....	6
A. S. M. Oakman c Archer b Johnson	....	10
*T. G. Evans st Maddocks b Johnson	....	47
J. C. Laker run out	....	3
G. A. R. Lock not out	....	25
J. B. Statham c Maddocks b Lindwall	....	0
B 2, l-b 5, w 1	....	8

1/174 2/195 3/288 4/321 5/327 6/339   459
7/401 8/417 9/458

Bowling: *First Innings* – Statham 6–3–6–0; Bailey 4–3–4–0; Laker 16.4–4–37–9;
Lock 14–3–37–1. *Second Innings* – Statham 16–9–15–0; Bailey 20–8–31–0; Laker
51.2–23–53–10; Lock 55–30–69–0; Oakman 8–3–21–0.

Umpires: F. S. Lee and E. Davies

AUSTRALIA

C. C. McDonald c Lock b Laker	32	–	c Oakman b Laker	89
J. W. Burke c Cowdrey b Lock	22	–	c Lock b Laker	33
R. N. Harvey b Laker	0	–	c Cowdrey b Laker	0
I. D. Craig lbw b Laker	8	–	lbw b Laker	38
K. R. Miller c Oakman b Laker	6	–	b Laker	0
K. Mackay c Oakman b Laker	0	–	c Oakman b Laker	0
R. G. Archer st Evans b Laker	6	–	c Oakman b Laker	0
R. Benaud c Statham b Laker	0	–	b Laker	18
R. R. Lindwall not out	6	–	c Lock b Laker	8
*L. Maddocks b Laker	4	–	lbw b Laker	2
†I. W. Johnson b Laker	0	–	not out	1
			B 12, l-b 4	16

1/48 2/48 3/62 4/62 5/62 6/73 7/73   84   1/28 2/55 3/114 4/124 5/130   205
8/78 9/84   6/130 7/181 8/198 9/203

Bowling: Lindwall 21.3–6–63–2; Miller 21–6–41–0; Archer 22–6–73–1; Johnson
47–10–151–4; Benaud 47–17–123–2.

*Laker's match, producing over five days a performance never likely
to be approached, least of all in a Test match. Note that he bowled
only 68 overs out of 191*

at Blackheath and he finished the season on top of the first-class averages
with 155 wickets against Jim Laker's 132. It was baffling.

Jim usually bowled with a deep square leg and a long on and one of
his wickets in the first innings, that of Benaud, was taken through a
catch by Statham at long on. In the second innings I remember being
rather pleased at the manner of Neil Harvey's dismissal, not only because
he made a 'pair'. We were always looking for him to try to play wide
of mid-on and I had Colin Cowdrey as a short midwicket. Harvey

jumped out to his first ball, reached it on the full pitch and hit it straight to Colin who held it well.

As I have said, the weather made the second innings, in complete contrast with the first, a long-drawn-out affair. When play was possible for a short time on the Saturday afternoon, I opened with Statham and Lock before bringing on Laker on a very wet sluggish pitch. Just before another deluge ended play, he had Burke caught at backward short leg.

Monday was a horrible day, cold and squally, and in two short periods of play in the afternoon we could not shift McDonald and Craig.

It was still pretty miserable next morning but the wind had dropped. I wanted to play. Ian Johnson, not surprisingly, was reluctant. The umpires settled for a ten-minute delay. Another strange feature of this match was that each of the batsmen who resumed, Ian Craig and Colin McDonald, was in the fourth day of his innings. McDonald, injured on Friday, had come back on Saturday when Burke was out.

As the pitch played then there did not seem much in it for Laker. I thought that he might have better luck from the Warwick Road end and tried him there. I tried Oakman, Bailey and then Statham, but at lunch, with only four hours of the match left, Australia had still lost only the 2 wickets.

During lunch the sun came out. I switched Jim back to the Stretford end, with Lock on at the other end, and after fifteen minutes things began to happen. Jim turned a ball to have Craig lbw and, as I had always hoped, the later batsmen could not offer the same resistance.

Within a few minutes Mackay, Miller and Archer had gone, but McDonald stayed, with Benaud in support, this time defending stubbornly. I took Jim off and tried the different off spin of Alan Oakman but no more wickets fell before tea and the pitch seemed to have lost its bite again.

I often think that too much is made of the influence of sun or cloud on playing conditions but there is no doubt that on the type of sodden pitch often met in those days the sun could change things very quickly. Having gone in before tea, it reappeared afterwards and at once Jim had McDonald caught by Oakman for a very fine 89.

It was when commenting on this burst of sunshine and other allegedly divine intervention by the weather on our behalf that Ian Johnson, nodding towards the Rev. David Sheppard, made his famous remark: 'It's not fair! You've got a professional on your side.'

Two more wickets followed which, if one had thought about it, put Jim on his own as the taker of 18 wickets in a first-class match. My own thoughts were directed at making sure we won. There was not much over an hour left and we were so accustomed to being stopped by rain and bad light that nothing was certain. The batsmen would

clearly have welcomed any opportunity to go off. Indeed, at one time
Ian Johnson complained that sawdust was blowing in his eyes.

There was absolutely nothing done to spare the last batsmen,
Maddocks and Johnson, until Jim could get at them. Tony Lock bowled
at the stumps, trying as hard as ever; I should have been chasing him if
he had not. Thus when Frank Lee's arm went up and Jim had Maddocks
lbw, he had really earned his wickets with no favours done to him.

There can seldom have been a less obviously emotional cricketer than
Jim Laker. The mere idea of his showing enthusiasm or leaping with
delight is absurd. And all he did now, after achieving a feat never likely
to be beaten in first class, let alone Test, cricket, was to take his sweater
from the umpire and, with his unhurried stride, walk in amid a tremendous ovation.

After this match there was an uproar about the pitches. Headingley
had not been all that bad a pitch. Our task was greatly eased by rain
and nobody could say for sure how the pitch would have played if it
had not rained. But the Old Trafford pitch was undoubtedly not of Test
standard. It had been too heavily marled.

There were some loose and utterly uninformed allegations of pitches
being 'rigged' to suit English spinners who, of course, were far better
equipped for them than their Australian counterparts. But the preparation of pitches has always been purely a matter for ground authorities,
and although I have read that selectors abroad sometimes give instructions about what type of pitch is to be produced I have no knowledge
of that ever happening in England. Cynics might say that that is fairly
obvious judging from the unsuitable bowling sides which the selectors
have sometimes picked!

By the time we chose the team for the last Test at the Oval we had
completed the party to tour South Africa that winter. To our delight,
Denis Compton had been passed fit to tour and we brought him into
the side for what was to be his last Test in England. It was the last
leg of Gubby's inspired hat trick – Washbrook, Sheppard and now
Compton.

It was not as easy a side to pick as had seemed likely, for there was
a lot of grass on the pitch and we at last had Tyson fit again to resume
his highly effective partnership with Statham. We had to leave out either
Washbrook or Bailey and, for once, we did without Bailey.

The Australians seemed so demoralized by Laker that the thought of
what he might do to them at the Oval, where he and Lock had bowled
them out three years before and again when playing for Surrey earlier

that season, raised unusually high hopes of an English victory. Not for the first or last time that summer the real winner was the weather.

I won the toss for the fourth time in five and entering the last half-hour of the first day we were 222 for 3. Denis Compton had come in at 6 for 3 and had played superbly. I doubt if I consciously set myself to play second fiddle to him but I always enjoyed batting with him and on this occasion it was a joy to watch from close quarters the one-kneed genius at work, or, in his case, at play. It was always a game to Denis. I was one of the many thousands praying that he would make 100 in his last home Test – on the ground where he had played his first, nineteen years and a world war before – when he glanced Archer firmly off the middle of the bat and was brilliantly caught at backward short leg by Davidson for 94.

The light was not good. Nor was the batting, and somehow we contrived to lose 3 more wickets to Archer and Miller before the close, having turned 222 for 3 into 223 for 7. However, it rained during the night and my chief concern while my remaining partners lasted next morning was to score as many runs as quickly as possible in order to bowl at Australia as the pitch dried.

After Tyson had taken an early wicket, Laker and Lock had them 47 for 5, but Harvey led a recovery which Miller and Benaud carried on with a wholehearted assault on the spinners. That night Australia were within 49 runs of our 247 with 2 wickets left, one of them Miller's.

It rained again in the night and I was not at all happy about our position next day when we batted again, 45 runs ahead but on a pitch from which the ball would sometimes lift impossibly. Davidson at reduced pace produced one such ball which Cowdrey could not avoid and an off break from Archer kicked and laid out Gil Langley, the wicketkeeper. But using fast bowlers to bowl cutters or to spin the ball is never the same as using specialist spinners. They generally bowl too short – or did in those days of uncovered pitches, when visiting countries bowled so much less well than England in wet conditions. Australians occasionally played on wet pitches at home but not of this slow turning type. They were well out of their element.

By contrast Richardson and Sheppard overcame the prevailing difficulties with great skill and were still there when rain stopped play, not only for that day but for Monday as well. It was after lunch on Tuesday, the last day, before they were able to resume.

The pitch then was too wet to have any life and, after Richardson and Sheppard were out, I had another happy partnership with Denis Compton, begun when we led by 153. While it was in progress, I had to consider a declaration. I saw no realistic chance of bowling Australia out quickly on the pitch as it was playing and with more rain threatening.

If Denis and I had attacked at once, we would probably have got out and nothing would have been achieved as on this sluggish pitch the later batsmen would have been unlikely to do much better. Anyhow, I had not the slightest intention of making a declaration which would give Australia a chance to square what had been a traumatic series.

So I waited until tea before declaring. When they lost 5 wickets for 27 before bad light and rain ended the match, there were, of course, criticisms of my failure to declare earlier. But I think that they lost some of those wickets through lack of concentration and because there was nothing left in the match.

I had now played in three successive winning series against Australia. Not many in the past could say that. In this last one my lowest score had been 43. I did not know as I spent the last days of September preparing to sail to South Africa that very soon I should be regarding a score of over 40 in a Test match as riches indeed. I was about to learn at first hand the meaning of the hackneyed old phrase about cricket being a great leveller.

9
Surrey under Surridge

That wet late summer of 1956 marked the end of Stuart Surridge's remarkable captaincy of Surrey. Five years, five championships won. Who could ask for anything more?

Yet at the start of the 1952 season Surrey had only won the championship outright once this century, in 1914. We had been getting near, with a half share in 1950 with Lancashire and a fourth place to Warwickshire in 1951. Michael Barton had done a good job in fashioning a promising youngish side along with two still successful old stalwarts in Laurie Fishlock and Jack Parker. But I doubt if it occurred to any one, except perhaps Stuart Surridge, that we might be champions for the next five seasons, indeed for the next seven.

On reflection, I realize that this is not quite true. It must have occurred to a former Surrey captain, Monty Garland-Wells, who had an accumulator on our winning for the next seven years. After four or five years the bookmakers took fright, justifiably as it proved, and Monty agreed a handsome settlement. He gave a splendid celebratory party at the Oval.

Between 1951 and 1952 three things happened which combined to have a profound effect on what followed. One was a change in the Oval pitches which in 1951 still retained some of their prewar perfection for batsmen. The ball began to move about, to turn by the second innings and to have a sort of rounded bounce, not especially quick but useful to good bowlers. The outfield, once rough and brown, was now lush and green, and the ball retained its shine longer. In fine weather not many matches were drawn.

Here, in haste, I must point out that the Surrey bowlers of the day were rightly indignant at suggestions that the pitches were made for them. These implied a subtlety, a prescience and a deviousness which Bert Lock and his staff did not possess. We were often told by the ground staff that they had a beautiful pitch for us that day, a promise which left us somewhat mystified when we found ourselves or our opponents 43 for 7.

We naturally expected a really good pitch for Alec Bedser's benefit match against Yorkshire in 1953. He had just taken 14 wickets in a

Test match against Australia, he was at the peak of his career and a highly respected figure. On the first day 21,000 were present but Jim Laker was turning the ball before lunch. We won, but the match was almost over in two days. The beneficiary, although our second top scorer with 45, was not amused.

The statistics show that our main bowlers – Alec Bedser, Peter Loader, Jim Laker, Tony Lock, Stuart Surridge and, when needed, Eric Bedser – took at least half their wickets away from the Oval. They may eventually have had an advantage in knowing better than visiting bowlers what was required on Oval pitches but they prospered, there and elsewhere, mainly because they were very fine bowlers capable of swifter execution than others.

The change in ground conditions had been to some extent coming on gradually and was accentuated by the rain of 1952 after the sunshine of 1951. The second development, a change in Tony Lock's action, took place in the winter of 1951–52. A technical analysis of this much discussed feature can wait until a later chapter. For the moment, it need only be said that he learned to spin the ball.

In 1951 he had by most standards been pretty successful, 89 championship wickets at 20 apiece, but he was no great spinner of the ball and for this reason was not widely thought of as a future Test bowler. In 1952 he spun the ball fiercely and in about the same number of overs took 116 wickets at 16 apiece. Certainly he had more wet pitches in 1952 but he turned the ball on almost anything and on wet pitches his faster ball, which was very fast indeed and well concealed, could be next to unplayable.

The third development in 1952 was, of course, the accession to the captaincy of Stuart Surridge. He was simply a great and inspiring leader. To be successful, a captain needs to have good players and Stuart inherited them, but it was his outstanding achievement that he consistently got the best out of them. His enthusiasm was unlimited and infectious.

'It's no good being second,' he would say – and he always tried to win in the shortest possible time. He was lucky in having four world-class bowlers plus an off-spinner, Eric Bedser, who in any other county side would have done the double every season. Yet there were times when either one of the other fast bowlers was injured or when they were held up. Then Stuart would seize the ball himself.

'As for me,' he would say by way of field placing and we duly took our places. Then, with uncanny frequency, he would take an important wicket. He was already thirty-four in his first season of captaincy and I suppose that in the early part of a career interrupted by the war he had looked on himself, as others had, as a useful amateur to have in reserve and a fast-medium bowler above the average in Second XI cricket.

He was, of course, renowned as a fearless close catcher and he was a robust late-order batsman good for a quick 40 or 50 when it was needed. I learned an enormous amount from him and not only about captaincy and cricket. In my young day I was a lively performer at the wheel of a red MG known as the 'fire engine'. Stuart Surridge taught me to drive safely, if still rather faster than seemed prudent to the chairman of selectors. Gubby Allen forbade me to drive at more than 50 miles an hour to Test matches!

In 1952 Stuart was the only member of the side to play in all twenty-eight matches in the championship. It was my last year at Cambridge and, what with the university season and four Test matches, I played in only eight matches for Surrey. Coming in for an important match against Kent in mid-July, I made my first 100 at the Oval. Stuart, who had taken 7 wickets in the first innings, and Tom Clark eventually won an exciting match for us in the last over by 2 wickets.

Tom Clark was a fine stroke-playing opening batsman, very near to international class, and, if he ever got on, an extremely useful off-spin bowler. He had a great memory for cricket records and train times and we used to call him Thomas Henry Wisden Bradshaw Clark. He came from Bedfordshire and returned there after retiring from Surrey. I always enjoyed reminiscing with him in later years and it was a great blow to all Surrey players of his generation when he died in 1981 in his fifties.

Tom played very well in the bank holiday match in August 1952 when the pitch was frequently freshened by showers. I batted with him for a time and remember being glad that Harold Butler, then nearly forty, was not ten or fifteen years younger. He was still pretty quick. As it was, we bowled Nottinghamshire out for 84 and 51, Alec Bedser taking 13 wickets, among them his 1000th in first-class cricket. As he was only in his seventh season, the figure gave some idea of what he had meant to Surrey and England since the war.

The three matches which we lost that season were during the last two Test matches when Bedser, Laker, Lock and I were all away. But, on the whole, our 'shadow side', as it was called, did us wonderfully well during those years. Our winning run of seven championships could never have been achieved without excellent reserves and we were indeed fortunate to have cricketers of the calibre of Geoff Whittaker, Dennis Cox, Alan Brazier, Derek and Ron Pratt, Ronnie Tindall, Roy Swetman, John Hall and Mike Willett.

After the last Test we only needed to beat Derbyshire at the Oval to win the championship on 22 August. We had the next three days off and there were joyful celebrations at the Oval, almost certainly more festive than when we had last won, for that was in the first month of the First World War.

We had a harder task in 1953 when, through being dropped by England, I played in twenty championship matches. This time we started quite well but fell away from the middle of June when Derbyshire beat us by an innings at Derby. In those days Les Jackson and Cliff Gladwin made Derbyshire a formidable bowling side if the ball moved off the pitch. They bowled us out for 81. On a pitch on which nobody else could bat, Surridge was in his element. This sort of situation seemed to inspire him to show the rest of us how it should be done. He made 51 of the last 55 runs with great violence.

I would happily have forgotten this match, which coincided with my being dropped from the Test team, but for the fact that Donald Carr occasionally recalls with a dreamy look of satisfaction in his eye that in the second innings he bowled me through the gate with a chinaman.

Donald was a most elegant batsman and among the best close catchers in the country. He was less well known as a left-arm slow bowler and I must admit that I was impressed the other day when, prompted by his son's success at Oxford, I looked up the family record and found that Donald had taken 328 first-class wickets.

Earlier in June we had played Derbyshire in a contest at the Oval which was much more typical of Surrey's cricket in those days. Jackson and Gladwin were a match for us on the first day on a damp pitch. We bowled Derbyshire out for 107, they bowled us out for 115. On the second day the ball turned and Derbyshire had no one like Laker and Lock. We bowled them out for about the same again and won comfortably by 8 wickets. It was the variety of the bowling as well as the swiftness of its working which was so effective.

An incident occurred in this match which I have never seen repeated. It made me think about the complexity of the Laws of cricket and the need for those playing to know the Laws thoroughly, even though they may barely cover incidents like this. Alan Revill was hit a nasty blow on the hand by a ball from Alec Bedser which lifted steeply. In the same movement he pulled his right hand off the bat and hurled it down again shaking off his glove in an instinctive reaction of pain. The glove knocked off a bail and he was given out 'hit wicket'.

The Law at the time said that he was out if 'while playing at the ball, but not otherwise, his wicket is broken by his cap or hat falling or by part of his bat.'

The 1980 Code of the Laws is more explicit. He is out if 'while the ball is in play, his wicket is broken with any part of his person, dress or equipment as a result of any action taken by him in preparing to receive or in receiving a delivery.'

I am not sure that even now the Revill incident is covered, as he was not exactly receiving the ball. He *had* received it. However painstakingly the Laws are drawn up and revised, cricket still throws up the odd improbable incident which is not catered for. At the time I thought that Alan Revill was unlucky. Even the bowler, who did not think that many opposing batsmen were unlucky, was noncommittal! We accepted the umpire's decision that he was out because there had been a continuity of movement in playing the ball and throwing the glove down. But it was the sort of situation in which, if we had been sure of the wording of the Law, we might have asked the umpire if we might withdraw our appeal.

Usually after rain at the Oval we would bowl sides out for 100 or less but we had a good pitch for the bank holiday match against Nottinghamshire and an exciting match in front of a huge crowd. We lost only 6 wickets in the match but met stiffer opposition than usual in an opening stand of 159 between Reg Simpson and John Clay. We eventually bowled them out just in time.

At about this time I used to hear that I was vulnerable to leg spin. Bruce Dooland, the Australian then playing for Nottinghamshire, was almost certainly the best leg-spinner in the world at the time and, helped by some benign pitches, I took quiet pleasure in making 135, 73 and 211 against Nottinghamshire in three successive innings, all not out. Vulnerable I may have been, but not all the time!

I suppose that it was during one of these innings at Trent Bridge when I had been hitting the ball as hard as I could through the covers that Freddie Stocks, a great character, came up to me between overs wringing his hands. He had just been paid and produced out of his hip pocket a bundle of notes.

'What's it worth to get out, skipper?' he asked. 'We're fed up with you in the covers.'

'It's a good pitch,' I said. 'You'll get your chance.'

He shook his head sadly. 'It's a different game when tha's bowling,' he said. The Surrey bowlers can rarely have had a more heartfelt compliment paid to them.

The last month of the 1953 season was interesting because we did not quite know where the main challenge to us lay. Middlesex were ahead of us but had played more matches. Then Leicestershire appeared on the scene having won their last three matches and it took 100 apiece by Raman Subba Row and Eric Bedser to give us the better of a draw with them at Loughborough. For a fortnight we did not win a match, by which time Sussex had emerged as the main threat.

After the final Test against Australia and the recovery of the Ashes we had a vital match at the Oval against Middlesex. We won it but my chief recollection is of a really great innings of 63 in fifty minutes by Denis Compton. When you talk about those days to him, he admits to having been rather pleased with this innings. His playing of Laker and Lock on a very nasty pitch, turning and lifting, was superb and I can still see him hitting Jim for a huge 6 at the Vauxhall end. On pitches like this he had a wonderful way of going out to the off-spinner, getting inside the ball and hitting it directly against the spin past cover's left hand.

By the time we played Sussex at Hove in our last match but one we only needed to draw to be champions – not a recipe for a good match. Rain took away several hours' play, and although Sussex led us on first innings their failure to win meant that we were safe. It was a time of double celebration in the May family. My brother John had been playing for Berkshire, who were that year's Minor County champions, and there had been one famous day when we each made 100.

Surrey's win in 1954 was unusual because it was belated, for we stood only eighth in the table in late July. Of the last ten matches we won nine and drew one and eventually overhauled Yorkshire to win by 22 points.

Stuart Surridge missed several matches in June including one against Hampshire at Guildford in which things really fell into my lap. The pitch was damp but I won the toss and put them in. They were soon 13 for 5 against Alec Bedser and Loader. A sixth-wicket stand of 72 between Colin Ingleby-Mackenzie and Mike Barnard gave the score an incongruous look, for the total was only 97.

By then the pitch was harmless but on Sunday night it rained again. We were 206 for 2, I was 117 not out and it did not take me long to decide that I would rather watch Bedser, Loader, Laker and Lock bowling at them than try my hand against Shackleton and Cannings, who would be an awkward pair if the pitch again played as it had on Saturday morning. The match was over before lunch, no spectacle, I am afraid, but a faithfully carrying-out, so I thought, of the Surridge policy of swift dispatch.

The stronger bowling side usually has the best of the weather, but not always. Soon afterwards we played Glamorgan at the Oval. Everything seemed to be under control when Tony Lock bowled them out for 95, but it rained overnight and the only innings played in reasonable batting conditions was Glamorgan's second in which they did well to make 217. On the last day the ball turned and lifted almost impossibly. I stuck it out for about an hour and a half but, having gone in at number three, had no partners left by then and was 17 not out. Jim McConnon

took 7 for 23, which probably had something to do with the selectors'
preference for him rather than Laker when they picked the team for
Australia a few weeks later.

We were drawing a lot of matches that season but the luck of the
weather was with us in a match against Essex late in July and we started
on our winning run. Ken Barrington had played only occasional first-
class matches previously but he had been given another chance in mid-
July and made two 100s in three innings. He made an invaluable 89 not
out against Essex and played a big part in the success of the next month.

I had a special interest in the young Barrington because, like the
Bedsers and myself, he was a Berkshire man. He had great determination
and was extremely brave against the fastest bowling. 'The Colonel', as
he was often called later, became a remarkable run-getter, but for all
the intense application of his batting he never lost his sense of fun. We
all miss him very much indeed.

Kenny's runs in August 1954 were the more valuable because during
our winning sequence I was not in great form myself. One who *was* in
form was Jim Laker who won us a low-scoring match at Kettering by
taking 11 Northamptonshire wickets and playing an innings of 33 not
out which saw us home by 1 wicket.

I did make 31 not out in an amazing match at the Oval which gave
us the championship. It was a perfect illustration of the speed with which
our bowlers worked and of Stuart Surridge's enterprise.

We started after lunch on the first day and on a wet pitch bowled out
Worcestershire for 25, mostly through Lock, who took 5 for 2, and
Laker. Worcestershire were short of spin in those days, the pitch seemed
easier and I was enjoying myself when to my astonishment I saw Stuart
appear on the balcony and declare. It was not yet half past five on the
first evening. Our score was 92 for 3.

In those days the amateurs still used the upstairs dressing room.
Downstairs among the rest of the side the general verdict was that the
captain must have gone mad. His explanation as he led us out was that
it was going to rain, which did not entirely clear up the misgivings.

One of the 2 wickets which fell in the last hour was that of Peter
Richardson who was out in a way which I have never forgotten. When
he played no stroke, he used to raise the bat high above his head out of
harm's way. He did this to the first ball he received from Jim Laker but
it turned and leaped so high that he was still caught at the wicket.

We finished the match in an hour next morning. We had batted for
only 24 overs but had won by an innings and 27 runs.

While playing in the last Test against Pakistan, I had missed another
of Stuart's finest hours but it was graphically described to me. On the
last afternoon at Cheltenham the Surrey bowlers, although at full

strength apart from Loader, were not making the progress to which Stuart was accustomed. Arthur Milton and Jack Crapp could be very obdurate. It began to rain with only 4 wickets taken and nothing in the sky suggested that it was likely to stop.

Stuart was in and out of the dressing room every few minutes examining the low cloud cover. Finally he came out and fairly glared in the direction from which the weather was coming. The rain stopped. Stuart lost no time in pointing this out to the umpires and hurried them out with the Surrey side hot on their heels.

Of the 6 wickets remaining he took 5 himself, including one with a ball which unkind eyewitnesses say would have missed the leg stump by a foot if the batsman's leg had not deflected it onto the wicket.

When the last man was out and Surrey had won, Stuart relaxed and the rain belted down. I may not have been present to vouch for every detail of the story but it is a fair illustration of the drive and inspiration of Stuart's leadership.

We were chased hard by Yorkshire in 1955, a much drier summer in which we did not draw a single match. Of the twenty-eight we won twenty-three and lost five. Yorkshire won twenty-one and lost by only 16 points. At that time points for lead on first innings were retained only in a match lost or drawn so that the difference between winning and losing could be only 8 points.

The first half of the summer was not as dry as the second and Tony Lock took 20 wickets in the first two matches. He had reached 100 wickets by the first days of July.

We had an amazing day's cricket, or rather hour's cricket, at Leicester on a Saturday in May when Charles Palmer took his 8 for 0. We had bowled Leicestershire out for 114 on a drying pitch and at tea were 42 for 1. I had already made 28 and was perfectly satisfied with the way things were going. As I came out after tea and passed Charles, he told me that he was going to have an over and with a laugh asked me to go easy on him as it was about the first time that he had bowled that season. He had had a troublesome back and I believe that he had in fact bowled only two experimental overs a fortnight before and not at all in the nets.

I realized that his intention was to bowl just the one over to allow his off-spinner Vic Jackson to change ends with Vic Munden and avail himself of the one damp patch remaining which was just outside the off stump. However, the third ball of the over hit the spot, came back smartly and bowled me.

At his trim medium pace Charles was always extremely accurate, so accurate, in fact, that when just occasionally he tossed up a high 'donkey-drop', he would flight it so skilfully that the batsman found himself in all sorts of a tangle trying to stop it dropping on the stumps. He bowled this ball very rarely but had a high striking rate with it.

On this occasion he hit the damp patch unerringly with his flat flight and every time that the ball passed the bat it seemed to hit the stumps. I was the first of seven whom he bowled and with our last pair together he had taken 8 for 0. He was then bowling to Jim Laker who saw his 8 for 2 of the 1950 Test trial being outdone and aimed a violent blow on the off side. He mis-hit and might have been caught in the covers but the difficult chance escaped and Charles had to be satisfied with 8 for 7.

After this incredible interlude the match took an unexceptional course and, with 200 odd to make, we won by 7 wickets.

We had two eventful matches with Yorkshire in the middle of the season. The match at the Oval was Arthur McIntyre's benefit and I was delighted that 45,000 were there over the three days.

Godfrey Evans could touch great heights of wicketkeeping especially on the big occasion, but day in, day out Arthur was the most reliable wicketkeeper of the 1950s. He should have played many more times for England. He kept superbly to Alec Bedser, Loader, Laker and Lock on most difficult pitches and made it look easy. He was never acrobatic. There was no need, as he was always in the correct position on his two feet.

His benefit match had an ominous start. The ground was soaked, Norman Yardley put us in and Appleyard and Trueman bowled us out for 85. Yorkshire did rather better and led by 46 runs but we had the best batting conditions for our second innings before it rained again, and we won the match.

This was the weekend when I took over the England captaincy from Len Hutton, who was out of form and out of sorts generally. He was twice out to Peter Loader, for 0 and 1, caught at the wicket in the first innings and bowled in the second. Loader was a very skilful swing bowler who varied his pace cleverly and who possessed a quick unpleasant bouncer. He had the ability to move the ball away not only in the air but off the pitch at a very fast pace and I can see him now dismissing Len with just such a ball.

A fortnight later at Headingley we lost a most unusual match. The gates were closed on the Saturday when Peteer Loader came in at 119 for 8 and, with support from Lock and Alec Bedser, made 81, so that we reached 268. On his day he could be a highly effective straight hitter.

Yorkshire were always struggling on the Monday and we led by 102 runs on first innings but unfortunately had to bat again for the last hour and forty minutes. The roller seemed to have brought up some moisture, for Trueman, Cowan and the fast, lifting ball were very nasty. What made it worse was that the light was the darkest in which I remember playing in England and the umpires stoutly refused to go off – to the delight of a large and noisily jubilant crowd. When I see them go off nowadays in what looks a perfectly adequate light, with medium pacers bowling and with far better sightscreens than existed in our day, I often think back to that Monday evening at Headingley. The light on the scoreboard was described in the Surrey dressing room as shining like a beacon on Eddystone lighthouse. We finished at 27 for 7. Mike Cowan was an underrated left-arm fast-medium bowler who, like his partner on this occasion, became in later years a brilliant after-dinner speaker much in demand.

Laker and Lock helped us up to 75 next day but the pitch rolled out mild. Yorkshire batted well and won by 6 wickets. They were a strong side at that time. Len Hutton was in his last few matches but they also had Frank Lowson, Vic Wilson, Willie Watson, the much underestimated Billy Sutcliffe and Norman Yardley to bat, and Trueman, Cowan, Appleyard, Wardle and Illingworth to bowl.

Briefly at the end of July Yorkshire took the lead in the championship but we had matches in hand and won seven of our last eight matches, which was good enough.

No county had ever won the championship outright five years running, so we had an extra incentive in 1956 – in fact, two extra incentives, for it was fairly certain that this would be Stuart Surridge's last season. My own contribution for Surrey that year was fairly modest. Subconsciously I may have saved my best for the Test series against Australia but, whatever the reason, my performance was the exact opposite of what it was in the following winter in South Africa when my Test form was so poor compared with that in other matches.

When we beat Australia by 10 wickets in May, we had already lost to Northamptonshire at the Oval and we were beaten by both Nottinghamshire and Gloucestershire in the next ten days. It is extraordinary to think that in the great year of Laker and Lock – when they took nearly 300 wickets between them, when Jim took his 19 wickets at Old Trafford and twice took all 10, and when Tony also took all 10 – we should have lost all these three matches on pitches which took spin. The explanation is that there were a lot of good spinners around in those days, among them the Australians, George Tribe and Jack Manning of Northamptonshire, John Mortimore, Sam Cook and 'Bomber' Wells of Gloucestershire, Bruce Dooland and the off-spinner Ken Smales of Nottinghamshire.

From the second half of July we won seven matches, which was a lot more than any other county won in seven miserably wet weeks. We met Lancashire, our main challengers, at the Oval at the end of August, but there was no play in the last two days and we became champions in the most unspectacular way – in the dressing room. There was no play at all in what would have been Stuart's final championship match against Warwickshire, so his five years of captaincy ended in damp triumph but triumph all the same.

Through those five years we had lost only two of the players who had launched us on the run – Laurie Fishlock and Jack Parker. They had been replaced by Micky Stewart and Ken Barrington. Micky, usually at square short leg, was a fearless close fielder in the same class as Stuart Surridge and Tony Lock. No helmets in those days. I doubt if it would have occurred to Micky to wear one if they had existed. He was a fine quick-footed opening batsman and a dedicated Surrey man who in recent years has brought pride back to the Oval as manager.

Dave Fletcher was a consistent opening batsman who nearly always gave us a good start – a particularly brave hooker.

Bernard Constable, small and neat, was one of those important but unspectacular players on whom most sides rely more than is usually recognized. He was a marvellous cover point, a brilliant player of spin, very tidy in anything he did. He was an amusing character to have around. His continuous, humorous battle with Alan Moss whenever we played Middlesex gave us a lot of fun. 'Don't you bounce 'em at me,' was usually his opening exchange with Alan. Whenever he had to cross from cover point to cover point between overs, he was ready with some piece of philosophy for the batsman.

Any side which included Alec and Eric Bedser was not short of characters. When I needed advice and consulted them, I would get the same advice word for word from each of them, although they had been in different parts of the field.

One of my favourite stories of the Bedsers is of the early postwar era when they were really very much alike. One day in Sydney Alec decided that he wanted a haircut and went into a barber's shop while Eric went to do some shopping. When Alec came out, Eric presumably approved of the job done and decided that he ought to have his hair cut too.

He went in and was greeted by the barber, 'Cor, mate, your bloody hair grows quickly.'

We had, of course, players of very different personalities, no pair more different than Laker and Lock. Jim Laker, quiet, withdrawn, undemonstrative, did not always seem to be enjoying the game as much as others, although he doubtless was. Tony Lock, by contrast, was flamboyant, full of action, aggressive, putting 105 per cent into all he did.

Yet the quality which I appreciate above all when I think back to the Surrey of the 1950s was the team spirit. This sounds like the usual platitude but it is more than that. I always had the feeling that if one of us made an exceptional individual contribution, its value to the side was uppermost in the mind of the others. And, for that, one man was responsible, Stuart Surridge.

He was very much the players' champion, insisting that we all shared railway carriages and stayed at the same hotels, which had not previously been the custom. With his boundless energy, his drive, impatience, often unconventional approach and touch of irascibility, he was regarded with profound respect, trust and indeed affection. His style of captaincy was unusual, but it worked – and we all knew it did.

10

South African Ups and Downs

I have mixed feelings when I think back to the 1956-57 tour of South Africa. It was a very happy tour to a lovely country of friendly people and immense hospitality. On the other hand, there was much uninspired cricket played and my own performance was an acute disappointment.

Sometimes people ask me, usually rather diffidently, how I came to average 15 in Test matches there and 85 in other first-class matches. As I had just averaged 90 against Australia, I could scarcely be charged with not having a 'Test-match temperament'.

My first reaction to the question is usually that I have no explanation. On reflection, I suppose that there were minor reasons. Early in the Test series I was out to some superb catches. Then, as a sluggish tempo dropped even further, I began to try to pick it up and took risks against tight bowling and brilliant fielding which did not come off. I do not accept that the strain of captaincy had anything to do with it. I had every help from the manager, Freddie Brown, and my vice-captain, Doug Insole. I think that a comparison can be made with Denis Compton's Test failures in Australia in 1950-51. It is a great and unpredictable game and these things happen.

As for the captaincy on my first experience of it overseas, I was lucky in my team – and in our opponents. The two South African captains, Jackie McGlew, who in fact was only fit to play in the Second Test, and Clive van Ryneveld, were old friends and opponents. For a captain it was hard work – I answered every letter personally – but it was not the most exacting of tours.

In retrospect, I think that one of the harder parts of it was the selection of the team beforehand. We had a surfeit of good fast bowlers and we took Statham, Tyson and Loader as well as Trevor Bailey. We left out Fred Trueman. Fred had played in only two Tests in 1956 and had not had one of his best seasons. We also left out Tom Graveney. This was a particularly difficult decision because he had finished top of the first-class averages. On the other hand, he had done little in the two Tests in which he had played. We wanted to fit in Doug Insole, who in fact did very well, and Alan Oakman, who was an improving batsman, a specialist close catcher and could be a reserve off-spinner. But what strength, to be able to leave out a bowler and a batsman of the class of Trueman and Graveney!

What made the cricket played so disappointing was that only eighteen months earlier we had had that marvellous series in England with South Africa. The difference now was that the pitches were generally helpful to good bowlers and there were plenty of those on both sides. They were nearly always on top and even more on top because of the athletic fielding on the South African side. We held many fine catches too.

Something of the strength of our bowling in the prevailing conditions can be gathered from two figures. Only one stand of over 100 was made against us on the whole tour and only two individual 100s, one by Roy McLean in the Third Test in Durban and one in Kimberley by Griqua-land West's opening batsman, Evans, who really earned the distinction the hard way. Not out 99 on Saturday night, he needed an hour on the Monday morning to make the last precious run. Our bowlers in that minor match were Tyson, Loader, Wardle, Laker and Lock.

By contrast, we made nineteen 100s on the tour, three in Test matches by Peter Richardson, Colin Cowdrey and Doug Insole. From this it might be deduced that we were the stronger side and should have won the series. So we should. But South Africa deserved all credit for coming back from two down, especially as they were without Jackie McGlew in four Tests. If fully fit, he would almost certainly have been the hardest man for our bowlers to dig out.

On our thoroughly enjoyable outward voyage I had time to think about some of the things required of a touring captain and, of course, to talk it over with Freddie Brown, who had done it all himself. It was also a great help to be able to talk about touring to our baggage master, George Duckworth, the Admiral as we called him. Some winters George, the great wicket-keeper of the 1930s, used to take his own Common-wealth sides overseas. They too must have profited from his fund of humour, kindly advice and solid sense.

By tradition, the captain in those days, however youthful, was much more of the senior partner than he is today. The manager looked after the managing and both press and public seemed to expect fairly easy access to the captain. The public were not satisfied with speeches by the manager, even by one as distinguished as Freddie Brown, and one of my first duties was to make a speech in Cape Town City Hall. Here I had a bit of luck. On board was a certain Professor Tomlinson. He was kind enough to equip me with several sentences in Afrikaans and to work on providing me with a passable accent. As it happened, I knew a little German, which helped. I duly fired off my few sentences in the City Hall. They caught public attention and they served me well subsequently. As I remember it, my theme was that we had come to play cricket which was a game and not a matter of international prestige.

We played our first match in lovely surroundings at Paarl, the centre of the wine-growing country, after which we beat Western Province by an innings. Though the Currie Cup champions, they were a young side and short of practice.

I made 162 in rather a long time, five hours or so, which was not quite what I had originally intended. I wanted to win the match and, as things worked out, I decided that the others had a better chance of playing an innings with the pressure off if I held one end. Some needed practice more than others. One who did particularly well but unfortunately did not fulfil his promise later was Alan Oakman. With his 6 feet 5 inches, he was a fine sight when driving but we used to laugh unbelievingly at the bat he used. It weighed 2 lb 9 oz. My own was 2 lb 4 oz. Denis Compton's was less. This will seem extraordinary to the young who now wield things weighing well over 3 lb.

One would think that there are few better ways of travelling to your next match than by driving up the Garden Route, but it rained all the way and we found Port Elizabeth very wet. Our match with Eastern Province was put back a day and, when we did play, we won easily in two days. Doug Insole began to work his way into the form which gave him a very good tour. I made another 100 and the spinners, Lock and Wardle on this occasion, took a lot of wickets.

Doug Insole, with his homely, highly unconventional, open and bottom-handed method, made the purists wince but he was a great collector of runs. He had a marvellous eye, was a very fine cutter, a magnificent slip and on this, his only tour, was a great asset to me both for his playing ability and for his sense of humour.

Gradually the batsmen found their form. Cowdrey and Oakman shared in a stand of over 300 in Bloemfontein. In Rhodesia Denis Compton, whose knee had been giving a little trouble earlier, began to make runs too. By his standards Denis may not have had a great tour but he played a number of valuable innings. After his final parting with his kneecap he was not very mobile and I had to be careful where I put him in the field. I did not want him near the wicket which, with bowlers of the calibre of ours, was where the action usually was.

In the First Test match I was setting the field. 'It's super to have you with us,' I said to him, 'but you struggle to bend down. Go to long leg and just stand there.' He departed to long leg where he doubtless missed the company and opportunities for conversation which, as a sociable chap, he had around the wicket. After two balls of the over he had moved quite appreciably in. By the fifth ball of the eight-ball over he was up among the short legs.

'Denis, what are you doing there?' I called out. 'I told you to go to long leg.'

He had a marvellously simple answer. 'I thought you needed help,' he said.

In Salisbury I had the privilege of sharing in a stand of 301 with Trevor Bailey which, I may say, took only just over three hours. I had moved Trevor up the order to number three as there were already signs that he might be needed to open. Colin Cowdrey was always a reluctant opener and was also needed to strengthen the middle batting.

We had already lost Jim Parks who had returned home with an eye problem. He was expected back and indeed started to come back but collapsed at London Airport. By then we decided that we could manage without him and did not send for a replacement. Jim was not a wicket-keeper in those days – we had Brian Taylor as second wicketkeeper to Godfrey Evans – but we had hoped that he would give a lively boost to the middle batting as he was to do in the 1960s.

There was a bad moment at the Wankie Game Reserve when Freddie Brown temporarily lost a Land Rover with four players in it, but so far on the field everything had gone unbelievably well. We had won every match by an innings. I myself, in five weeks, had played four first-class innings and made four 100s. Just before leaving Salisbury we attended a mayoral reception at which the mayor, Harry Pichanik, hauled me on the stage and said that there was clearly only one way of stopping this. He produced a live duck which flapped round the stage to the general amusement. Unfortunately it did the trick.

In Johannesburg against the Transvaal, MCC's first match on the new Wanderers' ground, we came up against Heine and Adcock, who bowled very fast and accurately, taking 13 wickets between them. Heine was the more aggressive and brought me down to earth with a bump, having me caught at the wicket first ball. I had only made 12 in the second innings when I met a similar fate.

My disappointment in the first innings was relieved by the fact that I was followed in by Denis Compton who made nearly 50 in an hour with all his old brilliance. After a shortened first day Brian Statham on the second morning performed a hat trick, which was remarkable because he hit the stumps all three times. We won the match but ended it on an unimpressive note, losing 7 wickets in our painful progress to the 67 needed.

Our first defeat was only delayed until the next match which was on a loose pitch in Pretoria against a strong South African XI including Hugh Tayfield, who took 12 wickets. Doug Insole lost the toss and though we bowled out the opposition for 138, that was comfortably the highest total of the match. MCC had never lost in South Africa before on turf. Loftus Versveld is, of course, better known as a rugby ground and the bare pitch had only been laid at the end of the rugby season.

We did not emerge with much credit from the match in any way, for there was a regrettable incident on the third evening. I had spent the day answering correspondence and arrived on the ground to find the place in an uproar.

It turned out that at six o'clock, with MCC 90 for 7, Jackie McGlew had left the field to inform Doug Insole that he was claiming the extra half-hour in the hope of finishing the match that evening. Bailey and Lock, the batsmen, having apparently decided that this was not in the playing conditions, went off too. There had, in fact, been a verbal agreement that 8 wickets should be down before the extra half-hour could be claimed and a written one which did not mention the 8-wicket requirement.

Play continued, however, and the match carried over into the next day before we lost by 38 runs. There was certainly an ambiguity in the playing conditions, or the way in which they were originally agreed, but we did not perform with the greatest credit. There had also been words on the field. We were not blameless and I had to make it clear to the team that I was not going to stand for anything similar in future. It was the only time that this was necessary.

I played against Natal in Durban and made another 100. Doug Insole made one too. We had much the better of a draw against one of the stronger provinces which included McGlew, Goddard and McLean. I stood down from the last match before the First Test and we sent Compton off to do a lap of honour at Benoni, scene of his 300 in three hours eight years before. He needed the practice, as it was nearly three weeks since he had batted on a decent pitch. He made 70 in not much over an hour before it rained, so the reputation of Compton in the Eastern Transvaal stayed untarnished.

Picking the team for the First Test was relatively straightforward. In England the choice between Wardle and Lock would usually have been different but Wardle, with the chinaman and googly to add to the left-arm spinner's conventional style, had been so much the more successful that he had to be picked. Tyson or Loader was a harder one. Loader was improving all the time, but while there still seemed a chance that a fit Tyson would recover his devastating form of Australia two years before we felt that we had to pick him.

The main decision that we had to make was to promote Bailey to open with Peter Richardson. It was not ideal. Trevor will remember that I always thought him overrated as a batsman and greatly underrated as a bowler. He could win matches as a bowler. But he was seldom easily removed and in case he became bogged down we moved Compton up to number three.

We were entitled to be fairly confident, even if the last three weeks had shown that, although South Africa had no great depth of first-class talent, their best players were pretty good.

I was not happy in having to leave Lock out, for he was a close catcher second to none. And although I had great faith in our bowlers, there was always a doubt about how they would react to the altitude in Johannesburg. Some people really feel the height there. Doubts existed too about the pitch. This was the first Test to be played on the new Wanderers ground. I was already worried, too, on the evidence of the tempo in the matches which we had already played, that we might become bogged down in a series of tedious draws.

That did not quite happen, although when on Christmas Eve in front of the biggest crowd ever to watch cricket in South Africa we made only 157 for 3, I really was depressed. Jackie McGlew's injured shoulder had caused him to drop out overnight and I found myself going out to toss with Clive van Ryneveld, a situation which neither of us could have envisaged when we played against each other in the University match of 1950. I always called tails and reckon that I had 60 per cent success. I got this one right, but after lunch we were only 48 for 3 and I was walking out after fending off a fast lifting ball from Adcock.

Apart from an innings of 100 in Rhodesia, Peter Richardson had made very few runs on the tour and he certainly played like a man out of form. But he was a great battler and he fought his way towards the slowest Test 100 then recorded, beginning with 69 in the six hours' play on the first day. Colin Cowdrey had one or two early escapes which subdued him for a long time. It was grim stuff but South Africa were at that time just about the most difficult side to bat against that I ever met. Heine and Adcock were at you all the time, banging the ball into the pitch at a genuine fast pace. When they were resting, you were having to cope with the wiles of Tayfield, a marvellous off-spinner of many subtle variations, and Goddard, left-arm medium-pace unfailingly accurate and at that time bowling a lot on an unhelpful length down the leg side. All this, and fielding of the very highest class.

On Boxing Day we were all out for 268, Peter Richardson having struggled away for eight and threequarter hours for 117. That evening South Africa were 91 for 1 with Trevor Goddard playing well. Next morning we had to do without Tyson who had tonsillitis but Bailey bowled at his best, Cowdrey held a marvellous catch in the gully off a full-blooded slash by Goddard and at one time we looked like having a lead of 100. With John Waite at number eight, South Africa batted a long way down and he and Tayfield kept our lead to 57.

Again our batsmen struggled against good fast bowling and Tayfield and some wonderful catching. The one-handed catch which Russell Endean took from me – diving to his left at midwicket when I thought I had played Heine off my legs for a certain 4 – was an incredible effort. But although we were out for 150 painfully earned runs and South Africa needed only 204, I had sufficient confidence in our bowlers on this fastish pitch of inconsistent bounce to be fairly hopeful.

As it happened, Bailey and Statham bowled superbly, Insole held two good catches at first slip – it was several months before he dropped anything there – and we had five out for 36 before the light faded and a storm stopped play. When the evening thunderstorm arrives on the high veld in summer, as it often does, that is the end of play for the day. This was the exception. The storm was a short one, the light improved and we returned for a few minutes during which we took 2 more good wickets.

It greatly eased our finishing off the match next morning when the mesmeric effect of Statham and Bailey was noticeably less. The pitch, too, had probably lost a little pace. Trevor had Tayfield caught by Godfrey Evans, his fifth wicket, but we were kept in the field for eighty minutes and it was May who finished the match with two runouts in successive overs.

Every victory is sweet, even one achieved in a grim cricket match like this, and I probably relished it more then than I do now in retrospect. But three days later another Test match, and indeed another year, was starting and everyone hoped for more colourful cricket in the incomparable setting of Newlands than had been played in Johannesburg.

Frank Tyson's tonsils had not fully recovered and we replaced him with Peter Loader, which we might have done anyway, for Loader relied less on sheer speed. I was a great believer in not worrying too much about the pitch and how it would play, but as I looked at this one on New Year's Eve I could not see that it would be of much use to Heine and Adcock. That at least was encouraging.

This time I went out to toss with Jackie McGlew who was pronounced fit. I won again and we made 214 for 5 that day. I had guessed right about Heine and Adcock, for our main opposition came from Tayfield who came on about midday and bowled for the rest of the day, 41 overs for 69 runs and 3 wickets.

Richardson and Bailey gave us a sound start but both were out soon after lunch, which left Compton and me together, he in sparkling form and myself hopeful. For a time I watched Denis firing off strokes against Heine and then I aimed to drive Tayfield on the offside. He was mostly floating the ball away from the bat and I was very well caught at the wicket off a thickish edge by John Waite.

Denis was out sweeping at Tayfield but Colin Cowdrey took root, Doug Insole played well in the evening and they may be said to have paved the way for a characteristic innings next day by Godfrey Evans, who with his twinkling feet made 62 with a freedom which was a blessed relief after a lot of our batting hitherto. To him Tayfield presented no problems. Colin took six hours over his 101, scoring his last 21 with the last man in. I do not, of course, speak from a strong position on the tempo of our batting because I was seldom in long enough to influence it.

Anyhow, we had 369 on the board and I was well satisfied, for I was sure that we were better equipped for bowling on this pitch. Sure enough, Laker was soon turning the ball more than Tayfield and had McGlew neatly caught at short leg by Cowdrey. Loader, with his changes of pace and movement off the pitch, was more effective than Heine and Adcock had been and soon had the left-handers, Goddard and Keith, caught at the wicket. Wardle tidied up the innings which had been conducted at a pace which made ours seem almost lighthearted.

There was only about an hour of the third day left and with a lead of 164 I had to decide whether to enforce the follow-on. Wardle's performance clearly provided the answer. He had turned the chinaman and googly a lot, the batsmen had not played him well and were not likely to play him any better in the last innings when the ball would almost certainly turn more. There was also the added attraction of batting with the pressure off for once and perhaps making runs in a way which would give us confidence to play strokes in the future.

Next day's batting was certainly an improvement. Richardson and Bailey made good progress although it was not easy against Heine and Adcock and defensive fields. After lunch I was caught at the wicket off Heine but Compton was playing well in a, for him, restrained way and I hoped would keep our score moving.

I had not long taken off my pads and was emerging from the shower when someone called out, 'Come and look at this!' I went to the window and there was the Cowdrey of Australia two years before, stroking the ball through the gaps as if it was the easiest thing in the world. Denis obviously enjoyed it too and contented himself with a supporting part. Cowdrey, the great enigma, made 61 out of a stand of 87 with Denis, a proportion which few others can have achieved, and I was able to declare at tea.

It was all over half an hour after lunch next day, as Wardle and Laker bowled them out for 72, Wardle 7 for 36. The pitch did not break up but he turned the ball huge amounts and, apart from Roy McLean, no one had much idea of how to play him. At the other end, Laker was not exactly easy and it was to his bowling, though not to him, that the most remarkable wicket fell.

Russell Endean had struggled for a long time without scoring when he shoved out his front leg at the ball which leaped up in the air and slightly back towards the wicket. Instead of padding it off, he knocked it away with his right hand almost absentmindedly, it seemed.

We all digested this strange action for a moment or two and then bowler and wicketkeeper appealed. Russell inevitably had to be given out 'handled the ball'. It was a weird coincidence that he was the wicketkeeper who had been obstructed at the Oval in 1951 when Len Hutton suffered that other rare form of dismissal. I looked round the field and tried to work out who else had been present then on our side beside myself. The answer was only two, Compton and Laker, although Freddie Brown, captain then, was in the Newlands pavilion as our manager now.

Two up, and the winners at Newlands by 312 runs, we were entitled to be fairly confident about the rest of the series. Nothing happened before the next Test in Durban to undermine our optimism. I played in the first two matches in the Eastern Cape and made runs each time. Denis Compton made 100 in a drawn match against Natal at Pietermaritzburg, which was important because we badly needed his fluency of stroke.

When the Third Test began, we made a splendid start. I won the toss again and at lunch Richardson and Bailey had made over 100 together. Yet that proved to be the peak of our achievement. I have always thought that it was our approach that afternoon which cost us the series. Peter Richardson was out for 68, having played very well, and ideally the stage was set for Compton, May and Cowdrey to exploit the advantage.

Denis certainly started promisingly but was bowled behind his legs by Heine. I nudged the ball onto the wicketkeeper's pad whence it rebounded for Trevor Goddard at slip to make a marvellous one-handed catch. Colin had been ill and was in no sort of form, although he hung around for a time.

The main problem was that Trevor Bailey, having played a most useful part in the opening stand and reached 50 soon after lunch, then made 21 in three hours. He was 71 not out when bad light stopped play for the day twenty-five minutes early.

I was asked, as one always was on these occasions, what instructions I had given – as if I would have told Trevor not on any account to play a stroke! I was also not going to say that one of our batsmen had disobeyed orders. We all knew what was required and I believed every one was doing his best according to his ability. Trevor was an intelligent cricketer who knew perfectly well what was needed, but he was very limited and was wont to become bogged down technically and mentally by good bowling and fielding. I think that here he saw himself as engaged in a personal duel with Tayfield and became so wrapped up in it that the momentum of the innings slipped away without his realizing it. It would have been nice to have been in a position to tell him to attack and not to bother if he was out. But the rest of us were not doing well enough for that.

On the second morning our innings subsided ignominiously and, with Goddard and McLean playing very well, South Africa finished the day looking set to take a big lead. But though McLean made the only Test 100 against us, Wardle and the fast bowlers passed quickly through the later batsmen and the lead was only 65.

In the second innings we again batted without distinction, except for Doug Insole whose 110 not out after some six hours of tense cricket meant that South Africa needed 190 in four hours ten minutes. We were by then without Bailey, who had a hand in plaster.

Tayfield had taken 8 for 69 but without turning the ball much and I was not confident that we could bowl them out unless they took risks. In fact, they never worked themselves into a position from which they looked likely to win. In the end, we were doing the attacking, and although we were not successful, a draw seemed not a bad thing in view of our 2-0 lead. In fact, it cost us the series.

On we went to Johannesburg to play the Transvaal again. Rain over the first two days spoilt it as a match but when we came to bat on the last two days we made nearly 600, Compton 131, Insole 192. I found myself batting with the same freedom and timing as early in the tour but, alas, not with the same luck. I had made 73 when I hit Tayfield wide of deep mid-on off the middle of the bat. It was a low skimmer going very hard, but deep mid-on, by name Pistorius, took off and held it right-handed at full stretch. It was an amazing catch, but after my recent Test experiences no catch surprised me.

After an innings win over Griqualand West in Kimberley we came back to Johannesburg for the Fourth Test. There was less grass on the Test pitch than on the one of a week before and I remember regretting that I was due to lose the toss. I did lose it. South Africa made 234 for 5 that day and we were glad to have them out for only 340. By the second evening we had made 87 for 2. Doug Insole, whom I had moved up to number three because he was in such good form, was 30 not out and so was I. With only 47 runs behind me in six Test innings I was not in a position to be confident but I played well enough that Saturday evening to hope that the bad times were over.

On the Monday morning we had to work hard, especially against Heine who bowled one of his fierier spells, but that had been safely negotiated when Doug was out in a most galling way. Tayfield appealed for lbw against him. The appeal was turned down. Doug, thinking that the ball had bypassed the wicketkeeper, started to run a leg bye. I had not thought of a run because I did not know where the ball was. In fact, Doug, who had been playing forward, and the wicketkeeper obscured it from me as it had gone to first slip who promptly advanced to the wicket and broke it.

This was just what South Africa needed. Even Denis Compton, not quite the nimble-footed player of spin that he had once been, could make no progress against Tayfield. Goddard was never easy to score off. Just before lunch Adcock was brought back and bowled me what I thought was one of the morning's few half-volleys. I drove at it and dragged it onto the stumps. I had made 61 and, in the sense that I had really begun to hope that I was out of my run of low scores at last, this was the bitterest blow of all.

Denis was not in form, although he battled on stoutly and the innings slipped away until we were all out just before the end of the third day, leaving South Africa with a lead of 89.

The next day was one of extraordinary contrasts, an opening stand of 62 by Goddard and Tony Pithey, which lasted until after lunch, being followed by the fall of all 10 wickets for 80. We knew only too well how difficult it was to attack on this pitch and when South Africa tried to accelerate against our bowling they suffered. Pithey, incidentally, had been brought in to replace McGlew in the previous Test. He was the opposite of the stroke-playing opening batsman whom I feared South Africa might produce but he was normally not easily removed, and Trevor Goddard was in such excellent form hereabouts that they usually made a fair start.

We went in needing 232 and made 19 that night, losing Bailey. Next day we so nearly won the series that it made the result, defeat by 17 runs, all the harder to bear. The consolation was that we batted more boldly than hitherto.

Richardson and Insole had some luck but played with a businesslike common sense and when Richardson was out I sent in Colin Cowdrey to continue the steady progress. That worked and the score rose to 147 for 2 at a pace not often reached in that series. Then Doug was out, not to Tayfield, who took all the other wickets in a spell lasting five hours, but to the nagging Goddard whom he tried to cut.

I was determined not to let Tayfield pin us down again and almost at once took a step to play him firmly to long on. I was caught off bat and pad.

At tea we needed 46 with 4 wickets standing, but Colin was still there, which meant that there was still hope. So was Godfrey Evans, who was capable of upsetting a spinner and winning the match in a few minutes. Not this time. Godfrey played on to Tayfield and Colin hit a hard return catch which the bowler held. Tayfield took the remaining 2 wickets, which gave him 9 for 113, and the crowd carried him to the pavilion. It was a marvellous piece of bowling, making the most of what the pitch had to offer.

Yet I felt that we should have won and I kept thinking of the great chance we had had in Durban after making our best start of all. We had allowed them to get back into the series and we already knew that Port Elizabeth would be unpredictable. Luck would play a big part there and luck has a way of turning against you when you have failed to take your chances.

We went down to the Cape and two days later played Western Province again. We had the better of a draw and infuriatingly, if that is the right word, I made 116 and 79 with some ease. Thus to Port Elizabeth and the final Test.

We had to go into this without both Statham and Wardle who were injured. With Tyson and Lock as replacements, we did not have to worry too much about that. What concerned us more was the newly laid pitch. The one on which we had played Eastern Province four months before had taken spin and this one had cracks in it which suggested an increasingly uneven bounce. It was going to be a good toss to win. I lost it.

Even when we had South Africa 41 for 4, 3 wickets to Bailey, one to Loader, I was not easy in my mind, for there had been a little moisture there for the fast bowlers and the ball had swung. I was afraid that batting could be at its easiest for the rest of that day and, unless we could bowl them out quickly, we were not going to be the ones who benefited. So it proved, although that did not detract in any way from Russell Endean's dogged innings of 70 which almost certainly was the matchwinner.

On the second morning South Africa lost their last 5 wickets for 26 but 164 was a healthy score to have in hand on a pitch now often producing the shooter. I do not remember another pitch on which the attempted bouncer would quite often creep along the ground.

I went in in the second over, in which Adcock had had Richardson lbw and had bowled Compton. Trevor Bailey and I then shared in a stand of 54. Trevor was in his element with improvisations on the theme of the forward defensive stroke. He played more fluently than usual while I played just about my best innings of the series. It ended in an exasperating way.

We were keeping firmly on the front foot not only as a defensive measure against the shooter but because the ball that could be driven was almost the only source of runs available. I received just about the only one which lifted. Trying to play it positively but, I thought, circumspectly wide of mid-on, I was caught off the edge at cover point.

Early on the third day we were out for 110, and although we kept them pinned down for the rest of a six-hour day, which produced only 122 runs, and took 7 wickets, it was certain that we would have to make an uncomfortably large score. It proved to be 189, Tyson having taken 6 for 40, mostly by cutting his pace for greater accuracy and bowling off a short run. He adapted himself well, but Statham with his accuracy and his low skidding trajectory might well have been deadly.

There was an air of inevitability about our last innings, although I went in number three and had another stand with Trevor Bailey which took us up to 41 for 1. There it ended in almost exactly the opposite way to my end in the first innings. It was now more than just the occasional ball which lifted and I had just coped rather well, so I thought, with one lifter from Goddard when he bowled a quicker one which straightened and shot along the ground to hit me on the right ankle.

We lost by 58 runs, and it was undoubtedly a great performance by South Africa to pick themselves up to draw the series. We had been lucky, perhaps, but we had had our chances in both the Third and Fourth Tests and we really should have won. I am convinced that the 1956-57 side to South Africa was better than the one which went to Australia two years later.

As a former captain in South Africa, I shall be expected to add something to the long-running controversy about whether or not their cricketers should now be ostracized. I do this with reluctance because this is a book about my enjoyment of cricket and I have not enjoyed seeing good men and good friends treated with contempt by critics often wilfully ignorant of the facts.

I have always gone on record as saying that we should play cricket with everybody possible in those relatively few countries in the world that play the game. This is even more desirable now that cricket in South Africa is non-racial and we are in a better position to help the Coloureds, Indians and Africans. They cannot claim British passports as do some South African games players who are able to come here and compete for England because of their British antecedents.

It seems to me, therefore, that those who wish to isolate South African cricket, and still more South African football and athletics, are harming the very people whom they profess to want to help. Moreover, by refusing to cooperate in the huge liberalization in sport which is taking place there, we are strengthening the hand of those who oppose change in South Africa.

It is a harsh reality that in international cricket few countries are free of governmental intervention and even England and New Zealand, whose sport is not under direct political control, are subject to the Gleneagles Declaration. The restraints which the threats and risk of financial loss put on the game in England create great difficulties for the Cricket Council and the Test and County Cricket Board. Yet I have no answer every time I am confronted with the wording of the Cricket Council's 1970 statement: 'No further Test tours between South Africa and this country will take place until cricket is played and teams are selected on a multi-racial basis in South Africa.'

The promise implied there has been broken and it gives me no pleasure to know that old friends in South Africa, who have done far more for the non-Whites than their critics in England and elsewhere have ever done, think that we have behaved dishonourably. I hate to see the good name of English cricket dishonoured.

I know that by modern thinking this makes me 'naive'. But I would rather be naive than bigoted and unfair.

11

Two English Summers

If I returned chastened by my Test record in South Africa, there was not much time to brood over it. In 1957 we had to face a West Indian team including many of the players who had given England such a beating in 1950 under the same captain, John Goddard. Moreover, I was now captain of Surrey, very keen, of course, that the end of their championship-winning run should not coincide with my taking over.

In fact, Stuart Surridge had left me with the best team of all, and although I myself had to miss nine out of the twenty-eight matches, I had an ideal right-hand man in Alec Bedser. I insisted that he was made vice-captain. Previously Surrey had never nominated one, certainly not a professional. Alec was thrilled and I was delighted because I knew how well and conscientiously he would do the job. When I hear of counties having domestic troubles nowadays such as clashes of personality and problems of selection, I remember with gratitude the harmonious way in which Alec and I ran things with, I like to think, the minimum of fuss.

Success helps, of course, and you cannot have success without good players. We had plenty of those. The strength and depth of our bowling become evident when one considers that although Jim Laker, in the year after his epic feat of taking 19 wickets in the Old Trafford Test, took 85 wickets in the championship at 12 apiece, three bowlers in the side – Lock, Alec Bedser and Loader – each took more wickets, not to mention Eric Bedser who took 60 at 13 apiece.

Nearly all the players were just about at their peak that year. I probably was myself. We usually played an extra batsman instead of Stuart Surridge and the other big gap which he left, as a great slip catcher, we filled by bringing Ken Barrington in from the outfield. He was to become one of the best slips of his time and with Mickey Stewart and Tony Lock made a tremendous contribution to the bowlers' successes.

We won the championship by 98 points, no less, winning twenty-one matches out of twenty-eight, drawing four and, when below strength, losing three. It must have been one of the easiest championship wins on record – we clinched it at Weston-super-Mare on 16 August – and I was especially pleased as it was Brian Castor's last year as secretary of

Surrey. I have already mentioned the backing which he gave in his own gruff way to the players.

I have cause to remember my first championship match that season against Glamorgan at the Oval. Batting at the Vauxhall end, I thought that I had been caught at mid-on by Bernard Hedges and set off for the pavilion. But Hedges, lying on the ground, signalled that he had dropped the ball which was somewhere under him. By that time, I was passing Ken Barrington at the other end and Wilf Wooller had the ball thrown to him and ran me out. Dear old Wilf, he was a hard opponent on the field but very likable off it and I always thought him a shrewd selector. He was a selector that year.

Another eventful match that season, or pair of matches, came in July when, having surrendered Jim Laker, Tom Clark and myself to Gentlemen and Players at Lord's and having injuries among Second XI players, Surrey felt justified in asking for Tony Lock to be released from the Players' side in order to play against Leicestershire at the Oval.

This was agreed and he took 11 wickets for 58 in a rain-affected match. But the same rain produced a very awkward lifting pitch at Lord's on the second day and I found myself captaining a Gentlemen's side which had the Players 46 for 9. Gentlemen v. Players was a splendid fixture much enjoyed by the public and participants, but those of us who were captaining counties often found our thoughts wandering to their progress if we had had to miss a championship match in order to play at Lord's. However, on this occasion we took the keenest possible interest in what was going on before us.

Our successful bowlers were all from Cambridge sides of different vintages – John Warr, Colin Smith and Ted Dexter. Colin Stansfield Smith of Lancashire, later to be kept busy as chairman of the Property and Works subcommittee of MCC, was a formidable fast bowler, the bane of an umpire's life in those days of the old back-foot rule, for he was a great 'dragger'. But here most damage was done by Ted Dexter who was in his second year at Cambridge and had not previously taken many first-class wickets. He took 5 for 8 in 5 overs before they declared. It made a nice change to have the Players' batsmen in trouble but the pitch rolled out easy on the last day and the match was drawn.

Something of the penetration of the Surrey bowling in those days can be gauged from John Wardle's benefit match at Bradford. Poor chap, he lost Saturday's play and it was three o'clock on the second day before we could start. But we were not far off winning even then. Having been put in, we mustered 196 for 7 against Appleyard, Trueman, Wardle and Illingworth, no mean attack in any conditions. I declared overnight. Laker and Lock then bowled them out for 91. Following on, they had

lost 7 wickets before they saved the innings defeat and held out for a
draw.

We had a very embarrassing match that season at Guildford when we
played Hampshire. The city was celebrating the 700th anniversary of
the granting of its charter by Henry III and on the second afternoon the
match was to be watched by the Queen and Prince Philip. Almost
everything went right for us and wrong for a royal visit.

Hampshire chose to bat on the first day and Loader and Alec Bedser
bowled them out before lunch for 66. The ball swung a lot. It must have
stopped swinging then, for Derek Shackleton, that model of medium-
paced accuracy and movement, did not take a wicket, nor did Jimmy
Gray, who could be a big in-swinger, and we had made 247 for 4 by
the end of the day.

Next morning I had to decide whether to declare, which I felt was the
right cricketing decision, or to bat on in order to make sure that plenty
was left for the royal visit. I decided that we were leading the championship and it was a first-class match which should be treated as such. So
I declared.

This time Hampshire were bowled out by Laker, and when Loader
finished off the match soon after lunch there were still several hours
before the Queen was due. An exhibition match was arranged, but our
second-line bowlers were almost as effective as their predecessors – I
remember that Eric Bedser looked like taking a wicket every ball – and
we had the greatest difficulty in keeping the second contest going for
long enough. We just succeeded but I am afraid that the royal party
watched some pretty contrived cricket which we gratefully interrupted
in order to be presented.

In their preliminary matches before the First Test the West Indians had
not looked the force of their last tour. The three Ws were still going
fairly strong. Sobers, Collie Smith and Kanhai were obviously young
batsmen of immense promise. But there was no opening pair of the
calibre of Stollmeyer and Rae and – something which strains belief today
– not much fast bowling.

Gilchrist, with his slinging action, was very fast but also very wild.
Dewdney did not look good enough, and although every one agreed
that the nineteen-year-old Wesley Hall had a lovely action, he was not
considered ready to play in a Test match and did not do so. Of their
faster bowlers, Frank Worrell was easily the best.

What we did not know was whether Ramadhin and Valentine, the
twin scourges of 1950, would again be as effective in English conditions.
They were still only twenty-seven, Valentine the older by three days,

and although we had played them with fair comfort in West Indies three years before, conditions there were very different. Another unknown factor was the pitch for the First Test, as this was the first Test match played at Edgbaston for twenty-eight years and the first five-day Test there ever. In fact, West Indies left out Valentine on the morning of the match. Our side was much the same as had played in South Africa but with Close for Compton, who had retired from Test cricket, and Trueman for Tyson.

The pitch looked a good one and I won the toss in fine settled weather. By tea we were out for 186 and Ramadhin had taken 7 for 49, better than anything he had achieved in 1950 or since.

Sonny Ramadhin was unusual with his quick loose wrist, rolled-down sleeves and, for a spinner, brisk pace and lowish trajectory. In English light it was hard to see the ball spinning in the air and no one could read him. He turned the ball just enough to do damage and won himself a big moral advantage by his accuracy allied to the doubt which he created in the batsman's mind. So it was that day. We were back in 1950, it seemed.

The rest of the Thursday, the whole of a hot Friday and more than half of Saturday were occupied by a West Indies innings which pressed home the advantage ruthlessly. The pitch, with its comfortable bounce, was no help to our bowlers – Statham, Trueman, Bailey, Laker and Lock – although they had five out for 197, including Walcott for 90. There followed what seemed an interminable stand for the sixth wicket between Collie Smith and Frank Worrell, begun in the middle of the second afternoon and not broken until Statham bowled Worrell for 81 with the last ball before lunch on the third day. They had added 190 and Smith went on, quick-footed and aggressive, until just before the innings ended for 474, a lead of 288.

By that time West Indies also had their troubles, although they seemed nothing compared with ours. Walcott had pulled a muscle, as had Worrell. This prevented Frank Worrell from bowling in the second innings, although some might say that the main sufferer was Bruce Pairaudeau who, having been yorked for nought by Trueman at the start of the innings, had to act as a runner for Walcott and Worrell for eight and a quarter hours.

As we prepared for the second innings I talked to the other batsmen about how to play Ramadhin. It was, of course, no new subject but I had not previously been prepared to instruct Test-class batsmen on how to go about it. I was dubious about theories that he lost heart if attacked as by the Australians in 1951–52. What worked in Australia was far from certain to work in England where he had more in his favour.

When a bowler has a moral ascendancy over you, there are two ways of regaining the initiative – by hitting him out of the attack and breaking his confidence or by taking no risks and wearing him down. The first policy had been favoured by several batsmen in the first innings with marked lack of success. It seemed even more unsuited to the situation in which we now found ourselves. West Indies had a huge number of runs in hand and could afford to give a lot away. If or when the assault failed, new batsmen would have to take it up and the difficulty which everyone had in picking Ramadhin made this aggressive approach unlikely to have more than passing success.

The second policy was clearly the one to follow, especially as there was hope of fairly easy runs at the other end. Worrell would clearly not bowl, the spin of Sobers, Smith and John Goddard was, on the evidence so far, unlikely to bother many on a pitch which had made Laker and Lock look fairly innocuous. That really left Denis Atkinson at medium pace as the main partner for Ramadhin and on this pitch he could only try to bowl a length, which in the event he did extremely well.

Our first resistance on the Saturday evening was encouraging. Peter Richardson and Brian Close batted without serious difficulty for an hour and a half. We were beginning to hope that we would reach the weekend without losing a wicket when Ramadhin removed Richardson and in his next over bowled Doug Insole. I came in at 65 for 2.

Brian Close and I had reached 102 for 2 by that evening, which gave us breathing space. I was encouraged that when, after I had been in about twenty minutes, I spotted a half-volley from Ramadhin and went through with the stroke not really knowing whether it was the off break or not, I hit it perfectly and the ball went past cover point at a great rate.

Over the weekend I thought a lot about playing Ramadhin, and the more I thought about it the more hopeful I was that we would put up a stiff resistance in the next two days. It was vitally important that we should not lose this first match of the series but, on a personal note, I knew that I had a lot of catching up to do. Memories are short, and although I had made runs against Australia the season before, I was only too aware that my shortage of them in South Africa could be said to have cost us the series. I felt on edge but I was reasonably confident that we had a chance of a draw if we played sensibly.

My optimism was somewhat dampened on the Monday morning when after twenty minutes Close was caught at slip off Gilchrist. Gilchrist was fast enough and unpredictable enough to cause an element of surprise when he produced a good one and we were undoubtedly helped when he limped off during the day.

For all my wishful thinking, it would never have occurred to me then that we would not lose another wicket all day. Yet Colin Cowdrey and I had few uneasy moments that I remember.

Colin and I had spent many hours discussing Ramadhin – as we discussed all aspects of the game. It is a fascination of cricket that one is always learning. We agreed that we must keep going forward and that he must be played as an off-spinner. If it was the leg break, we just had to hope it missed everything. Ordinarily one can work out a deceptive spinner sooner or later but the quickness of Sonny Ramadhin's arm made him unique in my experience. Sometimes we would decide that the leg break was the one which he bowled slightly slower or slightly higher or from slightly wider of the stumps. But we were never sure. I used to wonder how the wicketkeeper could read him so well. Was there a signal? One theory was that Sonny clicked his heels before bowling a leg break. But again we were never sure.

One stroke which I ruled out against Ramadhin was the one wide of mid-on to a ball slanting in towards the leg stump. It had only to straighten a little to have you in trouble. When you scored runs off him, he was adept at bowling the same ball again – but quicker. This, with the low trajectory which sometimes would make the ball keep rather low, accounted for the high proportion of his victims who were bowled or lbw.

Colin was a deep thinker on the game, which was unusual, perhaps, for one with such natural gifts. He was a great help in this partnership, never failing to urge patience on me when I passed a landmark and showed signs of taking a few more risks. Once I realized that I had nearly been in trouble, quite early in our stand, with the stroke wide of mid-on. Before the next over I made sure that Colin had noticed my mistake. I seem to remember telling him to tell me if he saw me playing it again and not to play it himself. But once Colin had committed himself to a policy of complete defence, his technique was so good that he made no mistakes in execution. The pity was that as he grew older he seemed to lose the confidence to use that technique in attack, which he could have done so well.

So we batted on and by that night had reached 378 for 3, 90 runs ahead. I was 193, Colin 78. Ramadhin had bowled nearly all day without taking a wicket but we still had no idea if the later batsmen would be able to cope with him. Next morning, therefore, we carried on with the same care.

By the time Colin reached 100 about half an hour before lunch we were able to allow ourselves more freedom. Colin played some fine strokes for another hour or so before he was caught on the long-on boundary after lunch for 154.

Our stand of 411 meant that we were 236 runs on. About three and

ENGLAND v. WEST INDIES at EDGBASTON
(First Test 1957)

Match Drawn

ENGLAND

P. E. Richardson c Walcott b Ramadhin	47	– c sub b Ramadhin	34
D. B. Close c Kanhai b Gilchrist	15	– c Weekes b Gilchrist	42
P. B. H. May c Weekes b Ramadhin	30	– not out....................................	285
D. J. Insole b Ramadhin	20	– b Ramadhin.............................	0
M. C. Cowdrey c Gilchrist b Ramadhin	4	– c sub b Smith	154
T. E. Bailey b Ramadhin	1	–	
T. G. Evans b Gilchrist	14	– not out......................................	29
J. C. Laker b Ramadhin	7		
G. A. R. Lock b Ramadhin	0		
F. S. Trueman not out	29		
J. B. Statham b Atkinson	13		
Extras	6	Extras	39

1/32 2/61 3/104 4/115 5/116 6/118   **186**   1/63 2/65 3/113 4/524   **583**
7/121 8/130 9/150 10/186   Innings declared

Bowling: *First Innings* – Worrell 9–1–27–0; Gilchrist 27–4–74–2; Ramadhin 31–16–49–7; Atkinson 12.4–3–30–1. *Second Innings* – Gilchrist 26–2–67–1; Ramadhin 98–35–179–2; Atkinson 72–29–137–0; Smith 26–4–72–1; Sobers 30–4–77–0; Goddard 6–2–12–0.

WEST INDIES

B. H. Pairaudeau b Trueman	1	– b Trueman	7
G. Sobers c Bailey b Statham	53	– c Cowdrey b Lock	14
C. L. Walcott c Evans b Laker	90	– c Lock b Laker	1
E. D. Weekes b Trueman	9	– c Trueman b Lock	33
F. M. Worrell b Statham	81	– c May b Lock	0
O. G. Smith lbw b Laker	161	– lbw b Laker	5
D. Atkinson c Statham b Laker	1	– not out......................................	4
J. D. C. Goddard c Lock b Laker	24	– not out......................................	0
R. Kanhai lbw b Statham	42	– c Close b Trueman	1
K. T. Ramadhin not out	5		
R. Gilchrist run out	0		
Extras	7	Extras	7

1/4 2/83 3/120 4/183 5/197 6/387   **474**   1/1 2/9 3/25 4/27   (7 wkts.)   **72**
7/466 8/469 9/474 10/474   5/43 6/61 7/68

Umpires: C. S. Elliott and E. Davies

Bowling: *First Innings* – Statham 39–4–114–3; Trueman 30–4–99–2; Bailey 34–11–80–0; Laker 54–17–119–4; Lock 34.4–15–55–0. *Second Innings* – Statham 2–0–6–0; Trueman 5–3–7–2; Laker 24–20–13–2; Lock 27–19–31–3; Close 2–1–8–0.

A draw – but one of consequence

a quarter hours remained. I thought about declaring then and during the next fifty-odd minutes while I batted with Godfrey Evans, but the strength and depth of the West Indies batting, and the fact that the pitch was such that only 2 wickets had fallen in the last nine hours' play, did not encourage a declaration.

Godfrey, of course, was the right batsman to have coming in then but it was Trevor Bailey who had sat with his pads on for about eight hours.

'There was no way I was going in when Colin was out,' Trevor said to me subsequently. 'I was mentally exhausted!'

Godfrey, on the other hand, was at his most irrepressible. 'Come on, skipper,' he said. 'We'll have some quick singles.'

'It's all very well for you,' I replied. 'I've been here for two days.'

The great thing was that we had saved a match which we had seemed sure to lose and had the conquerors of the first innings in retreat. Eventually I left us two hours twenty minutes' bowling and walked in weary but happy after the longest innings of my career, nearly ten hours, and the highest, 285. Somebody introducing me before I made a speech recently said that this was still the highest Test innings by an England captain. That was an easy one to follow. I said that as chairman of selectors I hoped that I would lose the record soon.

I think that in most ways it was probably my best innings as well as my highest. Too much is talked nowadays about the 'pressures' on players of all games but that particular time was undoubtedly very important in my playing career. I had to get going again after my barren series in South Africa. I had to show that the captaincy of Surrey was not weighing on me. Most important, we had had a feeble first innings, as a result of which the team was very down in spirits, and unless something was done, we were going to start the series with a heavy defeat. Thus its value to the side was probably as great as any other I played.

Nothing happened in the last hours of that First Test to persuade me that I was wrong in not declaring earlier. West Indies lost 7 wickets for 72 and Laker and Lock made the pitch look entirely different, but the way in which John Goddard defended convinced me that if they had had to bat for longer he and the other batsmen would still have held out.

In the second innings Ramadhin had bowled 98 overs for 179 runs and just the 2 early wickets. We had never fathomed him but he was never the same force again and took only 5 more wickets in the series. Whether or not he bowled less well is debatable. What is certain is that our batsmen played him better and with more confidence.

We were far better equipped for what was then a typical Lord's pitch. This was one of the matches when the 'ridge' at the nursery end was at its most pronounced. We held our catches. West Indies did not. Trevor Bailey bowled magnificently and took 11 wickets. Colin Cowdrey, coming in at 34 for 3 when Tom Graveney and I had been out in the same over from Gilchrist, made a very fine 152. We won by an innings.

We batted first on a beautiful pitch at Trent Bridge and made over 600 before I declared with 6 wickets down at tea on the second day. Tom Graveney played two superb innings in the series, 258 here and

164 at the Oval. Peter Richardson and I both made 100 and I was prepared for a long unrewarding bowl at the three Ws and others. In fact, they batted rather dourly on the Saturday and our bowlers kept control very well, especially Trueman and Laker. We never dislodged Frank Worrell, who batted through the innings for 191, but we held some good catches and on Monday morning they collapsed and followed on nearly 250 behind.

In the second innings West Indies were 89 for 5 soon after tea on the fourth day, but Collie Smith, that ebullient cricketer, played a spectacular innings of 168, a wonderful blend of aggression and sound judgement. What a loss to the game he was when he was tragically killed in a car crash only two years later, aged twenty-six. He was a cheerful character whose cricket, whether batting or bowling off breaks, seemed to reflect his personality.

For a long time we fielded well but we made a costly error by dropping Collie before he had made 50. It was unfortunate that the fielder was the substitute for Trevor Bailey. A regular member of the side has plenty of opportunity to atone but poor Jim Pressdee of Glamorgan did not. I felt very sorry for him. However, he was not alone, for several more catches went down while John Goddard and Denis Atkinson were giving Smith stout support.

When we eventually bowled them out, we needed 121 in an hour. Under the present sensible law which requires 20 overs to be bowled in the last hour, this might have been a feasible task, even though Gilchrist, whistling the ball high and wide at great speed, made contact difficult. In those days when the over rate could be dictated by the requirements of the fielding captain, we had to settle for a draw.

I was disappointed that we had not won but we had established ourselves by now as the stronger side and at Headingley in the Fourth Test we won the second of our three innings victories. The win here illustrated the depth of bowling available to us in those days. Brian Statham was injured, so we brought in Peter Loader who had not so far played in the series. He took 9 wickets in the match including a hat trick which finished off the first innings.

The ball moved about throughout the match but, for a side whose batting began with Worrell, Weekes and Walcott and the highly promising Sobers, Kanhai and Smith, West Indies did not bat with great distinction. Our bowlers were on top from the first morning when Tony Lock took one of his most brilliant catches at leg slip. This was from Sobers, who suffered at the same hands in the second innings when Lock, with a marvellous piece of fielding in the covers, left him stranded in the middle of the pitch. Our innings made an unconvincing start against Gilchrist and Worrell but from 42 for 3, Cowdrey, David Shep-

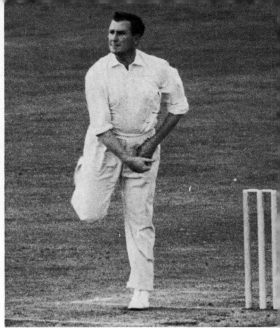

ABOVE LEFT: Tony Lock aggressive, always attacking the batsman . . .

ABOVE RIGHT: . . . and Jim Laker thoughtful, less obviously belligerent but even less accommodating

BELOW LEFT: Surrey – Middlesex matches could be sternly fought affairs but I seem to be on the receiving end of some ribald comment from Denis Compton as we leave the field during this one.

BELOW RIGHT: Two legendary Surrey heroes in 1958, Sir Jack Hobbs and Andrew Sandham

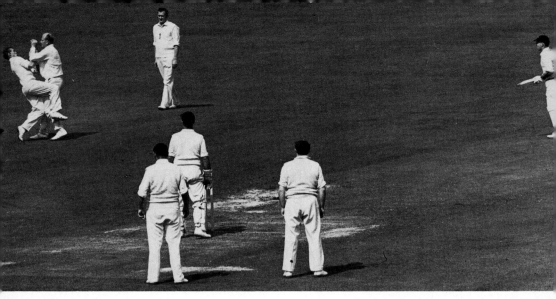

Lord's, the Second Test against New Zealand, 1958. Tony Lock catches Jack Hayes off his own bowling, knocking midwicket, Peter Richardson, out of the way in the process

Recriminations! Even the normally serious Jim Laker thinks it's funny

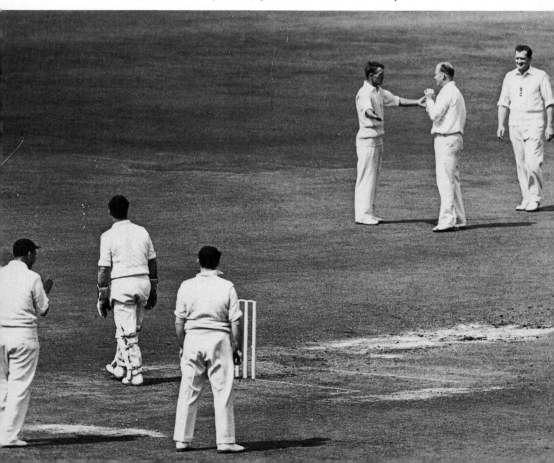

Martin Horton (Worcestershire) caught Stewart bowled Lock. One of the close catches which Micky Stewart and Ken Barrington (and very occasionally the fielder in between them) used to pick up towards the end of Surrey's seven-year winning run

Surrey in 1957, the year of our biggest win of all

Four formidable opponents – top left, Clive Walcott (West Indies), top right Neil Harvey (Australia), bottom left Hugh Tayfield (South Africa) and bottom right Vinoo Mankad (India)

Tossing with two distinguished captains. Looking up with John Goddard at Edgbaston in 1957 . . . and down with Richie Benaud at Scarborough in 1961

BELOW LEFT: One of the better moments in Australia in 1958-59. Hitting Alan Davidson back over his head in the drawn Third Test at Sydney

BELOW RIGHT: With Gubby Allen during the Oval Test of 1958, a worried-looking captain and chairman of selectors. Our immediate concern can only have been that it was about to rain again. There were only twelve hours play in the five days

24 April 1959, at Shamley Green, when the tour was over. The guests (from left): Tony Lock, Godfrey Evans, Tony MacGibbon of New Zealand, Eric Bedser, Alec Bedser, Peter Loader, Peter Richardson and Trevor Bailey

Convalescing at home in 1960 after my second operation

ABOVE LEFT: An almost unique picture of myself mounted – and hanging on tightly to the former Prime Minister of Ceylon, Sir John Kotelawala. Sir John had given a convivial lunch for the MCC at his home outside Colombo when we stopped en route for Australia in October 1958

ABOVE RIGHT: An unlikely opening pair at the Oval. Peter Sellers had expressed a wish to walk out to bat with me and the *Daily Express* 'fixed it'. We duly marched out together and then marched back again

With the May team ready for the new season. From left: Annabelle, Tessa, Nicola, Suzanne

Now a selector and still enjoying the game

Taking no risks with Derek Shackleton on a grey morning at Guildford in my last year as Surrey captain

pard, on his holidays again, and I helped the score up to 279, which was quite enough.

As a match the Headingley Test was disappointing in its one-sidedness but not as one-sided as the last, which was played on a reddish pitch at the Oval. I was accustomed to a variety of pitches at the Oval but I never remember seeing another like this colourful thing which was in garish contrast with the lush green outfield. Rain throughout the previous week had upset the preparation and left a layer of marl caked on top. The ball turned throughout.

In all four previous Tests we had had a left-handed opening pair – Richardson and Close at Edgbaston, then Richardson and Don Smith of Sussex. Now we moved David Sheppard up. He and Richardson put on 92, Richardson went on to make 100 and Tom Graveney his 164. On this sort of slow turning pitch Tom was a rare artist, helping the ball on its way with the spin. It was often said that Tom could have become a professional golfer if he had not chosen cricket. Having seen him recently in a television 'celebrity' golf match, holding his own with professionals, I am not surprised, although his rather quick three-quarters swing was in contrast with the high back-lift and leisured grace of his batting. Coming in at 238 for 2, I paid the penalty for hitting straight and was caught at midwicket when an off break from Smith turned a lot, but our score of 412 was obviously ample.

I soon had Laker and Lock on and despite stoppages for rain and bad light they had West Indies out for 89 that evening and for 86 on the third day.

Influenza prevented John Goddard from batting in either innings. I could not help reflecting on the two tours of England which he had led, the one a great triumph, the second seven years later a resounding defeat. I had the impression that he had not wanted to come but had been manoeuvred into taking on the captaincy through a lack of agreement in the Caribbean on any other candidate.

I had every cause to look back on the 1957 season with pleasure. I felt that I had played as well as ever. I was only twenty-seven but was a more commanding player now. What with Surrey's sweeping victory in the championship and England's 3-0 defeat of a West Indies side containing many good players, even if some were a shade past their best and others had not yet reached it, it had been a good year. On paper 1958 was not much less satisfactory. Surrey won again and were not seriously threatened. England won four and drew one of the five Tests against New Zealand.

Yet, in retrospect, it was thoroughly unsatisfactory. The weather was appalling, which had various effects. It weakened a New Zealand team already reduced by injuries and in a season when we were preparing to defend the Ashes in Australia it provided conditions which bore no resemblance to those that we would find there.

Surrey's performance in a season with little continuity was perfectly adequate. It was our seventh successive championship-winning season, and although I knew that it could not go on for ever, there were no positive signs that this would be the last win of the long run. I think that on the wet pitches our bowlers protected us from challengers because they would win matches so much more quickly than any other side's. In the following year when the sun shone and pitches were covered there was no such protection.

We made a curious start to the 1958 season. After a damp draw at Cambridge we played MCC at Lord's and the New Zealanders at the Oval in just about the only sunny week of the summer.

For MCC, the Smiths, M.J.K. of Warwickshire and Don of Sussex, began the Lord's season with an opening stand of 299. We were at full strength except for Alec Bedser, but on a lovely pitch our bowlers made no impression.

By the Monday, however, the bounce was irregular and we were bowled out for 116 by Alan Moss, who took 7 for 28, and Frank Tyson. Nothing was to be gained by defence and I made 63 fairly swiftly but was hit so frequently about the thighs that next day they were pretty sore and I decided not to bat. We were to play the New Zealanders on the Wednesday and I felt that it would be a discourtesy to miss that. In fact, Surrey batted rather better without me but still suffered their first innings defeat for five years.

I thought that, after experiencing the red Test pitch of the previous August, I knew all the types of pitch which the Oval had to offer. I was wrong. We played the New Zealanders on one which was fast and fiery, all right if you were in form but not to be recommended for most batsmen early in the season against good bowlers.

I was in form and found this sort of pitch more exciting than the slow turning ones which were a commonplace in the 1950s. Nobody else found it much fun, least of all the unfortunate New Zealanders who by the time they batted had already lost their captain, John Reid, with a split finger sustained in the field. He did not bat and we had them in and out twice by soon after lunch on the second day, Loader 8 for 33 in the first innings and Lock 5 for 9 in the second.

In the championship Surrey made an excellent start and I am bound to say that I had no complaints about my own form. I remember with great pleasure 163 in under three hours on Whit Monday at Trent Bridge and 174 two days later at Old Trafford, which took much longer because Brian Statham bowled so well to me.

This match had an extraordinary end because, after the pitch had been freshened by rain, David Gibson, Laker and Lock bowled Lancashire out for 27. Gibson was deputizing for Alec Bedser, who had had penumonia in April and did not play until July. Even then Alec was not fully fit and when neither he nor I was there Arthur McIntyre captained the side.

In Alec Bedser's absence the loss of Loader, Laker and Lock during Test matches was even more severe and it became increasingly hard to bowl sides out. We were almost at full strength when Yorkshire inflicted a heavy defeat on us at Bramall Lane. They had been suffering one of their domestic upheavals, and although in that first season under Ronnie Burnet they finished only eleventh, I suspected that when their problems were sorted out they would have the players to become a major threat to us. We were lucky to win against them at the Oval. I was becoming fairly used to dry dusty pitches and we made an adequate score on the Saturday. After rain Yorkshire had a difficult time on the Monday and lost by an innings. It was Eric Bedser's benefit and he had a very good match, making the second top score of 43 and then bowling them out twice with Tony Lock.

We lost to Kent in an excellent match at Blackheath in which I was out for 99, caught at slip off the leg-spinner, Jack Pettiford. Hereabouts I must have been getting rather above myself, for I remember driving Dave Halfyard straight for 6 in the second innings as my first scoring stroke and, against Nottinghamshire at the Oval, doing the same to my first ball, this from Arthur Jepson. We needed only 90-odd runs and had lost 2 early wickets. I went in determined to finish it quickly. At that time I was experimenting with setting myself up to play a certain shot to the next ball if it was of a reasonable length. If all went well, I was waiting for it. Arthur, bless his heart, bowled a perfectly respectable ball. I can still see the aggrieved look on his face.

We beat the wretched New Zealanders again by an innings, Alec Bedser, Loader and Gibson bowling them out for 54. From the end of June Hampshire, in the first year of Colin Ingleby-Mackenzie's captaincy, led us in the championship, but they faded away in August whereas we finished strongly. They had never won the championship, which made the final stages harder for them than for us.

Colin Ingleby-Mackenzie was a most entertaining captain to play against, an amateur of the old style with the gift of making you feel that the world is a cheerful place, however difficult it may seem. His cavalier reputation was such that he could keep two medium-pacers, Shackleton and Cannings, on for hours on end without complaints from anyone

SURREY v NEW ZEALANDERS, The Oval
(May 1958)

Surrey won by an innings and 163 runs

SURREY

T. H. Clark b Hayes	1
M. J. Stewart hit wkt b Hayes	25
B. Constable c Reid b Cave	10
P. B. H. May c Reid b Cave	165
K. F. Barrington c Sutcliffe b Moir	18
E. A. Bedser c MacGibbon b Moir	12
A. J. McIntyre c MacGibbon b Sparling	11
G. A. R. Lock b Moir	16
J. C. Laker not out	15
P. J. Loader c Sutcliffe b Cave	9
J. K. Hall c Miller b Moir	1
B 5	5

1/16 2/33 3/64 4/103 5/159 6/197   288
7/255 8/277 9/287

Bowling: Hayes 17–2–59–2; MacGibbon 20–4–77–0; Cave 24–6–63–3; Reid 5–1–19–0; Moir 10.4–2–45–4; Sparling 5–0–20–1.

NEW ZEALANDERS

T. Meale c Lock b Hall	2	– c Stewart b Loader	1
L. S. M. Miller b Loader	11	– c Hall b Laker	15
W. R. Playle b Loader	0	– c Loader b Lock	3
B. Sutcliffe b Loader	4	– c Barrington b Hall	5
A. R. MacGibbon c McIntyre b Loader	13	– c McIntyre b Hall	6
J. T. Sparling b Loader	13	– c McIntyre b Lock	0
E. C. Petrie b Loader	3	– b Lock	7
A. M. Moir c and b Loader	8	– st McIntyre b Lock	4
H. B. Cave not out	13	– not out	3
J. A. Hayes c Constable b Loader	2	– c McIntyre b Lock	3
J. R. Reid absent hurt	0	– absent hurt	0
B 5	5	B 2, l-b 2	4

1/8 2/9 3/14 4/19 5/38 6/42 7/51   74   1/1 2/14 3/26 4/31 5/33   51
8/70 9/74   6/40 7/40 8/45 9/51

Bowling: *First Innings* – Loader 15.4–4–33–8; Hall 11–3–21–1; Lock 3–0–14–0; Laker 1–0–1–0. *Second Innings* – Loader 3–1–9–1; Hall 6–0–13–2; Lock 7.2–4–9–5; Laker 11–6–16–1.

Umpires: L. H. Gray and John Langridge

The luckless New Zealanders were routed on a fiery Oval pitch
which produced an odd-looking score card

about dullness. His personality as a player and subsequently as a member of MCC committees has been a great asset to the game.

As for the Test series, the selectors, now Gubby Allen, Wilfred Wooller, Les Ames and Tom Dollery, foresaw the dangers lurking in the wet pitches and relative weakness of the opposition. With an eye on Australia they experimented but, in the weather which plagued us, not with great success. Peter Richardson had done us well for two seasons but we still needed an opening partner for him. M. J. K. Smith had undoubted qualifications. He had made 2000 runs the year before, his first as captain of Warwickshire, and although he was now batting at number four, much of his success at Oxford had been as an opener. He was picked to open for MCC against Surrey at Lord's.

Having made 160 there, he agreed to open for Warwickshire, probably with misgivings, for they already had a successful opening pair in Gardner and Horner. He opened in the first three Tests and in Gentlemen and Players but only once passed 20, and when he was left out of the Fourth Test he dropped himself down the Warwickshire order with, I imagine, a sigh of relief and certainly with better results.

We played the First Test at Edgbaston in dismal weather and on a well-grassed pitch, a depressing combination for a weak touring side. I felt sorry for the very likable New Zealanders who, under the same much respected manager, Jack Phillipps, had had such a great tour in 1949 with a strong side but were now in a recession. Their batting was especially weak. Bert Sutcliffe never really recovered from breaking a bone in his wrist early on and too much depended on John Reid, the captain. It is nice to think that only three and a half years later John led a team to South Africa which not only drew the series 2-2 but had a tour which, by all accounts, was on and off the field one of the most enjoyable ever undertaken.

New Zealand's moments of glory in 1958 were few. In the First Test at Edgbaston we struggled against the moving ball. Colin Cowdrey and I made 80 apiece but otherwise only the last pair reached double figures. Trueman, Loader and Bailey then bowled New Zealand out for 94. In our second innings Peter Richardson made 100, Colin played well again and I was able to declare. The match was over by soon after lunch on the fourth day.

Lord's was even more one-sided. The luck, as nearly always, favoured the stronger side. I won the toss and we batted on a good pitch, no more than adequately but with Cowdrey again in sparkling form. It rained that night and play did not start until mid-afternoon on the second day. Our last 3 wickets added some useful runs before the pitch began to dry and then Laker and Lock bowled New Zealand out for 47. There was more rain that night and on the third day, after a short delay, we bowled them out for 74.

It was that great occasion, the Saturday of a Lord's Test; the ground was packed and John Reid and I agreed to play an exhibition match. We tried to make it entertaining. I hit a 6 cross-batted over extra cover into the mound stand. I was rather pleased at the time to have contributed something unusual but I suppose that nowadays I would be expected to do it most Sunday afternoons. We did our best but these affairs were inevitably an anticlimax and must have been rather empty things to watch.

We again won by an innings at Headingley, although it rained so much that the match could not start until after lunch on the third day. The need to find an opening batsman for Australia was such that we asked Peter Richardson to stand down and brought in Arthur Milton to open with Mike Smith. They were a unique pair in one way, having played for England at soccer and rugby respectively. Their association on the cricket field was brief, for after Laker and Lock had bowled New Zealand out for 67, M.J.K. was caught in the slips.

The pitch had rolled out quite well on the Monday when I shared a stand of nearly 200 with Arthur Milton. When he reached 100 after tea, I declared 200 ahead. Arthur had done all that was asked of him but he was on the back foot nearly all the time and I could not help wondering how he would fare on the faster, bouncier pitches of Australia. It was in his favour that he was a brilliant close fielder, and as he missed the Fourth Test through injury we really took him to Australia on that one performance at Leeds.

Laker and Lock soon finished the Headingley Test off – they took 19 wickets between them – and it was over before tea on the fifth day, in other words in not much over two days' play.

We made six changes for the Fourth Test at Old Trafford, bringing in Dexter, Subba Row and Illingworth, all new to Test cricket. This was part of the search for players who might be useful in Australia. It made no difference to the result, for we again won by an innings, although we lost nearly all Saturday's play and the first half of Monday's.

I remember going out to bat with Raman Subba Row in a dull light on the Monday afternoon. 'We'll have a look at it for a while,' I said to him. That may have been the intention but one of the fast bowlers gave me a nice half-volley. It went sweetly off the bat for 4 – and two more after it in the same over. Raman, who was playing in his first Test, blinked at me through the gloom and looked mystified.

On the Sunday we had to pick the team for Australia, although there was still another Test match to be played. It was an unsatisfactory arrangement but necessary in those days when we sailed for Australia in September and players needed to be told as early as possible whether they would be needed during the winter.

The loss of nearly all Saturday's play plus the fact that New Zealand had batted until near lunch on the second day meant that by the Sunday we had very little fresh information except about Willie Watson's wellbeing.

On the Monday I made the fourth of five 100s against the New Zealanders that summer – the fifth was at the Scarborough Festival – and declared 98 ahead. The top was going off the pitch and I hoped for a wicket or two that night. I remember Bert Sutcliffe, that graceful left-hander, showing something of his old brilliance and we took no wicket that night. Next day I had Lock on at once and he bowled to the end of the match. Of the 10 wickets which fell for 55, he took 7.

The last Test was drawn but only about twelve hours' play was possible and that almost entirely on the first and fifth days. It did nothing to lift up a melancholy series which had been no help to us and must have been utterly depressing to the New Zealanders. They needed all the help from the weather that was going. They received none.

I much admired their cheerfulness in adversity. When I said to one of them that I was sorry that they had had such a miserable time, he told me not to worry. 'We are most of us amateurs,' he said, 'and a tour of England is a great experience whether we win or lose.'

12
Australia 1958–59 – Qualified Disaster?

I sometimes see the 1958–59 tour of Australia referred to as the greatest failure of my career as England captain. I myself often think that it may have been one of my greatest successes. At the end of it, England and Australia were still speaking.

A lot happened which could have upset Anglo-Australian cricket relations for some time. Freddie Brown, as manager, and I had to strike a balance between sticking up for our own side and avoiding friction so that controversial matters might be settled later, without recriminations, by administrators sitting amicably round a table. If we seemed to sit back and suffer rather submissively, I should say at once that I do not believe that it made any difference to the result. We were always going to struggle.

Australian cricket played on huge Ovals is a young man's game and we had too many players on their last tour. If you have lost the keen edge, Australia finds it out.

The need for diplomacy was, of course, inspired by the number of throwers to be found among Australian bowlers at that time. They seemed to appear almost everywhere we went and, as some were 'draggers' as well, they left behind them a wake of aggrieved batsmen. Having the ball thrown at you from 18 yards blights the sunniest disposition. We saw boys' matches in parks in which the bowlers were throwing without the slightest sign of discouragement from the presiding adult.

Freddie and I recognized that this was something which had to be sorted out at a much higher level than the one at which we were operating. The part eventually played by Sir Donald Bradman in the elimination of throwing in Australia in the early 1960s is history but for the time being the Australian Board did nothing.

In 1958–59 Australia was in a high state of nationalistic fervour about its cricket and understandably so. I remember Richie Benaud saying to me at the end in something like bewilderment, 'I've played three series against England over nearly six years and I've never know what it's like to win one before.'

Richie, with his enthusiasm, experience and shrewdness, had as much to do with the successful series as anyone. He was a very fine captain.

The Australian public was rediscovering cricket, which they had almost given away in 1956. The Olympic Games were then being held in Melbourne, their athletes and swimmers were beating the world and their lawn tennis players were just as successful. 'Why bother with a game at which we are losing' was the reaction of many. The Board foresaw that this series would set up cricket again in Australia and went out of their way to pooh-pooh suggestions that some bowlers' actions were unfair. 'I see no problem of throwing,' said Mr W. J. Dowling, chairman of the Australian Board of Control, more than once.

Not all the allegations of throwing came from the large English press party, although it was the English cricket writers who were read, through the prominence given to 'quote-backs'. This system provides for the more provocative comments to be sent back from London. Sometimes, I suppose, they appear out of context and the Australian reader thinks that the English cricket correspondent does nothing else but 'whinge'.

At this stage I should outline the recent history of throwing at that time and make it clear that we were far from blameless. Throwing in England had for long not been a major issue. Those of suspect actions had been nearly all spinners and no one had done much more than raise eyebrows. Cuan McCarthy was almost the only fast bowler of the early postwar years who was queried, but after the South African tour of 1951 and a year at Cambridge he departed to Minor County cricket. Umpires who had called a bowler for throwing were looked on as 'stirrers' or publicity seekers. The tendency was to sweep such unpleasantness under the carpet. A bowler banned for throwing would, after all, be deprived of his livelihood if he was a professional.

As it happened, I was on the field on the two occasions when a bowler was called in 1952. McCarthy, playing for Cambridge, was called by Paddy Corrall at Worcester. Tony Lock, playing for Surrey against the Indians at the Oval, was called by Fred Price. It was the first match in which I captained Surrey. I had just come down from Cambridge. What a baptism! I asked Fred what the problem was. He was in no doubt that Tony had thrown a faster ball. We were amazed.

In a successful attempt to spin the ball more, Tony had changed his action. His faster ball, which was usually the one in question, was a very lethal weapon indeed on soft turning pitches. In Australia it had much less effect, although it still claimed its victims because it was so well disguised.

The umpires, as I have said, had no wholehearted official backing and there was usually an element of humour in references by players to someone's suspect action. I am sure that some bowlers who were throwers or jerkers had no idea that they were because so little thought was given to the purity of actions in those days. The nearest that I can remember to a serious comment on a bowler's action was made by a batsman of abundant humour, Doug Insole, playing for the Rest against the champion county, Surrey, at the Oval in September 1955 He had been bowled by Lock's faster ball and as he passed the umpire at the other end he asked in a loud voice, 'Was I bowled or run out?' Everyone had a good laugh.

This, then, was the casual attitude to throwing in England. A fast bowler who threatened physical harm by throwing might have caused action to be taken but the fast bowlers of the day such as Tyson, Trueman and Statham were unarguably in the clear. Some doubts were expressed about Loader's action but I cannot remember that he was ever called.

No one can fairly leave the history of throwing in those years without pointing out that Tony Lock rectified his action after that series in Australia – as I remember it, when he saw pictures of it. To his great credit he abandoned of his own accord the action which had brought him so much success – long before the law began to be enforced more strictly. He went back to something more like his original action and bowled successfully with it in English and Australian cricket for many years.

The fact that we were not blameless did not stop our players from being astonished and indignant at what they found in Australia. They probably expected the captain and manager to lodge an official protest. We did not do so for several reasons. One was that we would have been accused of 'squealing'. I was very conscious that the Australians had not complained in England when they had plenty to complain about. I knew what Lindsay Hassett thought about the England leg-side bowling which stopped Australia from winning at Headingley in 1953. I knew what the Australians of 1956 thought about the pitches at Headingley and Old Trafford. They were understandably indignant at what they considered to be two thoroughly bad pitches. But they did not complain.

In 1958–59 we also thought that there was a chance that the Australian Board might themselves take action about throwing. They did not do so and before we left Australia Freddie Brown and I warned Don Bradman at a dinner that we intended to make a very strong report to Lord's once we had returned. It is history that in 1960 Sir Donald came to England, thrashed it all out with Gubby Allen and on his return home swiftly cleared the throwers out of Australian cricket.

We may not have complained to the Board about throwing but we did object, as was our right, to an umpire, Mel McInnes, after the First Test and asked that he should not be appointed again. He had had an honourable career but we thought that he was now past his best. Our objection was overruled, which I still find surprising. It has been customary for the home authority to accede to such a request by a touring management. I cannot remember an occasion when this has happened in England. But we were rebuffed. We accepted it but we certainly felt that the Australian Board were not being much help.

Some weeks before we left England we had had problems of our own. Johnny Wardle, who had already been picked, had had his invitation withdrawn after articles highly critical of the Yorkshire captain and committee had appeared under his name. MCC, the governing body, had to take action, but I was sorry that Johnny had been so ill advised as to write the articles and considered his a serious loss.

He was not the easiest chap to handle but in one of my first matches as captain I had made it clear that the issue was not whether he wanted to bowl but whether I wanted him to bowl. He accepted this and we got along famously from then on.

Australians were inclined to say that he was no great loss to our side. They were entitled to their opinion but not on the grounds that he had not done much four years before and had not been a regular choice in England. On the evidence of the South African tour two years before he would have been particularly useful in Australia because he was two bowlers in one. By this time he had developed the chinaman and googly to a high degree of accuracy. What had once been a sideline was now more important to us on tour than his conventional method. He had not been a regular pick in England because as an orthodox left-arm spinner on English pitches Lock was usually preferred. But Wardle had had one of his first successes with the chinaman in the final Test of 1954-55 in Sydney where he took 8 wickets and he was a far better exponent of it now.

One other event which probably had an indirect effect on the tour was Jim Laker's announcement of his forthcoming retirement, made when we were scarcely out of the English Channel. This seemed a pity because it suggested to the opposition that he for one thought that he was past his best. He could never hope to approach his English menace on Australian pitches but I knew that he wanted to get through without damaging his huge reputation. I also knew that the Australians were keen to get their own back on him and I had hopes that in trying to do so they might run into trouble.

Jim's announcement of his retirement was made exclusively to one paper. Its side effect was to increase the normal competitiveness of a section of the unusually large press party which we had with us. When the team that they are accompanying is not successful, they are expected to give reasons. The simple reason that the other side is stronger is not good enough. On this occasion they were under even greater pressure because they had been pretty confident beforehand that we would again be too good for Australia.

They were almost certainly more confident than the captain, although, of course, I kept this to myself for fear of lowering morale. I had faith in our bowling but I was very doubtful about the class and depth of the batting. In fact, we never made 300 in a Test match. I am a believer in success going in sequences. You have a run of good players and then, as they fade, the other side has its turn. The news from Australia, especially about the new young hope, Norman O'Neill, may have been exaggerated but it suggested that Australia would be tougher nuts to crack this time. They had, after all, just won 3–0 in South Africa where, a year before, we had only drawn 2–2.

When things began to go wrong on the tour there was a keener than usual hunt among the press for stories. Freddie Brown and I had distributed the duties rather differently on this tour because he had an assistant manager in Desmond Eagar, the respected and highly conscientious secretary of Hampshire, who looked after the finanical side and was known as 'Cash'. With George Duckworth, that great man, as scorer and baggage master and David Montague as physiotherapist, there was no shortage of help off the field. Freddie therefore took on the bulk of the press relations. Where I became involved unfortunately was through intrusions into my private life.

In the previous April I had become engaged to Virginia Gilligan. Her uncle, Arthur Gilligan, and his wife, Penny, were frequent visitors to Australia. Arthur had been the MCC captain there in 1924–25 and had subsequently done radio commentaries on numerous tours. He loved Australia and Australians, they loved him and as usual he was going to be in Australia during this tour. Penny and he kindly invited Virginia to go with them.

She made a promising start with the press, for in the first match after she set foot in Australia I made 100 in each innings. As things went less well, however, there were hints, or more, that the captain's fiancée was taking up too much of his time. Eventually a piece was written reporting that we had been secretly married.

This really was disgraceful and made me very angry. It is all right to look back on it now and have a good laugh. It makes us look rather dashing. But Virginia's parents, Marjorie and Harold Gilligan, were naturally horrified. They were preparing at Shamley Green for our wedding in the following April and wanted to know what was going on. Poor Arthur hastened to reassure them but it was upsetting for Virginia and it did not increase my respect for certain members of the press. I may not have been as at ease with the press or as forthcoming as my opposite number, Richie Benaud, but he was a journalist by profession. I had always tried to be helpful when I could and felt let down.

We began the tour more than usually short of practice. Two one-day matches in Ceylon had been almost completely washed out and the nets in Perth were too damp to be of much use. But we led both Western Australia and the Combined XI on first innings. Tom Graveney made 177 not out in the first match and both Colin Cowdrey and I made runs. As early as this there were murmurs about throwing. Western Australia had a bowler, Keith Slater, who played in one Test later and who was an off-spinner who could also bowl at a brisk medium pace. He bowled me for nought in the second innings and I was certainly late on the stroke but I do not remember thinking much about his action.

I made 100 in the second match in Perth where we were impressed by our first sight of the athletic Norman O'Neill. He also made 100. But I damaged a knee ligament while batting – this was the only occasion when I remember needing a runner – and did not play in either Adelaide or Melbourne.

We won in Adelaide on an early-season pitch bearing no resemblance to the one on which we would play the Fourth Test there three months later. In late October, only a few weeks after Australian Rules football had been played on the ground, the ball turned. Jim Laker took 10 wickets in the match and we won comfortably. We won again in Melbourne where Statham took 7 wickets in the first innings and Lock 6 in the second, the last 2 of them off the sixth and seventh balls of the final over.

It was an exciting finish but my clearest memory of the match is of looking out of the dressing-room window and watching the Victorian players practising in the outfield. One of them, a left-hander, whom we knew to be Ian Meckiff, was throwing the ball at a batsman. This seemed an odd way for a bowler to limber up. A few minutes later he was out in the middle bowling to Peter Richardson with exactly the same action. I was fascinated.

He soon removed Richardson but he was so inaccurate that he caused little concern. Arthur Milton and Raman Subba Row made what were to be their highest scores of the tour, and although Meckiff had played in the previous winter's series in South Africa, we could not believe that a bowler as wild as he was would be picked again.

I soon realized that one of the characteristics of the thrower is his wildness. But in this lies some of his effectiveness, for the batsman has few hits at the ball, even in an eight-ball over. There is no rhythm about the action, the line and pace are unpredictable – just a sudden jerk and the ball arrives.

After a three-week break I was fit to play against New South Wales in our first match in Sydney. They made nearly 400, after which we were bowled out by two leg-spinners, Benaud and Philpott. In the days when good leg-spinners abounded in Australia there was nearly always an innings early on when MCC gave an abject performance against them. Usually the furore about the feebleness and heavy-footedness of English batsmen against leg spin had scarcely died down before the same batsmen were making runs fairly easily against the same bowlers. That happened here. Although we followed on, we batted out the rest of the match comfortably, launched by an opening stand of 170 between Richardson and Milton.

This was our first meeting with the tall Gordon Rorke. He was erratic but he was the fastest we met and made the ball bounce a lot. His action, although not of the purest, was not as open to criticism as Meckiff's, but in combination with the amount that he was allowed to drag down the pitch he was the most difficult of all to play. I never batted in a cap except under a hot sun and I cannot believe that I would have taken readily to a helmet if helmets had then been in vogue. But if I *had* worn one ever, it would have been to Rorke. I knew that if he pitched it on the right spot, he would, as it were, hit double top and there would not be much I could do about it.

The match which followed against an Australian XI captained by Neil Harvey was untypical of the tour, a very amusing one on which to look back. They had a strong batting side, including Harvey himself, McDonald, O'Neill, Peter Burge and Bobby Simpson, but they were less well equipped with bowlers. I had been rusty in the New South Wales match but in this one I made 140 and 114. Our spinners were far better suited to the pitch than theirs and we won by 345 runs, Lock taking 6 for 29 in the second innings. The fast bowlers, theirs and ours, had been allowed to follow through too near the stumps and Lock bowled into the rough. This rebounded on us, for umpires subsequently were often unnecessarily fussy about keeping bowlers off the pitch.

The main contribution to the enjoyment of the match, as it turned out, was the decision of the *Sydney Telegraph* to extend to this contest the prizes for performances in the Test series to come. Among the prizes was one of £500 for 100 made between two intervals. On the third morning I went in just before lunch and moved pretty rapidly after lunch. With thirty-five minutes to go before tea I was 83 and excitement was running high in the dressing room. I think the Australians were keenly interested too. I myself knew vaguely that some prize was on offer but was not clear about the exact conditions. I am sure that I did not realize how well placed I was, for I accepted fairly philosophically a period of twenty-five minutes in which Raman Subba Row became well and truly bogged down and I received only the odd ball.

When I had a chance of another dart at the chinaman of Johnny Martin, I hit him for 13 in an over and then drove one of the fast bowlers through the covers to reach 101. At this point Barry Jarman behind the stumps said to me, 'You want 108.' I realized then the exact requirement. I had been 8 at lunch.

I hit another 4 and took a single to get up the other end for the last over before tea bowled by the other fast bowler, Barry Fisher. That made 106. I had to refuse two singles, which was all against my principles. But it would have put an intolerable burden on Raman and if anything had gone wrong – if he had got out or been unable to give me the strike – we would neither of us have been able to face the dressing room. Then I pulled one from Fisher for 4, cut him for another 4 – and got out.

It must have been the most generally popular innings I ever played. I gave a party with the proceeds and asked both teams and the press of both countries to it. It went very well.

There was not much joy in the Queensland match, the only one remaining before the First Test. It rained; Lindwall, now thirty-seven – the last of the straight-arm bowlers, as he called himself – made us look very moderate; and those who did not get out to him were out to 'Slasher' MacKay or to a leg-spinner, Wally Walmsley, aged forty-two. Raman Subba Row, our top scorer, broke a wrist fielding in the gully. Willie Watson, who had needed an operation after damaging a knee on the ship, played his first match but looked a long way from full form and fitness.

Trueman, who had back trouble, was another who could not be considered for the First Test, so the team did not take much picking. The injury to Subba Row, however, had caused us to send for Ted Dexter, who had been in our thoughts for some time. He took some locating, as he was working in Paris and fog kept him there for some days. But he arrived by the end of the Test match. An extra spinner, John Mortimore, had come out a fortnight earlier. We had found quite a few pitches taking spin and, in the absence of Wardle, had no back-up for Laker and Lock. Johnny Wardle, in fact, was not absent in the flesh, as he was a member of the press party.

The toss on that Friday morning at the Gabba was one which I would not have minded losing. There was green in the pitch and it was cloudy and humid. Yet the likelihood was that, as in the Queensland match, the ball would not stop moving about after the first day and there was the forbidding precedent of Len Hutton's decision to put Australia in there four years before. They made 600. So, on winning the toss, I batted.

The first two days produced some grim cricket with the bowlers well on top. That does not mean that they were unrelentingly accurate, for Meckiff had Wally Grout leaping from one side to the other and Davidson was not fully fit. But they had us out for 134 that day.

I can well remember the murmur in the crowd when Meckiff first came on. Queensland spectators were used to watching Lindwall, Fisher and Mackay, all of them with unquestionably legitimate actions. This was clearly something new to them.

The next day was sunny and very hot but after an opening stand by McDonald and Burke of 55, Bailey, Statham, Loader and the spinners kept them to 156 for 6 on a rather easier pitch. We batted again only 52 behind on the Monday and from then on gave a pretty awful performance.

Peter Richardson was out almost as soon as Richie Benaud came on, well caught high and left-handed by the bowler. I had Trevor Bailey ready for such an emergency and he went in at number three. This was not, in hindsight, an inspired piece of captaincy, but it seemed sensible at the time. The whole day's play, including 30 added by Australia in the morning, produced only 122 runs. A day's play then was of five hours and the match of six days.

Arthur Milton was frequently in trouble against Davidson but after he was out Bailey and Graveney stayed together for the rest of the day, for much of which Benaud bowled. They were still bogged down next day – only 19 were added in an hour and a half. It was certainly not easy, and when Tom was run out I went in, restless and perhaps careless, and was lbw to Richie's googly, which he did not bowl often and I liked to think I could read. Richie bowled very well in this match, indeed throughout the series, 31 wickets at 18 apiece. He was at his best now and it was bad luck that he was bothered by a shoulder injury during the 1961 tour of England. But that is another story.

If there was a bright spot on that awful day in Brisbane when we lost our last 8 wickets and scored only 106 runs, it was towards the end of Colin Cowdrey's innings. But he was out to a controversial catch which he and even adjacent fielders seemed to think had pitched short of Kline at square leg. The umpires – McInnes was at the bowler's end – seemed unsure too and subsequently gave conflicting accounts of their discussions but Colin was given out. I was asked for a statement and merely said that we did not question the umpire's decision. 'Richie Benaud asked Kline if he had caught it, Kline said that he had and I am satisfied with that,' I said.

It was not McInnes's decision that bothered us but his indecision. He made what we thought were several other mistakes and misjudgements and, having known him well in the past, Freddie Brown and I thought that he was over the top. Hence our objection to his appointment for the next Test. In fact, he was kept on until after an embarrassing error over a runout in the Fourth Test.

Trevor Bailey went on to make 68 – in seven and a half hours – but we were all out for 198, which meant that Australia needed only 147. Jimmy Burke then scored 28 at a rather slower rate than Trevor had achieved, but Norman O'Neill made everything that had gone before look even more wretched by making a sparkling 71 not out and Australia won by 8 wickets.

It was clear that our whole approach needed changing. Our batting, I knew only too well, was not strong but strokelessness was not going to improve it. We had had a terrible match.

Between the first two Tests we went to Tasmania. Ideally the two matches in Tasmania should be played later in the series as partial relaxation and not at a time when the Test team is still unsettled and needs tougher opposition than was usually met in Tasmania in those days.

The only other match was the second one against South Australia who, since we played them before, had found two new bowlers, Trethewey and Hitchcox, both with highly suspect actions. The introduction of these two when there was already a lot of talk of 'chuckers' in the press was particularly disappointing, as was the quote from the chairman of the Australian Board of Control that allegations of throwing were 'grossly exaggerated' and that he did not think that any such problem existed.

Willie Watson made a few runs in all three matches and we brought him in for the Second Test in Melbourne instead of Arthur Milton. I went out to toss with Richie on the morning of my twenty-ninth birthday. Again I won it, again I looked at a grassy pitch without enthusiasm and again I felt that I had to bat. Shortly afterwards we were 7 for 3.

The ball moved about but no more than might have been expected on a first morning. Alan Davidson bowled a very fine opening spell and in his third over accounted for Richardson, Watson, with a full toss, and Graveney. Yet at the end of the day we had recovered to 173 for 4. Trevor Bailey, who had opened the innings, played much more positively than on other occasions to make 48 and Colin Cowdrey stayed with me for the rest of the day when I was 89. I had had one big piece of luck when, in a bit of a tangle with Richie's first ball, I gave him a return catch which was not difficult and which I imagine he still remembers with less pleasure than almost everything else in the series.

Next day I reached 113 and was thinking that there were plenty more to come when Meckiff, with the new ball, produced an absolute thunderbolt from somewhere. My bat was still in the air when it shattered the wicket.

We were out for 259, after which Neil Harvey played an innings of great quality, repaying Jim Laker for a few of the indignities suffered in 1956. Colin McDonald held the other end safe. Next day, before a Friday crowd of over 70,000, Statham had McDonald caught at slip but Harvey went on playing beautifully until they had almost reached our score. Then from 255 for 2 they collapsed, losing 4 wickets in the last hour, Harvey's to Loader, the other 3 to Statham. It was the more remarkable because the first eight overs with the new ball were played with perfect safety. There was no pause in the collapse next morning. Statham and Loader carried on as before and had them out for 308, a lead of only 49.

Our delight at this turn of events was short-lived. In the first innings Alan Davidson had taken 6 wickets to Meckiff's 3. I was certainly surprised by the way I had been bowled by Meckiff when well set but it is fair to say that he was so uncontrolled and bowled so many wide ones that we still found it hard to see him as a major threat.

Suddenly on that Saturday afternoon it all changed. He got it right and his method was such that he had a devastating effect. I saw much of it from the other end, for, with the help of some brilliant catching, he took 5 of the 6 wickets which we had lost for 57 by tea. He was very, very fast. Somehow one was mesmerized. It was an extraordinary feeling.

By tea, of course, the match was lost beyond reasonable doubt. Afterwards Richie withdrew the field to give me singles and to let Davidson and Meckiff fire at the other batsmen. I was eventually caught in the gully, slashing at Meckiff, and we were all out on a good pitch for 87, Meckiff 6 for 38. Early on the Monday morning they won by 9 wickets. We were two down.

In those years we seemed to have a perpetual problem with opening batsmen. For the Third Test in Sydney later that week we tried Bailey and Milton. Ted Dexter played his first Test against Australia, as did Roy Swetman, Godfrey Evans having broken a finger in Melbourne.

For a time events went much as usual. Having won the toss, I again had to hope that our opening pair would survive the first hour, during which there would be a little moisture in the pitch. This proved beyond them. However, Tom Graveney and I settled in and were approaching 100 when we were out to two superb catches by Mackay and Harvey.

I thought that I was the unlucky one, for I doubt if Mackay ever caught a better catch than the one he held diving forward at cover point off a pretty fair stroke hit very hard off the back foot.

The bowler was the West Australian, Keith Slater, in the first over of his only Test. Dexter, playing no stroke, and I provided him with his only Test wickets. I hope he remembers us kindly. To be scrupulously fair to him, I should add that although mentioned in the same breath as some famous 'chuckers', he was only called twice, the second time six years later, long after the purge of throwers had taken place.

We did not bat very well, especially against Benaud, and we had our problems in the field. When play eventually started on the Saturday, delayed by inadequate covering of the square, we dropped catches and had our fast bowlers upset by McInnes's fastidiousness about their follow-throughs. Brian Statham was the tidiest of bowlers in every way and I doubt if he had ever before been told that he was running on the pitch. In fact, on the slow pitch I had Laker and Lock bowling for most of the innings. The ball scarcely turned but Australia lost 6 wickets before they passed our score on the fourth day and it was a big seventh-wicket partnership between the left-handers Mackay and Davidson which gave them a lead of 140-odd.

We lost 3 wickets for 63 but Colin Cowdrey and I both made a good start on the fifth afternoon. We had barely cleared off the arrears when the Australians went on the defensive and seemed prepared to settle for a draw. Colin and I put on 182 together before I was bowled or, as Jack Fingleton wrote, thrown out by Burke for 92. Colin made 100.

It was just conceivable that we could have won this match but for the shortened second day. Laker and Lock took 9 wickets in the first innings and after six full days the ball might well have been turning enough for them to have Australia in trouble.

Before the Fourth Test in Adelaide we played both Victoria and New South Wales. Colin Cowdrey captained the side in Melbourne where we won in tremendous heat. I made 100 in Sydney in a match restricted by rain. We rested Jim Laker from both matches to make sure that his spinning finger, with which he was having trouble, would be fit for Adelaide.

This will be remembered as the Test match in which I put Australia in and they made nearly 500, thus settling the series and the destination of the Ashes beyond all reasonable doubt. I have never questioned that in the circumstances I did the right thing. We were two down and two to play. A draw was of no use to us and we were most likely to avoid one if we could bowl Australia out on the first day while there was still

damp in the pitch. Adelaide Test pitches had the reputation of being
still pretty good on the sixth day. Any doubts about what I should do
if I won the toss were finally removed when Jim Laker came back from
the nets on the morning of the match and told me that his finger would
not allow him to play.

It seemed such an obvious decision in our obviously desperate situation that I was surprised at the reaction of, amongst others, Richie
Benaud when I told him he could bat. He seemed amazed as well as
gratified.

In fact, two tours later there was an Adelaide Test match which
endorsed my line of thinking. Graham McKenzie took 3 England wickets
when the pitch was a little lively on the first morning and England under
Mike Smith never quite recovered. They lost the match and only halved
a series which they had looked like winning.

With one quite extraordinary exception the pitch produced nothing
with which the Australian batsmen could not cope. The very first ball
of the match, bowled by Brian Statham, pitched well outside the off
stump and passed over the top of the leg stump. It was an amazing
ball. Yet nothing remotely like it happened again. Colin McDonald, the
batsman concerned, made 170 and his opening stand with Jimmy Burke
was worth 171. We made 240, which was about our par for that tour,
followed on and were beaten on the sixth day by 10 wickets. Richie
Benaud took 9 wickets and Ray Lindwall, recalled in place of Mackay
for his first Test since 1956, took 3 and bowled very well.

The match marked not only the return of the Ashes to Australia but
also the end of Mel McInnes as a Test umpire. He had made a lot of
mistakes, and although players are usually sympathetic with senior
umpires whom they have learned to respect, McInnes lost some
sympathy by what had become a rather dictatorial manner. I think that
it would have been kinder if the Board subcommittee on umpires had
stood him down after the First Test as we had requested. Their refusal
to do so was all the more unusual because only five and a half years
before, after the Headingley Test of 1953, Lindsay Hassett had objected
to Frank Chester, who was at a similar stage in a distinguished career
to McInnes now. Chester was withdrawn from the remaining Test in
which he was due to stand.

We had been asked by the subcommittee to supply instances of
umpiring mistakes. We were not prepared to do this. We would have
been labelled as 'whingers' and it should have been enough for us to
have said that we had lost confidence in McInnes.

The particular incident which led to his replacement for the final
Test and his subsequent retirement was a marvellous muddle. Colin
McDonald had been rubbing a knee and at lunch on the second day,

Saturday, when he was 149 not out, he asked me if he might retire. I agreed, although apparently it was an old injury. I wondered if I had been too scrupulous in not asking for a substitute for Godfrey Evans who had aggravated an old finger injury and was still keeping under handicap and in a temperature of over 100 degrees. I was told later by Australians that I had been overgenerous but, never mind, I agreed, and we next saw McDonald at the crease on Monday when a wicket fell and he reappeared with Burke as runner.

Before long, McDonald drove Tyson to Statham at mid-off. Burke, somewhat unusually running on the off side, set off for a run. McInnes had moved out to the off side and when, from Statham's return, Tyson broke the wicket, he promptly raised his hand as no batsman had crossed his field of vision. Burke, of course, was behind his back.

I had been well placed to see the incident from around mid-on and watched what followed with keen interest. Burke would have been out by a yard or two but he knew very well that McInnes had not seen him. He asked McInnes what his decision was and McInnes, realizing his error with horror, had no option than to reverse his decision and give McDonald in. It was an incident which had a unique blend of tragedy (for McInnes), frustration (for us) and humour (for almost everyone). The matter was resolved by Colin McDonald who to his great credit gave his wicket away a few minutes later.

While we were in New Zealand McInnes's memoirs began to appear in the press. I started to read them but immediately came on a reference to myself which was wholly untrue. I decided to read no more and keep unsullied my memories of a very nice man and, until this last series, a first-rate umpire.

We had a splendid week before the last Test, the highlight being the Prime Minister's match in Canberra. This would have been a memorable occasion at any time but when the Prime Minister was as knowledgeable and enthusiastic a cricket lover as the Right Hon. Robert Menzies, it made it just about the best day of the tour. He had the ideal captain for his side in the irrepressible Hassett.

The Prime Minister gave a wonderful dinner and made one of his most brilliant speeches, relishing the chance to comment on the performance of Sam Loxton, the former Test all-rounder but now a Liberal MP in Victoria. Hassett had already warned him that with the sometimes fiery Loxton about to go to India and Pakistan as manager, war was likely to break out there at any moment.

I was cheered up too by the fact that on our way between Adelaide and Canberra we played before large and appreciative crowds of country people at Wangaratta and Wagga. It was nice to think that they were still keen to see us although we had been so thoroughly beaten.

There have been series before and since in which, with the rubber decided, the winning side has relaxed and the losers, with nothing more to lose, have recaptured a little esteem.

Not in Melbourne in February 1959. First Statham and Loader were put out of the match by a car crash. Just what this meant can be assessed from the fact that in the previous Test played in Melbourne over the New Year they had taken all but one of the Australian wickets which fell, 11 out of 12. Willie Watson broke his finger in the nets the day before the match, which gave us a chance to play Ted Dexter again. He had done very little since he arrived out of a European winter but the class was there and if he ever settled in he would bring a badly needed aggression to our middle batting.

We gave a first Test to John Mortimore who had not bowled badly in the second match against Victoria and had been making his 30s and 40s at number eight or nine. Generally our off-spinners have been more successful then our left-arm spinners against the best players in Australia, and although it hurt to leave out Lock, he had taken only 5 wickets at 75 apiece. We were so infrequently on the attack in that series that his close catching was not of the same importance as it usually was. Godfrey Evans was kept out by his injured finger and the casualty list was augmented during the match when ailments stopped Bailey and Laker from bowling.

I had been told often enough since Adelaide that it was nearly fifty years since a captain who put a side in had won a Test match in Australia. That did not stop Richie Benaud from putting us in when he won the toss for the first time in the series. As the Melbourne pitch was usually lively on the first morning and as the selectors had loaded him with fast bowlers – Davidson, Meckiff, Lindwall and Rorke – it seemed inevitable. Bailey was soon out to a lifter; so was I, and although Peter Richardson played his best innings of the series and John Mortimore made 44 not out, we finished, as usual it seemed, with a score of not much over 200. With dismal consistency we repeated it in the second innings and Australia won by 9 wickets.

The three weeks in New Zealand were a relief rather than an anti-climax this time. New Zealand cricket was in one of its troughs and we won the first Test comfortably, Ted Dexter making his first Test 100.

I had one particularly enjoyable, if somewhat exacting, interlude when Frank Gilligan, Virginia's uncle, who was headmaster of Wanganui Collegiate School, asked Colin Cowdrey and myself to play against the boys there. Frank had been a fine wicketkeeper-batsman, captain of Cambridge in 1920 after which he played quite a bit for Essex. He was a famous figure in New Zealand educational circles but, alas, died a year later.

I had only just started to make the runs expected of me when I played a ball off my legs, not too badly, I thought, and to my dismay was miraculously caught by a small boy at short leg.

This was clearly not in the script, but Frank, umpiring at the bowler's end and prepared, no doubt, for just such an emergency, rose to the occasion and sang out, 'No ball.' I have always hoped that the small boy, who must be in his forties now, was not too disappointed.

I was coming home to be married and although the weather was miserable for the Auckland Test, it made a nice end to a long tour to score 124 not out in my final innings as a bachelor.

The series in Australia had been a clear example of how in their own conditions a vibrant and youthful Australia will be too much for an experienced and relatively ponderous England. The difference between the two sides in the field was alone worth hundreds of runs over the series.

Yet I still balance the many disappointments by a feeling that we achieved something worthwhile by contributing to the harmonious atmosphere which enabled throwing to be so swiftly eliminated from the game. When Ted Dexter's side went four years later, I believe there was not a suspect action in sight.

My memories of the tour are also warmed by the most generous and understanding letter which I received during the final Test from the Prime Minister of Australia. We had seen him quite often during the tour and he had been in great form when he came to dine in Adelaide with Colin Cowdrey, Peter Richardson, George Duckworth and myself.

Ordinarily I view with suspicion books which include letters written to the author telling him what a fine chap he is and I give this one here, with some trepidation, only as an illustration that there were deeper issues at stake then than the winning and losing of a series.

14th February, 1959

My dear Peter,

My duties having called me back to Canberra, I saw only one hour of play on the first day of the current Test Match.

I imagine that you must be feeling a little disappointed about the results of the series, in the course of which you have enjoyed the benefit of the critical advice of a great number of people who know less about cricket than you do. But I would like to tell you that not only has your batting been an unfailing source of pleasure to all of us, but the obvious good relations which exist between the two teams owes a great deal to your constant example of courtesy and good humour.

It is, I think, a good thing that the 'Ashes' should move around from time to time and from that point of view one should not be unduly agitated about any current results. I am writing merely as one to whom you have given great pleasure, to thank you for your own great work, and to tell you what agreeable memories you leave behind you for all cricket lovers.

With very kind regards,

Yours sincerely,
Robert Menzies

So I came back to England knowing that I had at least one friend left! And a marvellous man at that.

13
Illness Intervenes

Virginia and I were married at Cranleigh on 24 April 1959 and went off on honeymoon to Cornwall in blissful ignorance of the troubles which were to beset our first year of married life.

By the time we returned and moved into a house on the green at Cranleigh I had missed Surrey's first three championship matches but played against Somerset at the Oval in the third week in May. This was an unusual match in which we only just avoided the follow-on but bowled them out for very little in the second innings, Loader 8 for 48, and won by 9 wickets. Stewart and Barrington made nearly all the runs in the first innings, Stewart and John Edrich in the second.

With three young batsmen of their calibre now reaching their best, Surrey were entitled to expect to win their eighth successive championship. There were doubts about the bowling, not so much on the grounds of advancing years, although Alec Bedser was now forty, but because pitches were now covered except during the hours of play. The speed with which our bowlers had finished off the opposition on wet pitches had always been one of our strengths. We also did not know how effective Tony Lock would be with his revised action. Yet, although none of our first three matches had been won, I thought we should still be good enough.

Fortunately I never needed much practice and, in fact, had only one more match before the First Test against India. That was against Kent and, having made runs in both innings, I departed for Trent Bridge to play the First Test with what was widely hailed as a new team. We had only six survivors from Australia – Cowdrey, Evans, Milton, Statham, Trueman and myself.

That year's Indian side was full of paradoxes. They had plenty of good players – Contractor, Roy, Umrigar, Manjrekar, Borde, Nadkarni, Gupte and, after the Oxford season, Abbas Ali Baig – but they did not make up into a strong team. They had a superb, almost cloudless summer, which should have helped them. But they went down 5-0 and gave little opposition.

On our side, the selectors had to find a team to go to West Indies at the end of the year without being influenced by performances against a side lacking the fast bowling of West Indies.

We won the First Test in four days by an innings. I had a partnership with Ken Barrington, who was recalled after four years for what was to be an almost permanent presence over the next ten years or so. I was delighted with my own form, although if I had known that the 106 on the first day was to be my last Test 100, I should have been less happy.

At Lord's India lasted only three days. Lancashire had produced a leg-spinner, Tommy Greenhough, who was very much seen as a symbol of a new era. At Lord's in the first innings he took 5 for 35 but after that we lost him for a time in the most frustrating circumstances. He had such difficulty in avoiding following through on the pitch that he had to drop out of first-class cricket to correct it. It was not until the Fifth Test that he could play again but he went to West Indies that winter. Colin Cowdrey and I finished off the match on the Saturday afternoon with a stand in which he played absolutely beautifully.

The Third Test at Headingley was my fifty-second in succession, which apparently equalled Frank Woolley's record. I read this with mild interest but, again, if I had known that it was the end of the sequence my feelings would have been very different. By now we had only five of those who had started the series – we tried twenty-one players that year – but this match also lasted only three days. India were bowled out by Fred Trueman, Alan Moss, a good accurate bowler who moved the ball at just below top pace, and Harold Rhodes, whose action was to cause a lot of argument over the years until it was adjudged by cameras to be more legitimate than it looked because of 'hyperextension' of his elbow. Colin made 160 at his best.

Surrey meanwhile were in a winning run. I went down to Cardiff after the Headingley Test and made 60, which was well above the usual. I fear that the fact that Wilf Wooller was not playing may have had something to do with it. Bernard Constable, who always made runs against Glamorgan, scored 168. We won by 10 wickets and by the same margin against Kent at Blackheath the following weekend when I began to feel below par. At Bradford over the weekend I felt more and more down.

Yorkshire and Surrey were at the top of the championship table and the gates were shut on each of the first two days. I had to work hard to make 54 on a pitch which gave all bowlers a chance, but our 153 soon looked a good score when Loader and Bedser bowled them out for 91. We eventually left them to make 222 to win but Peter Loader, who had taken 6 wickets in the first innings, took another 6 in the second and we won by 48 runs. This was the second time that season that we had beaten Yorkshire but they finished the season better than we did and our seven-year run as champions was over.

Towards the end of that match I felt so awful that I handed over to Alec Bedser and went off the field. I had never had to do anything like that before and I was very depressed as I drove over the Pennines to Lymm where the England team was staying for the Fourth Test at Old Trafford. I wondered if I would feel any better in another thirty-six hours, but I soon realized that I had to make a decision that night. The obvious replacement as captain was Colin Cowdrey, who had been my vice-captain in Australia, and he had not been picked for this match. He had been left out not through any loss of form, far from it, but in order that the selectors might give another chance to Mike Smith who had just played two big innings for the Gentlemen at Lord's. So I rang Gubby that night and he was able to divert Colin to Old Trafford from Maidstone where he would otherwise have been playing for Kent.

When Gubby arrived, he asked me if I wanted to stay and watch for a day or two. I stayed for two days but by then all I wanted to do was to go home.

Our doctor in Cranleigh called in a specialist who diagnosed an ischiorectal abscess and arranged for me to go into the Central Middlesex Hospital almost at once. Virginia drove me up. My state of health by now was such that when a nurse offered me 'a nice cup of tea' while we were sitting in the reception room, I said that I just wanted to go to bed, nothing more.

I could not understand it. I had never been ill in my life and still thought that I would be out and about again in a few days. It was some time before I learned that recovery from this particular operation was a slow business because the wound was deep inside and the tissues had to heal from inside out. Apparently they tend to do it the other way round.

In the following year I was told that this operation often had to be done twice for that reason. I think that if I had realized this and anyone had told me that I was unwise to go to West Indies that winter I would certainly not have gone. But once the operation was over and I had left hospital I went home to convalesce, watched cricket on the green in the late summer sunshine and felt perfectly well. In the autumn I was back in the office and, as December approached, having the odd net at Alf Gover's school in Wandsworth. It was nearly five months since the operation and I felt entirely fit.

I should add at this point that in those days we had different ideas of fitness. To me the best preparation for batting, bowling and fielding was batting, bowling and fielding. I doubt if any of my contemporaries, especially the older ones, did many exercises. I have often tried to picture

Evans and Compton doing press-ups in the outfield before the day's play but so far have failed miserably.

It was therefore a novelty when, before we set off, we gathered at Lord's for a demonstration of something called circuit training by the AAA chief coach, Geoffrey Dyson. This was designed to harden us up while we were on the SS *Camito* and it worked pretty well. We were also addressed by Harry Altham, that year's President of MCC, whose wide-ranging services to the game were tragically cut off by his sudden death five years later. He was a most understanding man and an inspiring talker who had a command of the English language which made him a joy to listen to whether he was talking about a forthcoming tour or the coaching manual.

Colin Cowdrey was again my vice-captain and the manager was Walter Robins. It is widely believed that Walter and I were at loggerheads on that tour. That is totally untrue. We were certainly not on the same wavelength but there was never the slightest friction between us. We came of different generations and he, although considered unconventional in his time, had more of the old type of amateur outlook than I did. On his first tour as manager he was also probably more sensitive to criticism than I was by this time. I had had plenty in Australia and elsewhere and the only time when I took criticism to heart was when I thought it fair and justified.

The side picked was unusual, especially in those days, for at twenty-nine I was very nearly its oldest member. Keith Andrew was the oldest and there is only a fortnight between us. To that extent the lessons from the year before had been learned. But most important of all to our success was the fact that we had strengthened our middle batting with such as Ken Barrington, Ted Dexter and Mike Smith. Raman Subba Row also made runs and so did Jim Parks when he was called in from a coaching job in Trinidad to play in the last Test.

We had also found an opening pair in Geoff Pullar, a solid left-hander, and Colin Cowdrey. I had told Colin as long ago as 1956 that he was the best opener in the country but he was never happy about opening. As I have said, he liked to put his feet up after fielding and to think about the batting to come. But he played the fast bowling with so much more time than anyone else and on this tour, when there was a lot of short, very fast bowling, he was magnificent. One other important contribution was that of Fred Trueman. Brian Statham always bowled well but this series was, I think, the best of Fred's career – 21 wickets at 26 apiece compared with Wes Hall's 22 wickets at 30 apiece.

Besides Colin Cowdrey the team contained three other future England captains who were to bring widely differing qualities to the job. Ray Illingworth came under the heading of shrewd Yorkshiremen, Mike

Smith was completely unflappable and Ted Dexter brought a touch of brilliance to almost anything he tackled. In the side there were also two future managers of England touring teams, Ken Barrington and Raman Subba Row, so I might be said to have been in command of a highly responsible body of men.

During our practice in Barbados we took a three-day excursion to Grenada just before Christmas for a match on the mat. Even in these days of swift air travel, teams coming from an English winter need a month before they can hope to be near their best and we were well beaten by Barbados. Seymour Nurse and Gary Sobers put on over 300 for the third wicket and just about the best thing we did was to stay out in the rain while Cammie Smith and Conrad Hunte hammered Statham and Trueman for 58 in 6 overs to enable Barbados to win by 10 wickets.

This match gave us our first sight of Charlie Griffith who played in only one Test in that series but formed a highly successful fast-bowling partnership with Wes Hall a few years later when his action was the subject of much comment. It was his first first-class match and I was one of his first victims, caught in the gully off the glove.

I was not disheartened by this defeat which was no great surprise at that stage of the tour. Barbados were captained by Everton Weekes and their strength was such that he was not required to bat.

It was nice to walk out to toss in the Test match which followed with an old friend of Cambridge days, footballing as well as cricketing, in Gerry Alexander. It was a strange thought. The West Indies captain had played soccer for England in amateur internationals. Three years before, the South African captain had been Clive van Ryneveld who had played rugby for England.

I was not so pleased with Gerry when he caught me brilliantly on the leg-side off Wes Hall, but Ken Barrington, who had started the tour in tremendous form, and Ted Dexter each made 100 and we mustered nearly 500. West Indies made even more and that was about the end of the match, which was not a bad preliminary. It gave the batsmen confidence and the bowlers some idea of what would be needed.

We had been fortunate to have our first taste of really fast bowling from Hall and the very aggressive Watson on so plumb a pitch. But in two matches in Trinidad the problem was spin. We won them both, although the first was after a declaration by our opponents and after we had only just avoided the follow-on. The gratifying part was the general form of the batsmen – all except myself. Mike Smith and Ted Dexter knocked off the runs against the clock in the first match, Colin and Geoff Pullar started the second match with a stand of 174 and Colin made 173 himself.

So we came to the momentous Second Test at Queen's Park, Port of

Spain. When I went back there as President of MCC in 1981, I found the memories flooding back with a clarity which defied the twenty-one year gap.

Brian Statham had been unable to play in the First Test but was now fit, which was important. I won the toss again and we had to endure a fiery attack by Hall and Watson. Both were warned at some stage. When I was caught at second slip for nought just before lunch we were 57 for 3.

From there, however, the innings was picked up by Ken Barrington and Ted Dexter in a splendidly positive way. Next day Ken went on to make his second 100 of the series and Mike Smith made one too, a brave effort because I know that, wearing glasses, he found the glare of West Indian pitches a problem.

After two days we had made 382 and Hunte and Solomon 22 for no wicket. The next day, a Saturday, was one of the most remarkable I experienced.

Almost at once Statham had Conrad Hunte caught off bat and thigh at short leg. Kanhai was soon lbw playing across a ball from Trueman. Sobers was out third ball. The ball was flying very fast over my head at third slip, I only just reached it with my right hand but knocked it up conveniently to first slip.

This stroke of Sobers was just about the last attacking one, but the luck was with us, as when Solomon was run out after a misunderstanding with Frank Worrell. West Indies batted on doggedly but Trueman and Statham bowled superbly. When I wanted to rest them, I used the spinners, of whom we had three – Barrington, Allen and Illingworth. It was a very good pitch and I was afraid that Ted Dexter's not always accurate medium pace might give them a chance to recover. As it was, Ken Barrington performed one of his proudest feats as a bowler, 16 overs for 15 runs.

The West Indies struggle achieved so little that soon after tea when Singh, a young left-arm bowler who had only just come into first-class cricket, was run out by a quick piece of fielding by Ted Dexter, West Indies were 98 for 8. Within a few seconds we were wafted back six years to British Guiana, to a similar incident with a similar sequel. Then as now it was a local batsman who was run out – and by a yard or more.

First, bottles were thrown on the ground and then beer cans, fruit and anything else which came to hand. Then the crowd began to swarm on. I tried to persuade them to go back, Sonny Ramadhin, a Trinidadian, standing beside me, and we made no attempt to leave the field. But they came on in increasing numbers.

It was quite frightening. Fred Trueman grabbed a stump and placed himself in front of me. 'They won't touch you, skipper,' he said. I appreciated the thought but was not quite sure that this was the way to restore peace. By then, however, it was clear that the situation was hopeless. The ground authorities had been caught completely by surprise, so we had no alternative but to retreat and await the riot squad.

When they came, they turned a hose on the popular side where a crowd was besieging the broadcasting box. Inside were Jeff Stollmeyer and Rex Alston who were indignantly saying how disgraceful the scenes were. This inflamed those with radios even more. Unfortunately the hose was soon out of action as someone turned the water off behind the stand.

At that time the Federation of West Indies was in being. The Governor-General, Lord Hailes, was present. So were the Governor of Trinidad, Sir Edward Beetham, the Premier, Dr Williams, Learie Constantine, who was Minister of Works and Transport, and many other senior figures on the island. They sat helpless and before long play was officially abandoned for the day.

On these occasions the cricket tends to seem of secondary importance but we were bitterly disappointed at having been cut off when we were having a tremendous day in the field.

That night the Governor and the Premier broadcast bitter condemnations of the behaviour. Next day Sir Errol dos Santos, chairman of the Queen's Park Club (and still chairman when I went twenty-one years later) apologized on behalf of the club to MCC. Walter Robins made a suitably sympathetic reply. By the Monday morning the dust had settled and, as usually happens, those present – there were 10,000 or more – were models of decorum. We were loudly applauded when we took the field and I myself received quite an ovation when I went out to bat later.

Trueman and Statham soon finished the innings off. West Indies had been bowled our for 112 on a good pitch. Although we led by 270, I had already decided to bat again. An extra half-hour was being added to each of the remaining five-hour days and it seemed that we would have an easier task later on when our spinners, who had not taken a wicket in the first innings, might find the ball turning a little on a rather bare pitch.

We did not find runs easy to score in the second innings but with such a big lead that was encouraging. Nor would the opposition. Illingworth and Trueman had a rousing partnership towards the end of the day and next morning I was able to declare 500 ahead with 9 wickets down and 10 hours left.

The spinners did most of the bowling in the last innings. I tried to keep Trueman and Statham fresh for emergencies but in fact it was Ted Dexter who removed the main obstacle, Rohan Kanhai. At this time we used to call Ted the 'fruit-box bowler' – Liquorice All-Sorts. On this occasion he produced a full toss which Kanhai whacked straight at midwicket. We won with nearly two hours to spare. It seemed a great landmark, the first match won with a new team.

We moved on to Jamaica where we played the Colts in Sabina Park, the Test ground, and then played the Island in nearby Melbourne Park. We scored over 500 against Jamaica, with 100 from Mike Smith, big scores by Subba Row and Dexter and even 124 by May. But I did not really play well and I was beginning to feel pretty rough.

However, I won the toss again when the Third Test started and we ran into some short dangerous bowling by Hall and Watson. I was not at all sure that I had done the right thing by batting, for it was here in Sabina Park six years before that Trevor Bailey's bowling on the first morning had done so much to win the match. Fortunately Colin Cowdrey played a heroic innings, heroic because he took all sorts of bruising blows but was still there at the end of the five hours, 75 not out. Next day he made this into 114 and we were out for 277, the next top score to Colin's being David Allen's 30 not out.

Colin's innings had given us a respite but from that first day we were always struggling to save the match. West Indies passed our score with only 2 wickets down before collapsing. Gary Sobers made 147 but it occupied over six hours. When he was established on one of those supremely good pitches, we used to spread the field and give him a run, not primarily to slow him up but to goad him into taking risks. It did not work on the third day, for West Indies did not lose a wicket. Next day they lost their last 8 for 54 – to five different bowlers.

We owed a great deal that afternoon and the next to Geoff Pullar and Colin Cowdrey. Colin made a really brilliant 97. The rest of us found it hard going, and when we were all out on the last morning after a priceless last-wicket stand of 25 between Allen and Statham West Indies needed only 230 to win in about four hours.

The main credit for saving the match – West Indies finished it at 175 for 6 – goes to Fred Trueman. I told him that whatever he did, he must bowl at the off stump. No one could have followed instructions more faithfully. He hit the stumps four times. It was marvellous bowling. This, and a great piece of luck when Sobers was run out going for a run which Kanhai refused, undoubtedly saved us.

This was the day when there was a bit of a rumpus about my refusing Rohan Kanhai a runner. I heard it said at tea that he was tired and was going to have a runner. My reaction was that if some of our fielders who were showing signs of exhaustion in the heat had to keep going, he should not be spared the discomforts either. When he asked for a runner, I said that it did not have my approval. He said he had cramp and I sent for a glass of water and a salt tablet. I suppose, if the cramp persisted, that it came under the heading 'injury or illness'. In that case my consent was not required and, if the umpires had wished, they could have agreed to his having a runner. In fact, they disagreed and Gerry Alexander who was batting was not sure of the form either.

After the match I decided that to avoid further discord or misunderstanding I should apologize to Gerry and to Rohan Kanhai. In some parts of the world, unfortunately, to apologize is to lose face. I am a believer in apologizing if you think that you may have been in the wrong. There were plenty of people prepared to say I had been wrong here. So I apologized.

I was due for a few days off, a sort of mid-tour sabbatical. Virginia had come out with her parents and we all went off on a cruise to Caracas. It was a welcome break from a cricket environment but I was becoming increasingly uncomfortable. At the end of the cruise Virginia announced that she was staying on and not going home as planned with her parents.

Although this upset all plans, 'I don't care,' she said. 'Peter is not at all well and I am staying with him.' It was one of her best decisions, one for which I was profoundly grateful in the next two weeks.

So far I had thought that the wound, which was open and bleeding again, would heal. I had not mentioned it to anyone, although I had been to one or two doctors in recent weeks.

Virginia went to Barbados to await developments while I rejoined the team in Georgetown, British Guiana, and played in the colony match. I lost the toss and we fielded for nearly two days. It was this ordeal in the humidity of the Demerara River estuary that finished me. This time the doctor told me that I could not go on playing. I told Walter Robins and next day he announced that I would play no cricket for a fortnight, which meant missing the Fourth Test.

I had had the trouble for so long that I myself doubted if there would be much improvement in the next fortnight, especially in the sticky climate of that part of the world. However, Virginia joined me and we watched the Test match, which was a dull affair on a lifeless pitch. As before, we were led on first innings but Raman Subba Row, who replaced me, and Ted Dexter made 100s in the second innings and we kept our 1-0 lead.

It was a depressing week for me and, I am sure, for Virginia. Georgetown is an interesting old place built by the Dutch but it is no holiday resort, as one realizes on seeing the brown waters of the Demerara River surging out to discolour the blue of the ocean. At the end of the match I was no better and, encouraged by the doctor, I decided to go home as soon as possible, preceded, as it happened, by Brian Statham. He, poor

chap, had been increasingly worried by news about the health of his
son, who was in hospital. Brian would obviously be badly missed in the
final Test but his presence at home was far more important.

Colin was left in charge of a slightly depleted team but one which
was still batting well and was now reinforced by the inclusion as wicketkeeper-batsman of Jim Parks. He made 43 and 101 not out in the last
Test in Trinidad. Colin himself made 119 in the first innings and saw
to it that we did not lose our hard-won lead. It was always going to be
a draw and, if anything, West Indies, having lost the toss, had rather
the worst of it.

By that time Virginia and I had flown home and I was back in hospital
having another operation. Among the kind letters which I received while
I was recovering was one from the President of MCC, Harry Altham,
who wrote personally to every player in the side expressing the club's
appreciation of their effort in being the first MCC side ever to win a
series in the Caribbean. His letter cheered me up a lot.

This time I had no doubt about what I should do after the operation.
I put aside all thought of playing again in 1960 and concentrated on
making sure that the wound healed completely. I am happy to say that
it did and I have never had any trouble since.

During the summer I went to the Oval occasionally and I saw a bit
of the South Africans of that year. They were between generations and
not very strong, although just over the horizon lay a host of great players
such as Barlow and the Pollocks followed within a year or two by Barry
Richards and Mike Procter.

Towards the end of that winter, nearly a year since I had last held a
bat, I began to have a few nets at Alf Gover's school. The Australians
were coming in 1961, which was an exciting thought, but I also wanted
to contribute something towards Surrey's building of a new team. Alec
Bedser had retired and I knew how much he would be missed. I myself
had no intention then of retiring in the near future. I was only thirty-
one.

My keenness to start playing again took me to Fenners in April. We
had a pleasant game which the university saved with their last pair
together. They included a freshman called Mike Brearley playing in his
first first-class match and keeping wicket. He batted very well at number
eight to make 76 before we ran him out. I made runs in each innings
and another 70 at Lord's against MCC who included Gary Sobers and
Fazal Mahmood.

It was to be a hard season for Surrey. Loader and Lock were still
good bowlers and, now that Jim Laker had gone, it was nice to see Eric

Bedser having the chance to show what a good off-spinner he was. But on covered pitches we no longer had the bowling to rout sides as we had in the fifties.

In our first championship match I made 3 and 99 against Worcestershire who were just starting on some good years which included winning the championship twice. I was playing quite well and was satisfied with my form and fitness until we played the Australians in mid-May.

The Australians, very keen to revenge their defeat five years before, made a big score on a good pitch. This was the innings which impressed on us the ability of Bill Lawry, who made 165. When our turn came against what was not on paper a great Australian bowling side, I played rather well but pulled a muscle in the groin. Without this I would probably not have been run out for 58. The groin felt slightly easier next day and I batted again when we followed on but after a time had to retire. We had already lost David Fletcher with a broken finger and were facing certain defeat, so there seemed no point in aggravating what I hoped was only a passing strain.

In fact, it kept me out for two and half weeks and it was not until the Saturday before the First Test that I played again – at Northampton. I made 30 and the groin stood up to it but I realized that this injury following an absence of over a year from the game meant that I could not be fit yet awhile for a five-day Test. I rang Gubby Allen that night and asked him not to pick me.

Instead I played for Surrey at Taunton, which provided an ideal pitch for a batsman needing practice, and made 153 not out. This was Bill Alley's great season when, at the age of forty-two he made over 3000 runs and bowled 600 overs for 62 wickets. I do not remember having much trouble with his bowling on that pitch but I had to field while he made 183 not out and 134 not out. I wisely missed the return match at the Oval in August when he made 150 not out. A year later he bowled me out for 1 at the Oval and he always delights in reminding me of this dismissal whenever we meet.

I was pleased with my progress at Taunton but in the next match against Lancashire I damaged a calf muscle and did not play again before the Second Test at Lord's. The First at Edgbaston had been drawn. They had led us by over 300 on first innings but in the second innings Raman Subba Row had made 112 and Ted Dexter 180.

I had told Gubby at the weekend that I should be fit for Lord's but, as there was still some uncertainty, we agreed that Colin should retain the captaincy.

We picked the wrong side for Lord's and Australia picked the right one, though neither set of selectors could be blamed or complimented. Australia had only four fit bowlers – Benaud was an absentee – and so played them all. Davidson, McKenzie, Misson and Mackay proved ideally suited to the pitch. Alan Davidson bowled particularly well. He was a very high-class all-rounder and, incidentally, one of the few top Australian cricketers to have committed themselves later to the game's administration.

England had an option as in our thirteen we had David Smith of Gloucestershire. After a good look at the pitch, the selectors left him out and played two spinners, Illingworth and Lock. In the event, the ball moved off the seam throughout and Smith, who never played in a home Test match, would have been invaluable in addition to Trueman, Statham and Dexter.

Over the last two years Colin and I had excelled ourselves with the toss. This was the twelfth successive time that England had won it, Colin's contribution being nine. On this occasion he probably did us no favours. Australia took the initiative and never lost it, although Statham and Trueman gave them an uneasy few minutes on the fourth and last morning when, needing 69, they were 19 for 4. The ball bounced erratically and I was twice caught at the wicket off lifters.

It was not an auspicious return to Test cricket but I resumed the captaincy at Headingley. I look back with special pleasure on those days, not only because Colin and I could pass the captaincy to and fro with absolute harmony but because we both got on so well with Richie Benaud and indeed all the Australians. Before my playing days there had been periods when it was not done to fraternize much with the opposition. In the era of such Australians as Hassett, Lindwall, Miller and Benaud, relations between the sides were of the happiest and I like to think that we made a contribution to that.

At Headingley I was confronted with a mottled brown pitch on an otherwise green square. Richie and I looked at it and I expect that he thought, as I did, that England's thirteenth successive winning toss might be one of the most valuable. I lost it, he looked relieved, Australia batted and dust flew almost at once.

Statham had not been fit for this match and we had called up Les Jackson of Derbyshire who had played for England only once before, against New Zealand in 1949. In the intervening twelve years he had been pushed aside by a flood of other good bowlers but, at forty, he was still a magnificent bowler with a sort of slinging action. No batsman played him with ease. He never bowled badly and was most unlucky not to have gone to Australia in 1950–51 and perhaps later. Having looked at this remarkable pitch, the selectors were in some doubt whether to play him but I was all for it and we left out Brian Close.

For a long time everything went as expected. Lawry and McDonald found it difficult going on a low slow pitch. Trueman and Jackson gave

ENGLAND v AUSTRALIA, Headingley
(Third Test, 1961)

England won by eight wickets

AUSTRALIA

W. M. Lawry lbw b Lock	28	– c Murray b Allen	28
C. C. McDonald st Murray b Lock	54	– b Jackson	1
R. N. Harvey c Lock b Trueman	73	– c Dexter b Trueman	53
N. C. O'Neill c Cowdrey b Trueman	27	– c Cowdrey b Trueman	19
P. J. Burge c Cowdrey b Jackson	5	– lbw b Allen	0
K. D. Mackay lbw b Jackson	6	– c Murray b Trueman	0
R. B. Simpson lbw b Trueman	2	– b Trueman	3
A. K. Davidson not out	22	– c Cowdrey b Trueman	7
*R. Benaud b Trueman	0	– b Trueman	0
†A. W. T. Grout c Murray b Trueman	3	– c and b Jackson	7
G. D. McKenzie b Allen	8	– not out	0
B 7, l-b 2	9	L-b 2	2

1/65 2/113 3/187 4/192 5/196	237	1/4 2/49 3/99 4/102 5/102	120
6/203 7/203 8/204 9/208		6/105 7/109 8/109 9/120	

Bowling: *First Innings* – Trueman 22–5–58–5; Jackson 31–11–57–2; Allen 28–12–45–1; Lock 29–5 68–2. *Second Innings* – Trueman 15.5–5–30–6; Jackson 13–5–26–2; Lock 10–1–32–0; Allen 14–6–30–2.

ENGLAND

G. Pullar b Benaud	53	– not out	26
R. Subba Row lbw b Davidson	35	– b Davidson	6
M. C. Cowdrey c Grout b McKenzie	93	– c Grout b Benaud	22
*P. B. H. May c and b Davidson	26	– not out	8
E. R. Dexter b Davidson	28		
K. F. Barrington c Simpson b Davidson	6		
†J. T. Murray b McKenzie	6		
F. S. Trueman c Burge b Davidson	4		
G. A. R. Lock lbs b McKenzie	30		
D. A. Allen not out	5		
H. L. Jackson run out	8		
L-b 5	5		

1/59 2/145 3/190 4/223 5/239 6/248	299	1/14 2/45	(2 wks.) 62
7/252 8/286 9/291			

Bowling: *First Innings* – Davidson 47–23–63–5; McKenzie 27–4–64–3; Mackay 22–4–34–0; Benaud 39–15–86–1; Simpson 14–5–47–0; *Second Innings* – Davidson 11–6–17–1; McKenzie 5–0–15–0; Mackay 1–0–8–0; Benaud 6–1–22–1.

Umpires: J. S. Buller and John Langridge

*My first Test as captain after my illness. A match of collapses which
ended abrutply on the third afternoon with a win which put England
level in the series, though not, alas, for long*

nothing away – Jackson in the match bowled 44 overs for 83 runs –
but the only wickets were taken by Lock. At tea, with Harvey and
O'Neill accelerating, Australia were 183 for 2.

The first new ball had done nothing but I took the second after tea
mainly because I believed in subjecting the batsmen to change when
possible. To everyone's amazement they began to get out to Trueman
and Jackson in a rush, seven of them for 21 runs, and it was almost

reassuring to the side batting next when Davidson and McKenzie put on 29 for the last wicket without much difficulty. Trueman and Jackson bowled very well, Cowdrey and Lock held some smart close catches and we had fifteen minutes to bat that night.

We now had a left-handed opening pair in Pullar and Subba Row and they gave us a good start in an innings which followed a similar course to Australia's. The early batsmen had to work hard but Colin Cowdrey played extremely well for 93 and we reached 190 for 2. Soon after tea the new ball was taken and the innings began to subside. I tried to drive Davidson but on this pitch there were always likely to be hazards in driving. The ball stopped and lobbed gently back to him.

On the third morning Ted Dexter steered us past Australia's 237 with only 4 wickets down, but of the last six batsmen only Lock, with a priceless 30, reached double figures and our lead was only 62.

One significant development that morning had been Alan Davidson's switch to bowling left-arm spin. With this he had Ken Barrington caught at slip, bowled Dexter and had Trueman caught at long on. I had already thought of asking Fred Trueman to reduce his pace and try cutting the ball but at the start of the second innings there seemed no occasion for such an improvisation. McDonald played on to Jackson, and when I brought Lock and Allen on Allen turned a ball to have Lawry caught at the wicket and gave O'Neill such problems that I thought I would let the spinners carry on.

It was really Neil Harvey, a brilliant player of spin, who forced me to turn back to Trueman. Neil made his second 50 of the match so well that I had awful pictures of his playing an innings which could soon give Australia a winning lead in a low-scoring match. So I brought on Trueman. His third ball stopped, much as mine from Davidson had done, and Harvey was caught at cover point.

Fred now announced that he was going to shorten his run and bowl off-cutters. I had hesitated to ask him to try something unusual but I had underestimated his accuracy. From then on he kept getting batsmen out and a match which only a few minutes before had promised to be a long hard struggle was suddenly racing to a finish. Beginning with Harvey's wicket, taken in his normal method, Fred took 6 wickets for 4 runs in 45 balls.

Soon after tea on that Saturday evening their 99 for 2 had become 120 all out and we needed only 59 to win. We won by 8 wickets, utterly bemused by the speed of it all.

Much has been written about the Old Trafford Test and a wealth of arguments put forward about how we came to lose it and Australia to win it after they had looked the likely losers for all but the last few hours.

I have never been in any doubt that the man who had the most influence on the result was not within 200 miles of Old Trafford. That was Colin Cowdrey, who had dropped out with a throat infection. Irrespective of the number of runs he might have made, he would never have dropped the catches which we put down at slip in that match.

That apart, the decisive factors were the last-wicket stand of 98 between Davidson and McKenzie, begun when Australia were only 157 ahead, and Ted Dexter's brilliant innings of 76 which, with Raman Subba Row's support, gave us ideas above our station.

Rain took away half the first day's play but our fast bowlers, notably Statham, bowled Australia out for 190 and by the second evening we were 187 for 3. I was 90 not out, having played as well as at any time that year, and was very disappointed next morning when, at 95, I gave a hard chance to the wicketkeeper who knocked it up for first slip to catch.

Ken Barrington and the later batsmen extended the lead steadily to 177, after which Bill Lawry made 100 and we had cause to regret that we had gone in with only one spinner, David Allen. However, he bowled very well and when the ninth wicket fell early on the last morning after all the batsmen had been in trouble against Allen, I was reasonably confident that we could make the runs needed in the last innings.

Early in the marvellous stand between Davidson and McKenzie I took off Allen when Davidson hit him for 20 in an over. This was long a matter for widespread criticism, which may or may not have been justified. What decided me was that the strokes had been hit with confidence from the middle of the bat. If they had needed some luck, I would have left Allen on. But it seemed to me then that 200 was all we could reasonably expect to make in the last innings and another over played with the same resounding success would have finished our chances of winning.

When we found that we had to make 256, I thought that, short of a miracle, it was unrealistic to consider it seriously on that pitch, especially as only three hours fifty minutes were now left. Ted's innings of 76 in 85 minutes changed all that. At 150 for 1 we had to go on.

Even before Ted was out I foresaw our dilemma. So did Richie Benaud, who came on, not trying to spin the ball – his shoulder made that difficult – but bowling round the wicket into the rough to slow things up and perhaps force a mistake. He knew that if he could break the second – wicket stand, the rest of us would be in a predicament, honour-bound to press on but having to take chances on a worn pitch and without time to settle in.

So it turned out. Ted, trying to cut Richie, was caught at the wicket. I was bowled round my legs ignominiously, for just about the only time that I can remember, and we went rushing to defeat. A lot was made of Brian Close's swing across the line, but, to my mind, it was irrelevant. We should never have had to make as many as 256. We lost by not holding our catches.

It was a tremendous win by Australia, a lasting tribute to Richie's enterprise. The Ashes stayed in Australia and we never promised to square the series in the last Test at the Oval. They led us by more than 200 on first innings and we batted out the rest of the match, Raman Subba Row making his second 100 of the series. He was a sterling example of a batsman who by judgement and determination used 100 per cent of his ability. He had steadily improved since our Cambridge days ten years before when he was a middle-order batsman and leg-spinner.

I batted quite well in that last Test but I was having trouble with minor injuries and did not play again until Scarborough where I went to play my last match against the Australians. The days were over when the Australians could complain, not without some justification, that they were playing an additional Test match at Scarborough. This was not a very serious affair. We enjoyed it. So, I think, did the 15,000 who came each day. I made 100 and 41 and went home to consider my future.

My views had changed since the spring. On top of my two operations had come injuries which I had never had before. I realized that I now had to work harder at keeping match fit for Test cricket. I had never really played as well since my illness and somehow I was not enjoying it so much. There were business and domestic considerations too. We were starting a family and I had no intention of going on another long tour. I had also always promised myself that I would give up at the top.

Surrey was a different matter. I had only played in twelve matches that season, which had been their worst ever. There were good young players coming on and I thought that I owed it to the club to play for another year or two while they developed.

So, that December, I asked Bob Babb, Brian Castor's successor as Surrey secretary, if he would invite the press to a meeting. And on a dark winter's night at the Oval I formally announced my retirement from Test cricket.

14
Selecting

Before the 1962 season I told the Surrey committee that I would not be available for every match. Suzanne was barely a year old, Nicola was on the way and in my semi-retired state I did not want to be away from home too much. I did, in fact, play in seventeen of the championship matches, more than for some years, as well as against both universities and Pakistan.

On the whole that season I played fairly well, beginning with 82 against Glamorgan made with rather more ease than in the days of Wooller. I made a century against Warwickshire at Edgbaston and against Pakistan and Middlesex at the Oval. I must add that in the other match against Middlesex I was bowled Titmus nought, so I finished my career at Lord's with three noughts, which must be some sort of record.

I usually went in after three very good players in Micky Stewart, John Edrich and Ken Barrington. Bernard Constable was still consistent and we did not often go short of runs. The bowling would doubtless have been stronger if David Gibson, a very useful all-rounder, had stayed fit, but our two opening bowlers, Peter Loader and David Sydenham, both took over 100 wickets. Tony Lock was still bowling well and we found a useful partner for him in Ron Tindall, although he had scarcely bowled a ball in the days when we had three other off-spinners in Jim Laker, Eric Bedser and Tom Clark.

Thus, having finished fifteenth in the championship in 1961, we found ourselves still in with a chance of winning it in the last week in August when we played Yorkshire at the Oval. There was some congestion at the top of the table but Yorkshire were best placed and first-innings points were the height of their ambition in this match. They made certain of them by batting for about nine hours during which I damaged a hand fielding in the gully. I took no further part in the match. So, on a disappointing note, my season finished. There was no more cheer in Surrey's final match at Southampton which was drawn. We finished fifth.

I went home and reviewed the position. It had been quite an exciting season but I felt that I was not enjoying the game so much. Perhaps it was anticlimax after the glorious years of the 1950s, beer after champagne, as it were. Perhaps I was not playing up to the high standards which I had always set myself.

It seemed the moment to retire in almost every way. Many of my colleagues were retiring. I felt that I had done all I could to help pick Surrey cricket up again. I had an able successor in Micky Stewart. Two personal considerations were a growing family and impatience to develop my career in the City. As when I had given up Test cricket the year before, I was not influenced by any one factor but by a number.

So I resigned the captaincy of Surrey that autumn while telling the committee that I would be glad to play while on holiday if required.

I had no complaints. I had been lucky enough to do almost everything that a player could wish to do. I suppose that if I regretted anything it was that I was foregoing a chance of making a hundred 100s, which only one other batsman, W. G. Grace, had done as an amateur. But I never saw the game as a personal thing, which was why I enjoyed it so much. I was always more interested in how we did as a team. This may sound prudish, and today perhaps, when so many careers depend on it, it is a different story, but that was the thinking in the era in which I grew up.

There were two popular misconceptions at the time of my retirement. One was that I had retired as a result of harassment from the press. That is quite untrue. I never let criticism bother me to that extent. In fact, if it was constructive I would often appreciate and act upon it. The other prevailing belief was that I would make a comeback to Test cricket as Washbrook and Sheppard had done. That was never in my mind.

My subsequent cricket was interesting in that, to my mind, it contradicted the theorizing about the structure of the game which prevailed at the time. One-day cricket was being mooted – the Gillette Cup was just starting – and one of its great virtues was said to be that it would allow recently retired players or amateurs to play when they could not afford the time to play three-day cricket. In fact, it was soon established that one-day cricket required a fitness and an amount of practice which was well beyond most players emerging from a City office.

No subject has been more thoroughly examined in recent years than limited-over cricket and its virtues and failings. My views on it are not exactly novel. I recognize the rise in the standard of fielding to which it has contributed. I realize its attractiveness as producing a definite result in a day. I think the recent institution of 'circles' has been a big help in avoiding the ridiculous field settings of former years. But I shudder for the coaches whose pupils see on television so much cross-batted batting and negative bowling, especially by spinners. And it goes against all the basics of the game that a side can win without taking a wicket.

I was never asked to play for Surrey in a limited-over game but I realized soon enough from a short experience with the Charterhouse Friars in The Cricketer Cup, which had also just started, that, for me anyhow, cricket was not a game to be approached casually.

I made 100 for the Friars against Harrow at Charterhouse. It was great fun to make runs there again after all that had happened since my schooldays fifteen years or more before. But I came down with a bump in the next round when we played Repton on a neutral ground in the Midlands and I was quickly bowled out by Sir Leonard's younger son, John Hutton.

There was no dishonour in that and I could not have asked for a more estimable executioner. But it confirmed what I had come to realize in the three matches which I played for Surrey in 1963, two at Guildford against Cambridge and Sussex, one at the Oval against Northamptonshire when there was a shortage of players through injuries and Test claims. I made 85 against Sussex but only 5 runs in the other innings. Because of everything that had gone before, a great deal was expected of me and I knew that, without the constant competitive cricket on which I had thrived, I would not be able to produce it. It was like having a golf handicap of 14 and being expected to produce the results of your younger days when you played to 3. I did not enjoy the idea of letting people down. It seemed to me that I would soon be keeping out younger players on false pretences. So I restricted myself in subsequent years to matches for charity and for friends. In relaxed conditions I usually made the runs required, though once or twice I privately winced at being out to someone who I did not think could bowl at all.

I resumed my links with Test cricket in 1965 as a selector. Doug Insole was the new chairman, the others were Alec Bedser and Don Kenyon, captain of Worcestershire.

In England the selectors have an especially difficult job because there are seventeen first-class counties as against about half a dozen first-class sides in other countries. The hardest thing is to know whether in-form county players will be successful in Test cricket. It depends so much on temperament because in home Tests they are subjected to intense criticism and are thrown into a new environment for nearly a week with tension building up. It is an enormous jump. The guiding principle, of course, is when in doubt pick class. The most notable coup in this respect is probably the selection for Australia in 1954–55 of Colin Cowdrey, who had not previously played in a Test match, although he had made runs against some of the stronger bowling sides he had met.

I found the meetings of selectors interesting. It is not always realized that they pick not only a team but the reserves, in case anyone drops out. This avoids collecting everybody together again for an emergency meeting. The reserves are often more difficult to pick than the team itself, for it depends so much on who drops out. There have been times in recent years, for example, when we had to work on a hypothesis that Ian Botham might withdraw, which would need far more rejigging then if a specialist batsman or bowler had to be replaced.

I enjoyed the travelling round and being back in the game but it has many frustrations in England that are not experienced in other countries. We do not have players on our front doorstep, as it were, as selectors living in Sydney or Melbourne would. We have to set off early in the morning to drive across the country and, when we get there, we may find that if we want to look at a batsman he is fielding or, if it is a bowler we are after, his side is batting. It may be raining.

My most frustrating experience was when I drove down to Swansea in 1965 to see the young fast bowler, Jeff Jones. I went down the night before. Happily the next morning was glorious and I went out on top of the pavilion before the start of play, looked out over Swansea Bay and breathed in the sea air, full of goodwill to all men, my satisfaction completed by the fact that Glamorgan were in the field.

As they came out, I looked for the red-haired Jones. 'Where's the great fast bowler?' I asked a committee member standing nearby.

'We've left him out,' he said. 'The boyos think the ball will turn.' I was speechless, although in fact the boyos were right about it turning.

In England it is physically impossible for selectors to watch players time after time, except where the selector is a current player as Don Kenyon was in 1965. But we did a lot of talking then – and still do – to coaches and umpires. Umpires see a lot. Charles Elliott was very helpful to us in the 1960s and became a selector himself later. Information received from coaches who are experienced cricketers themselves is also welcome. After all, it is the county coaches on whom we rely to find us the players from whom to choose. There is a popular misconception that coaches and county captains tend to favour their own players unduly. I have seldom found this. If anything, they know a player's weaknesses better than an occasional watcher and set these alongside his strengths.

We had M. J. K. Smith as captain in my first season as a selector. He had just won a series in South Africa and led by example. In committee he gave a balanced view of the qualities of the players under discussion.

This was the first season of the two-tour arrangement. New Zealand and South Africa were the visitors. This system, sold overseas by Gubby Allen, was prompted by several debacles in which weak visiting sides unused to English conditions had been swamped. It was badly needed. Three one-sided Test matches are infinitely preferable to five, unless they are one-sided against England in a home series. Then the selectors have a chance to experiment and the English public, unlike that of Australia and West Indies, still goes to watch, as it did when England were swamped by West Indies in 1984. But interest swiftly fades if the opposition is weak.

Some countries such as New Zealand and South Africa were happy to come for half a season because their players were mostly amateurs who had difficulty in obtaining leave from their jobs for more than three months. To other countries who might see the shortening of their visits to England as a loss of face, Gubby, in his year as President of MCC, had to explain the situation clearly and diplomatically and had done so with much tact.

At the time I joined the selection committee the accent was strongly on greater enterprise with the bat. It was a policy which was rewarded within eighteen months by the extraordinary feats of Bob Barber who hammered his way round Australia with huge success. But it led us into almost immediate difficulties when Ken Barrington batted for seven hours to make 137 against New Zealand at Edgbaston. He had certainly been out of form so far that season but the fact that others played fluently on the pitch and that when in the 80s he spent an hour without scoring before speeding up after reaching 100 forced us to take action. We had to show that our call for a more positive approach was not just talk. So we left him out of the Lord's Test. This caused something of a furore but he was such a splendid chap that he took it well. He was back for the Third Test in which he made a fine 163.

It was not exactly a quiet time for selectors. In 1966 we had three captains against West Indies – Mike Smith, Colin Cowdrey and Brian Close. We made numerous changes after each defeat. One of the more successful was to bring back Tom Graveney, who was probably a sounder player at the age of forty then ever before.

With the series decided, we won the last Test at the Oval under Close. In the next season, 1967, India and Pakistan were not the sternest opposition and the season was relatively peaceful for selectors – until near the end. Just after the last Test against Pakistan Brian Close, as captain of Yorkshire, was severely censured for what many thought to be a gross piece of time-wasting a fortnight before when Warwickshire had looked like beating Yorkshire at Edgbaston. He was given a chance to apologize but refused and MCC, not being prepared to send to represent them on an overseas tour an unrepentant captain whom they had just had to censure, instructed us not to pick him as captain.

It may sound trivial now but it did not seem so at the time and, knowing the sensitive nature of tours of West Indies and being greatly in favour of maintaining standards, I thought it was an inevitable decision. But I was sorry for Brian.

The selectors had no part in the decision, of course, and merely had to act on it. We turned back to Colin Cowdrey who, as it proved, did a great job and won the series.

Colin was our captain throughout the 1968 series against Australia, which we eventually squared at the Oval but should have won. England had the better of all three previous Tests but were almost certainly thwarted by rain in two of them. We lost the First Test at Old Trafford after what at the time was hailed as a classic piece of selectorial misjudgement. We took fourteen players to Old Trafford but left out three bowlers, David Brown, Tom Cartwright and Derek Underwood. This left us only three bowlers – Snow, Higgs and Pocock, plus Barber and d'Oliveira, who had taken only a handful of wickets that season.

The reasoning behind this was that we were bothered about the batting – Ken Barrington had had to drop out – and were concerned about making enough runs on a dubious pitch. In fact, Australia won the toss, made 310 for 4 on the first day when the pitch was at its best and had settled the match by then. We might have got away with it if we had won the toss but, in retrospect, I doubt if we were very bright to discard the accuracy of both Cartwright and Underwood.

We ended the 1968 season – and my four years as a selector – heartened by our win at the Oval. Some good bowlers, notably Snow and Underwood, were coming on the scene and England's Test prospects for the next year or two looked rather good. But almost at once we, as selectors, involved ourselves, although with the best possible motives, in a sad controversy. We had had to find a late replacement at the Oval for Roger Prideaux, who was ill. I thought that Phil Sharpe, the designated reserve batsman, would be called up but Basil d'Oliveira was summoned because the captain had become worried about the suitability of our chosen bowlers for late summer conditions at the Oval. Colin had played for Kent there the week before, the ball had swung a lot and he did not think that Ken Higgs, who was in the twelve, would be particularly effective.

Since playing in the First Test Basil had taken 40-odd wickets for Worcestershire but he had not done much with the bat. He had also not had a great tour of West Indies the previous winter and as the summer passed we had ruled him out of the team which we were pencilling in for that winter's tour of South Africa. We were already overstocked with batting candidates. After Basil had made 158 at the Oval we reconsidered the position but, as he had been dropped twice early on, came to the conclusion that his innings, valuable though it had been in its context, did not alter the judgements made over the cricket of the past year.

It was, of course, entirely the decision of the selectors plus the one or two others who, *ex officio* and not all with voting powers, sit in on the selection of a touring team. No instructions were given us by MCC – the TCCB was not yet born. They never were given except on those rare occasions when for disciplinary reasons we were told that players were not available for selection. Close as captain in 1967 was one example. Wardle in 1958–59 was another and, more recently, the banned players of the 1982 team in South Africa.

We were not so ingenuous as to ignore the likely hubbub which might follow the non-selection of Basil. We knew that it would be easier to pick him than to leave him out. But I myself thought – and I believe that the other selectors did too – that it would be grossly wrong and utterly against the principles on which our selectors work if we allowed ourselves to be influenced by considerations outside cricket. We included Basil in the list of reserves who would replace any of those who dropped out before or during the tour. Thus, when Tom Cartwright withdrew in September, Basil came into the side in his place as a similar type of bowler, indeed an all-rounder.

The subsequent reactions of the South African Government and of MCC are too well known to need elaboration here. I thought some of the criticism fired at us, much of it from people entirely ignorant of the cricketing arguments, was incredible. We were, for example, called 'politically naive'. Heaven help the world if selectors of cricket teams have to be politically sensitive or are instructed from above to select on political grounds.

As for whether we were right or wrong on cricketing grounds, that is impossible to say. Tom Cartwright was a very high-class bowler at the time. Basil became a tremendously useful Test cricketer over the next few years. But for that particular tour, who knows? The large number of batting candidates available meant that somebody was going to be very unlucky and amid the fuss about d'Oliveira it was almost unnoticed that we also left out Colin Milburn. He had made a brilliant 83 in the Lord's Test against Australia on a wet pitch but had then dropped out with an injury. It may be remembered that, towards the end of the substitute tour of Pakistan, Milburn was sent for and after a long journey from Australia made by all accounts a very fine 100 in Karachi on a completely different type of pitch from those on which he had been playing. He was just becoming a batsman of the highest class but two months later he had his calamitous car accident and lost an eye.

This made a wretched footnote to a sad chapter in international cricket. Even the substitute tour of Pakistan had been curtailed by riots.

But by then my term as a selector had ended and I had retired into private life again with nothing to divert me from my main preoccupations, the family and Lloyds.

When I returned as chairman of selectors fourteen years later, in 1982, Test cricket was very different. It was big business, not least for the players, and it had multiplied. I was immediately confronted with the TCCB ban which prevented us from considering fifteen of our leading players. How many of these we would have wanted to pick is hard to say, but even if only two or three had been regular choices, two or three players can turn an average side into a strong one. There was a period, for example, when Greg Chappell and Lillee added up to much more than two elevenths of the Australian side.

There was also the handicap of having the counties persevering with overseas players whom we could not consider and who, whatever their contribution to their county's wellbeing, were taking the places of young English players who might have been gathering experience. Certainly the Board had learned its lesson and had introduced legislation to reduce the number of overseas players to one per county but that could only work slowly.

Since that legislation I have been particularly disappointed that some counties who had to surrender an overseas player for a season to his country's touring side should have hunted around for another overseas player as a replacement for one season. Not only were they missing an opportunity to bring on a young batsman or bowler of their own but they were giving an overseas player a chance to come on a future tour of England as a more complete cricketer.

I fully appreciate that the counties feel that they need instant success to satisfy members but a major part of their income stems from Tests and in the long term it is not in their financial interests if England selectors are operating under handicap. This has been stressed by Alec Bedser over many seasons. Test-match receipts are an enormous, life-saving sum to the counties in some years and, as a selector, I would like to see them graded according to the number of players available for England which each county had used. Yorkshire, who have stuck to their principles, would have the maximum.

On my rounds of the counties I have been much impressed by the high standard of wicketkeeping. So has Alec Bedser. I think that it may be significant that since the days of Farokh Engineer and Deryck Murray no overseas wicketkeepers have been taken on. The counties have had to rely on local talent and have done very well.

When I was asked to succeed Alec as chairman, I told the Board that

I would not be able to give the job the time which he had devoted to it. Willis, Faber and Dumas, my employers, were extremely sympathetic but I was not prepared to take any more time off than was absolutely necessary. I took on the press relations and I did my share of travelling to see players. But I was lucky to have Alec still available with his experience of the off-the-field detail of modern Test matches. We took it in turn to look after the daily problems which arise and which seem to be more numerous than in the Test matches of the 1950s.

One other difference now is that there is less first-class cricket to watch. Counties sometimes play only three first-class matches before the selectors choose the first Test team. If it has rained during May, there has been almost nothing to go on. In 1981 Gloucestershire did not bowl a ball in the championship until 3 June.

I realized that more than ever we must rely a lot on coaches. Coaches and managers see far more of likely players than selectors on fleeting visits and they see them in opposing sides as well.

Thus I have written to coaches before each season giving them my home and office telephone numbers and asking them to tell us if they have any players whom we should watch. We will then come and have a good look. I sometimes cross-check with the coach of another county against whom a player has recently been in action.

All this is not to spare selectors travelling but because there are limits to what four selectors can cover in the time and weather available. If four selectors cannot see everything, how much harder would it be for the one-man supremo who is sometimes advocated.

Of course, we make mistakes. All selectors do. When I think that we may have been unwise, I comfort myself by recalling the famous story of Arthur Mailey who, when asked to pick a Test side for his paper, neglected to include a wicketkeeper. His editor was furious and asked Arthur if he realized what he had done. Arthur, that impish and delightful man, blandly replied that he had picked no wicketkeeper because the bowlers selected would never get the ball past the bat!

I admit that there are times when one looks at players in the nets on the day before a Test match and detects what looks like a fairly basic technical eccentricity. But if a coach has allowed a player to develop in a certain way, it is nonsense for us to tell him otherwise, risking upsetting his confidence and overall method. He has made his way into Test cricket by his performances achieved in his own particular way.

I have said that I was not keen on too much net practice myself but I do believe that it should be undertaken seriously, even though the season may be well advanced. Match practice, of course, is the best practice, but when there are sometimes gaps of a week in mid-season in a county's programme and when a player may be preparing for a Test match with no recent match practice other than a Sunday afternoon skirmish, a good net is highly important.

There is no easy way to the top and most players require very hard practice. This is one respect in which I have been impressed by overseas players. Whenever I have watched them, even the best among them seemed to work very hard in the nets. I think that it may derive from the less concentrated first-class cricket at home which has given them more time for practice there and indeed created a need for it.

Before I returned to the selection committee, Alec Bedser had tried to clarify the Board's brief to the selectors in relation to the role of the captain on the committee. In other countries the captain has little or no say in the choice of his team. He is presented with it by the selectors. I believe that in the context of English cricket the tradition of coopting the appointed captain onto the committee with full voting powers is the right one but his influence needs to be kept within sensible bounds. Not all captains are as wise and experienced as others.

I certainly believe that it is undesirable for a captain to take the field with a side in which he has no confidence. I value his opinion, as I like to think mine was valued when I was captain. On the other hand, if the selectors allow the captain the final say on every issue, he would finish up picking the team. What then would be the point of having selectors? There have been cases in the past when captains have made both inspired and ludicrous requests for certain players and the selectors have yielded. When the choice has been unsuccessful, it has been the selectors who have taken the blame for what they had not wanted. That is fair enough, the penalty of weakness. It is their responsibility. But it seemed to me that we should always strive to achieve a happy medium and that it was the chairman's delicate task to determine what weight should be given to the captain's view where it differs from that of a majority of the selectors.

The idea that selectors work by a rigid system of voting is in my experience as chairman quite unfounded. In fact we always try to avoid voting. We exchange views, and if we reach an impasse we leave the subject for a while and come back to it. Then we talk it over again and eventually reach an agreement.

The TCCB's normal practice is to appoint selectors for a four-year term, based on the old reckoning that this would cover one home and one away series against Australia. I think that a four-year term is about right in ordinary times. I have enjoyed mine as chairman but would naturally have enjoyed it much more if we had been more successful.

None of us nursed any false hopes when we took over in 1982. We knew that we must be weakened to some extent by the ban and we knew that there was a dearth of top-class bowlers, especially fast bowlers. The mere fact that Bob Willis in his middle thirties was clearly the most effective fast bowler was painful evidence of the shortage. However, a chance has been given to young players, some of whom will be a force in the future, and we did start off by winning home series against India, Pakistan and New Zealand, none of them a pushover nowadays. We also played some very good cricket in the 1983 World Cup until we, like West Indies in the final, fell victims to India's brilliant use of the prevailing conditions.

I thought that it was a particularly good win over Pakistan, for they were a strong side in 1982, better balanced than we were. But successes are soon forgotten when the next defeat comes along, especially when it is as severe a defeat as that by West Indies in 1984, followed by an indifferent performance against Sri Lanka.

In January 1985, on the invitation of the TCCB, Virginia and I took a fortnight's holiday in India which enabled us to watch the Madras Test. We saw one of England's best Test victories for a long time. To win is always nice but to win on a thoroughly good pitch by better batting, bowling and fielding is a joy.

I was staggered by the hospitality which we received, by the enthusiasm for the game and most of all by the knowledge of my own performances on the field. What did you think about when you were batting at Edgbaston in 1957, I was asked by complete strangers. How is Len Hutton? There were questions about Cyril Washbrook's come-back at Headingley in 1956.

Nearly all the questions concerned matches in which India were not involved. When I was asked why I had not myself played in India, I had to explain – countless times – that in 1951–52 I was still at Cambridge and unable to take two terms off from my last year. The next England tour of India was not until 1961–62 and by that time I had retired from Test cricket. I was greatly impressed by the very sporting crowd who clapped our players just as much as their own.

I was impressed, too, by the fitness and stamina of the players in hot and humid conditions. I was delighted by the double 100s of Graeme Fowler and Mike Gatting, two players who have had to stand up to a lot of criticism, Gatting especially. It was splendid to see a young English bowler, Neil Foster, breaking through and bowling beautifully to take 11 wickets in the match.

Above all, England looked a happy side, much keener than many nowadays to discuss and analyse the day's play.

Having set out with no pats on the back from any one and with the memory of five defeats by West Indies and a feeble performance against Sri Lanka, they suddenly found themselves breaking records. They were understandably thrilled and the chairman of selectors counted himself very lucky to have come to Madras really by chance – it was the only time I could get away – and to have been present at such a refreshing occasion for English cricket.

15
Off the Field

I used to be rather surprised when people asked me what I did when I was not playing cricket or selecting, but the insights on television nowadays into the private lives of sportsmen are such that I realize that I was lucky not be interrogated more closely on my skill at washing-up and other domestic pursuits.

In fact, during my playing days while I was still a bachelor, I used to spend many winter evenings at cricket dinners. In 1957 I went to seventy-five, speaking at nearly all of them. This was not through any great desire for oratory or for convivial society but because it seemed a part of my duties as captain of Surrey and indeed of England. I still believe that it is very important to keep oneself informed and there is no better way of doing so than by meeting cricketers of all levels and perhaps others whose knowledge of the game may not match their enthusiasm for it.

There were, of course, some sticky evenings. Recently I was at a dinner at which Jim Swanton was speaking and he recalled a similar function during my years as England captain when the first two speakers went on interminably. When my turn came, I got up and said that I wished that our Test team was blessed with openers who would stay on their feet as long as the opening pair that evening. I think they were rather pleased.

Otherwise, since I married, my days have been devoted to a full family life, jobs about the house and property – I have recently become an expert planter of beech trees – commuting to the City, an occasional game of golf and sundry cricket interests at various levels.

There was never a time between my two terms as a selector when I was completely divorced from cricket. I was usually on the MCC committee or the Surrey committee. I chaired the Surrey cricket committee and I was president of the Surrey Supporters' Association. I was involved in various fund-raising projects. It was a great time for fund-raising. But as the years passed and the girls grew up, horses began to play a part in my life which would have been inconceivable to me as a boy.

Before I go any further, I should perhaps answer the question which I have been asked hundreds of times: 'Do you ride a horse yourself?'

The answer is that I learned on a pony with an uncle when I was very little but have not ridden since.

If this seems extraordinary coming from one living with five talented horsewomen and a floating population of about twelve horses, I find it easy to explain. I was not brought up with horses. I am not exactly the right shape for a jockey. I have no reason to believe that I would ride particularly well. If I had had an only daughter, I would probably have taken up riding to be company for her. But Virginia and the girls are company for themselves. I would merely be an encumbrance, more liable to falls than some one born in the saddle and of less use to them all with a leg in plaster then I am in full working order.

That does not mean that I have ever been uninterested in the world of three-day eventing. I may not be too brilliant at identifying parts of a horse's anatomy but I am as keen on the riding careers of the four girls – Tessa, although still at school, has been winning Pony Club events – as they are on cricket, which they follow with great fervour. They have their favourites, and if they picked the England team it would usually differ quite a lot from the one that takes the field. They feel a defeat deeply. The difference between my interest in eventing and theirs in cricket is that I am sympathetic if they make a mess of their dressage or fall in the cross-country section, whereas they give me severe stick if England have a bad match or we pick the wrong team!

Anyhow, it seems to work all right. When available to attend events, I keep a low profile and regard myself as the handyman or back-up. I am not allowed to drive the horsebox. That requires a heavy vehicle driving licence which Virginia and Suzanne obtained after taking the tests. They have my heartfelt admiration. Driving the huge machine through narrow country lanes, muddy car parks and sometimes for hours on end to and from events in Norfolk, the Midlands or the West Country is an exacting job for any one. Stabling for horses is available at events but is in short supply for humans, so the box sleeps four and has a cooker.

The girls do their own entries, quite a tricky job, for there is a profusion of events from which to choose in the season and different classes for different age groups and for horses of different experience. Virginia commands the operation. In the 1950s she was on the short list for the British team in the European Championship in Turin but her horse went lame. The girls' records have been a great tribute to her guidance.

Suzanne was a junior international at dressage. I flew to Vienna with my mother-in-law, Marjorie Gilligan, to watch her in the European Championship. Nicola followed by getting into the British junior three-day event team for two years. On the first occasion she won the indi-

vidual gold medal in the European Junior Championship held that year
in Ireland at Punchestown.

That was a great occasion with an uncomfortable prelude. Virginia
drove the horsebox up to Holyhead with Nicola and two other girl
members of the team plus three horses. When they arrived there, they
found the crossing had been cancelled because of rough weather. They
were diverted back over the Menai Bridge, cleared with only inches to
spare, to a friend's farm behind Carnarvon for the night. Eventually,
after more coming and going across Anglesey, they embarked and
reached Punchestown.

As in Vienna, the supporters' club of Virginia's mother and myself
flew over. The excitement of it beat any Test match. Nicola needed a
clear round in the cross-country and show jumping to give Britain a
chance of winning the team event and to give herself the individual title.
She did it, and although France just edged us out of the team title,
Nicola, aged sixteen, was the European junior champion. The long drive
back to Surrey was a joyful affair.

In the following year in Austria Nicola was only seventh but Britain
won the team gold medals. In 1984, Annabelle almost followed her into
the British junior team with a horse which she had not been riding for
long. She was first reserve for the European Championship in Poland.
Although one reserve at least had been called on in previous years, she
was not required this time and had to wait another year. Tessa is
immensely keen and knowledgeable, a great help to her older sisters and
as determined as the others to do well.

The snag about all this is the financing of it. It is a very expensive
occupation and even though Virginia and the girls work long hours at
it and do it all themselves, we could never afford it without the sponsorship which early in 1984 we were lucky enough to receive from the
Happy Eater chain of restaurants. They have been extremely kind and
understanding and I hope are pleased with the results so far. Their
colours incidentally are the same as MCC's, so any one seeing a red and
yellow, splendidly equipped horsebox on the road would be wrong to
think that there was any cricketing significance in its appearance. Indeed,
what pleased me especially about the launching party of the sponsorship
was that it was the girls who were the important thing and the cricketing
notoriety of their father was not touched on.

If they are going to try to compete at the top level, they have to buy
good or promising horses and the costs are enormous. Each rider ideally
needs two or three horses of roughly the same ability. Otherwise, if her
best horse is wrong, she will be completely on the sidelines, perhaps for
another year. Horses have to eat, and there is no National Health for
horses. They run up veterinary bills. Horseboxes are expensive to buy

and to run. Two are needed, for one girl may be competing in Devon and another in Northamptonshire. Virginia always says that if we had four millionaires behind us we would be all right.

The income, apart from sponsorship, is derived from prize money, which is welcome but not lucrative. This is a different world from the heavily sponsored, frequently televised professional world of show jumping. We like to defray expenses by taking in horses on livery if we can and the girls sometimes buy a young horse, work with it and sell it as a more mature animal at a profit. To that extent, we run a business. Suzanne, incidentally, does the VAT.

Although we have to part with horses which prove unsuitable rides for a girl, which are clearly not going to be good enough or are only on lease, there are inevitably family favourites. One such was Coppa Captain, a chestnut pony ridden by all four girls in Pony Club trials during his long and honourable career. He won many prizes and when Nicola rode him in Sweden in the 1977 Pony Dressage Championship, he was the best British pony in European dressage.

One morning in the summer of 1984 he was found in his paddock with a broken leg. He had been kicked by another pony and there was no alternative but to call the vet and have him put down. We had had him for ten years since he was a four-year-old. There was much sadness in the household, tears all round.

But there are many happy and rewarding days. The enjoyment of it is the main thing and the girls are doing something they love. The one on duty gets up at 6.30 and feeds the horses. From then on they exercise, groom, muck out, sweep up and work hard at it all day.

I am always thrilled to watch them go well across country. I get much the same satisfaction as seeing someone stand up to really fast bowling. There are, in fact, many similarities to me in the philosophy of cricket and of eventing.

Cricket is said to be a great character former. Think of the disappointments to be borne by the batsman who receives a bad decision, is out to a freak catch or to the only ball which keeps low all day; who struggles through a loss of form only to be run out by a reckless partner; who is dropped from a team. The bowler has to bear the frustration of beating the bat without reward, of having catches dropped off him. Cricketers may have nagging injuries which have to be brushed aside with a lot of resilience and the minimum of self-pity.

But I have found that the torments of the event rider are infinitely greater. For one thing, the rider does not have just to keep himself or herself fit but also the horse – and however carefully horses are looked after, they have an infuriating way of knocking themselves and putting themselves out of action just when it is least wanted.

Suzanne has had a full share of bad luck. In her last year as a junior, Commodore, on whom Nicola won the European Championship a year later, was kicked and could not compete. In 1982 Suzanne broke a leg. She tried three years in succession to get Clowne to Badminton. He knocked himself the first year, the second year she had to withdraw him when he developed colic after the dressage. He did very well to finish fourteenth at Burghley that autumn and hopes were high for Badminton the following spring. But, having thrived during the winter, he struck into himself on the Sunday before Badminton.

Nicola has had her bad luck too. She was picked for the British Young Riders team to compete in the European Championship in Germany in 1984, but although Jolliaventa had been tenderly nursed over the hard ground of that summer, he had several setbacks as soon as he was selected and had to drop out.

The young anywhere feel disappointments more acutely than their elders who have become used to the ups and downs of life. The letdown is the more severe when the event for which the horse is being prepared is the culmination of months of hard work, of early rising, of lonely hours spent exercising in all weathers, of meticulous practice in the dressage arena and so on. But there he is. The horse which you left perfectly sound last night is unsound this morning.

A batsman at least has another chance in the second innings or perhaps next day in another match. A horse may not be fit to compete again for months. If the rider can raise a smile, forget the past and carry on again with the future in mind, he or she must be learning one of the more valuable lessons of life.

I have said that I often have to answer questions about my equestrian record. One other question which I have sometimes been asked by ardent cricket lovers is 'Aren't you disappointed that you haven't a son to carry on the cricket tradition?'

There is an easy answer to this. I have four super daughters, all fit, and I could not be more delighted. I have also been spared the responsibilities of a cricketing father and the diplomacy required of him. I have followed with interest the approach of those of my contemporaries who have had sons with cricketing ability and I have wondered how they hit the right balance between offering every encouragement and yet not overdoing it. Some boys get put off by parental enthusiasm and by well-meaning people who ask them if they are going to follow in father's footsteps.

Obviously every case is different but I suspect that it is a help if the father genuinely does not think that his young are particularly good cricketers. The pressure is off them, playing stays a pleasure, and if they have a real talent it will flower naturally.

If I had a son, I would see that he understood the basics and leave it at that. For a young batsman, I believe that the basic dictum of coaching should be: 'Play forward, play back, stand still and get on with it.' These are the fundamentals. I am no admirer of the modern habit of standing with bat raised. Great batsmen of the past made thousands of runs against all types of bowling without doing it and I was glad to read Sir Donald Bradman's stern condemnation of it.

I blame a lot on the weight of the modern bat, often a whole pound more than the one I used. I am not surprised if some batsmen have trouble in picking it up quickly. I imagine that it is for this reason that they prefer picking it up before the ball is delivered. Few can cut with a bat weighing well over 3lb and I think that when they play fatally across the line although well in, it is often because they are tired and late on the stroke.

Mercifully I am spared having to tell a son how heavy his bat should be – and telling a daughter what sort of saddle she should use is well outside my province!

16

Cricket's Problems Today and Tomorrow

I was not directly involved with the Packer descent on cricket in 1977, although I have had plenty of opportunity to assess at close quarters its after-effects. At the time I was distressed by its divisiveness and by the way that in some cases it destroyed traditional loyalties, especially those to one's country.

To my knowledge there had been no discontent among players in England. There may have been some in Australia, where cricket was not a fulltime occupation for so many, but the state captains had just thanked the Board for what was being done to improve the players' lot. It was still in most cases not a game to be played purely for money, but ideally by players qualified for other jobs beside cricket.

In England the Cricketers' Association had been consulted on every major issue affecting players. The Association, just as much as the Board, must have deplored the covert way in which the defections were achieved, though I suppose that in any business move like that – and this one basically concerned exclusive Australian television rights – secrecy is all important.

What has it left behind? On the profit side, more sponsorship. There had been no shortage of sponsors before, but, stimulated by this new commercial invasion of the game, they were prepared to put more money in now. Where this penetrates to the grassroots, that is a thoroughly good thing; and I have said that I do not grudge the leading players their greater rewards so long as they do not allow fringe benefits to interfere with the main reason for their prosperity, which is their cricket.

I am not entirely sure that the average county player is much better off than he would have been without the Packer business and indeed there has been at least one season when the Cricketers' Association has asked the TCCB not to increase the fees for Test matches because they were getting out of proportion to what non-Test players could earn.

But with the big rewards there came, so it seemed to me, a changed approach to the game. Some of the reports of behaviour on the field in Australia and by West Indies in New Zealand have appalled and disenchanted those brought up in days when the courtesies and manners of the game were observed by everyone, not least by the professionals.

Even in England where players and administrators run things in general harmony, disciplinary action has to be taken far more frequently nowadays. Sometimes the authorities overreact, sometimes they are too weak. It is very hard to hit the right degree of punishment for infringements of the game's code of conduct. For one thing, if suspension seems the proper punishment for a leading player, the Board or relevant authority must not allow itself to be influenced by knowing that this would upset the sponsors.

The intense way in which the so-called instant cricket is played has much to do with excesses. Matches, and the rewards attached to them, engender a heat of excitement in which umpires' decisions are questioned in a manner which would never have been tolerated once.

This is an area of the modern game about which I am particularly concerned. One of my first acts on becoming chairman of selectors was to ask the new captain, Bob Willis, to do his best to stamp out bad behaviour and dissension on the field. He made an excellent job of it but it is not easy to eliminate unruly behaviour in your own side when their opponents are behaving badly – and sometimes profiting by it, for example by excessive appealing which can bully umpires into making mistakes.

The burden on the umpire has become depressingly heavy, heavier still because his decisions are subjected to playbacks on television. However sympathetically these are done, people forget the decisions he gets right and remember the few which he gets wrong.

We pride ourselves in England on having the best umpires in the world, partly because they are either former first-class cricketers themselves or because, through standing in a full first-class programme, they have absorbed the thinking of first-class players. If an international panel of Test umpires is ever formed – to eliminate not biased umpiring, which I believe is a rarity, but bad and inexperienced umpiring – I would expect a high proportion of its members to be English.

But it is unrealistic even in England to expect all our umpires to tackle the wide range of duties now required of them and at the same time to have the toughness of character to resist the pressures put on them by ill-behaved players. They may unanimously agree at meetings in the quiet of the close season on what action should be taken on bad behaviour and unfair play, but that is very different from deciding in the heat of battle, perhaps when weary at the end of a long hot day, the exact degree of a player's transgression and whether he has overstepped the mark.

I have always admired Dickie Bird's handling of difficult situations. He does not duck away from them but brings an element of humour to the scene and has the respect of players. He is often considered to be an eccentric and to that extent reminds me of Alec Skelding of Leicestershire, a veteran umpire in the 1950s. Alec was not as good an umpire as Dickie Bird. For one thing, his fading eyesight prevented it. He made many mistakes but got a lot right by cricket instinct and he was such a lovely character that the players did everything they could to help him.

A big difference between my time as a player and today is that the umpire is now required to do much of what should properly be the captain's job. Control of short-pitched bowling is one example.

The best fast bowlers of my day did not bowl a succession of short-pitched balls. The odd bouncer was considered a legitimate weapon in the fast bowler's armoury and also added to the variety for the watching spectators. But there was horror if one was bowled to an inept, ill-equipped late-order batsman.

I well remember Ray Lindwall's words on the subject: 'If I can't bowl out nine, ten, jack by pitching the ball up, I shouldn't be in the side.'

Apart from the dangerous and bullying aspects, an excess of short fast bowling in not only ineffective against stout-hearted batsmen but downright boring. It cheats both crowd and opponents, for the batsman has few chances to play strokes. The drive becomes almost extinct. The game loses its character and its attractiveness. Who, apart presumably from the bowler, wants to play or watch a game in which batting for the majority (I except the most skilful and the really tall batsman) is largely a struggle to survive without injury, not a duel of strokes and subtlety with the bowler? It is a poor game when four fast bowlers fire away with next to no relief from spin. The ideal remains two fast bowlers, one medium-pacer and two spinners, which must make it a more interesting game to watch and play.

There is no easy solution. One country may lay down special conditions, as did the TCCB when, following an International Cricket Conference suggestion, it limited bouncers to one an over, but if visiting sides refuse to abide by this, the home players are put at a disadvantage. The most feasible solutions lie in the hands of captains, who must realize that the spirit of the game is being infringed by intimidation by their bowlers, and of umpires, who must be firm in acting on what is now a clear directive from the Laws.

The hope that this may one day come about no doubt stamps me as an impractical idealist, but I see no legislation at the moment, in the present climate of differing world opinion, which can both maintain the game's variety and curb excesses.

I appreciate that the captain, like the umpire, has a harder task today, in his case because he does not have the same authority as the amateur captain had. After the Second World War the amateur had a hard time establishing himself in first-class cricket. Bowlers would run up with appreciably greater zest when they saw a 'fancy cap' at the other end. But once an amateur had made his mark as a good enough player and a good leader, his stoutest supporters would be the professionals who appreciated the spirit in which he played and recognized that, not earning his livelihood from the game, he was in a stronger position to represent them with the committee.

Professionals of my generation still wag their heads sadly at the demise of the amateur, although I am sure that for the sake of the game's reputation and for economic reasons it had to come. An amateur might not have been paid for playing but if, through advertising and writing for newspapers, he earned more than the professionals and indeed deprived them of their perks, his position made a mockery of amateur status and was understandable cause for resentment.

I myself think that the game lost a lot with the fading from the scene of the old position of senior professional, the captain's chief of staff, who looked after dressing-room discipline and whose word was law. Every county seemed to have the knack of finding the right man for the job.

One other respect in which I believe the game has lost some of its charm and unpredictability is through the now total covering of pitches. I freely admit that it they were uncovered the spinner would not nowadays have the opportunity which he once had of bowling on sticky pitches. The fast bowlers would be given the job. Whether this is because captains think they they will do it more economically than the spinners or because the texture of pitches has changed is hard to say without more evidence of wet and drying pitches.

Yet uncovered pitches would lead to less stereotyped cricket and although I appreciate the arguments for covering – it keeps England on equal terms with other countries who all cover and it provides more cricket – I would vote for its abolition if required to do so.

When my year as President of MCC began in October 1980, I was well aware that nowadays the job carries very considerable responsibilities and sometimes disagreeable tasks. Some of my recent predecessors had been drawn into leading delegations or travelling round the world on delicate political missions. As it happened, my immediate successor, Hubert Doggart, had to take the chair at an extraordinary general meeting called on a motion that MCC should send a team to South Africa.

My own year was mercifully free of contentious issues, indeed was blessed by the series against Australia which turned on the historic win at Headingley and two other exciting Test matches at Edgbaston and Old Trafford.

In so far as a President can set himself targets in just one year of office, I had two objectives. One was to meet members and listen to suggestions. The membership is the most important part of any club and I thought that anything which I could do to show that the President was not a remote unapproachable figure must be a good thing.

I found a lot of goodwill on all sides. By the end of my year, of course, everyone was in an excellent humour because of the way that the Test series had gone. But even before that, for example, at the AGM in May – potentially one of the most difficult days for any President – I felt that the members were somehow on my side. I think that a President who has been well known as a player has a big advantage. He is regarded as a cricketer first and foremost with no political axe to grind and with no reputation as a shrewd businessman to uphold. A President from the City without a known background, however worthy and brilliant, has to work a lot harder to establish himself in the eyes of the membership. Few know how invaluable his work has been to the club on committees and how lucky the club is to have at the helm for a year someone who is probably used to steering big organizations. He has, of course, not only to be the president of a private club which has special responsibilities for the Laws and is the owner of the world's most famous cricket ground, but he has to be the chairman of the International Cricket Conference.

Ideally, I believe, the presidency should move around from cricketer to businessman and to men from other walks of life. The main requirement should obviously be a love of cricket and, where possible, service to it. I had this in mind when I nominated Hubert Doggart as my successor. Although for many years a busy headmaster, he had never ceased to involve himself closely with youth cricket as president of the English Schools Cricket Association and in many other ways. He was known to members as a former captain of Cambridge and Sussex who had played for England and I like to think that they realized what he had done for the National Cricket Association and non-first-class cricket. I know that he was a most conscientious President, who did his homework painstakingly throughout his year in office, whether it was chairing an important meeting at Lord's or speaking at the dinner of a cricket club with which he had had no previous contacts. He has recently added to his responsibilities the chairmanship of the subcommittee organizing MCC's bicentenary in 1987.

My other aim was to do anything I could to preserve the priceless heritage of Lord's. Rebuilding is constantly under review and I did what I could to keep moving the process which should ultimately lead to the replacing of the Mound stand by 1987.

The business side of cricket today needs most careful handling. Mistakes can be very costly. The biggest mistake that MCC have made in my recollection was to cave in to a small but vociferous group of members who protested against the original plan of two tiers of boxes in the new Tavern stand. It was claimed that this would deprive members of seating on big occasions and would involve extra cost. The number of seats lost would not have been great and the amount saved was only £30,000. That would have been recovered several times over in a single season, such is the demand for boxes. Surrey sold the boxes in their new stand before it was built.

If boxes were to be let at the present high rental, it seemed to me desirable that they should be as well equipped as possible. My own small contribution as President was to have television sets installed in them.

The administration of cricket nowadays is a complex and time consuming business. Just as the qualifications required of a golf club secretary have grown out of all proportion in the last thirty years, so they have for administrating MCC and the counties. Surrey now have Raman Subba Row as executive chairman working with a small committee who meet regularly and run the club, reporting to the full committee at routine meetings during the year. The TCCB does roughly the same and I am sure that this is the way to run the game nowadays. A secretary of MCC is not really a secretary in the old sense but a chief executive who needs a fair working knowledge of the law, finance and property as well as the ability to look after the social and cricketing side.

The President's role has often been under consideration. One year may not be enough, but one year is all that most men of the right age group are likely to be able to spare for a job which requires far more day-to-day attention than was once the case. But should it? With the secretary as a sort of chief executive, some believe the President need not be so heavily involved. I think myself the distribution of duties is probably just about right as it is.

At the heart of MCC affairs in my time was always Gubby Allen. He was chairman of selectors when I became captain of England and twenty-five years later, when I took the chair for my first committee meeting as President of MCC, there he was sitting at short square leg and contributing to the business on hand from a wealth of knowledge which no one else could match. He had done everything himself. He had been President, treasurer, in and out of Lord's as player and administrator for over sixty years, and he lived – as he might say, mixing his sporting metaphors – no more that a five-iron shot from the square at Lord's. He was a great help.

In his younger days he had, of course, been a great fast bowler and had captained England. Though he was playing first-class cricket seven years before I was born, I batted against Gubby's bowling once. On his annual visits to Cambridge with the Free Foresters in the early 1950s he usually made a lot of runs but in my first year he also opened the bowling and had David Sheppard caught at the wicket for nought. I am glad to say that I did not share the same fate – I should be hearing about it still! – but with his beautiful action he was still sharp at the age of forty-seven.

Later, during our harmonious partnership as chairman of selectors and captain, he gave me some good advice on selection which I have often had cause to remember. 'Distrust labels,' he said. 'If you hear that a good player is vulnerable against spin or fast bowling and you see him fail once, don't rely on that one impression. Go and have another look.'

I suppose that the most worrying part of my connection with the presidency was just before I took office. If the Centenary Test of August 1980 could have been staged at Lord's again with the benefit of hindsight, measures would doubtless have been taken to lessen the risk of harm being done to cricket in what should have been one of its showpieces. But as regulations and attitudes were in 1980, the match unfortunately earned itself a dismal place in cricket history.

Obviously it was going to be hard to follow the huge success of the Melbourne Centenary match of three and a half years earlier. In fact, the TCCB's social arrangements went remarkably well and were much appreciated by the old players of both sides. Nothing was more appreciated than the marquee for old players erected in the memorial garden behind the Warner stand. They sat in there for hours availing themselves of the hospitality. The innings played and the wickets taken were legion. It was a marvellous atmosphere. The tragedy was that the match itself, which is what the public remembers, was a big disappointment even allowing for the bad weather which blighted it.

At the time I was not only President-designate of MCC, due to take office in about a month's time, but chairman of the TCCB cricket subcommittee. I had no official part in the organizing of the match but had indirect interests through being on the MCC committee and through my contacts with umpires and captains at regular meetings with them.

It will be remembered that rain took nearly an hour's play out of the first day and rather longer out of the second. On the Friday night the ground dried out but was soaked again by rain early on Saturday morning. The skies then cleared and the packed crowd sat in sunshine while the umpires, Messrs Bird and Constant, came and went at intervals throughout the morning and into the afternoon, deciding each time that the ground was unfit for play. The unfit part consisted of two worn patches at the lower end of the square which had been left uncovered.

To make a depressing situation worse, a few members of MCC shouted abuse at the umpires and jostled them as they returned to the pavilion with the captains after one inspection. It was a disgraceful incident. The culprits were identified and two and a half months later, as President, I wrote to members telling them that appropriate disciplinary action had been taken.

But the damage had been done. The good name of MCC had been smeared on just about the last occasion one would have wanted anything like this to happen. There are always people keen to depict MCC as an exclusive citadel of privilege and smugness and they not surprisingly had a field day.

Inexcusable though the behaviour was, it arose from the lack of action on the field and that, in turn, arose from the attitude of mind of the four parties most closely concerned in the conduct of the match – the umpires, the players, the TCCB and MCC.

The umpires worked by the Laws of the game and the regulations governing first-class cricket and which are drawn up to ensure that as far as possible they are fair to both sides and to the public. They thought the patch of ground was still unfit and they said so.

The players considered that the Centenary Test match was still a Test match and that any decision to treat it as some special festive occasion not to be approached with the usual sternness of matches between England and Australia would devalue it. They could have told the umpires that they wanted to play even though the ground was not strictly fit, but for that the two captains would have had to be in agreement. And as England were in very much the weaker position, Ian Botham made no attempt to influence the umpires to play.

The TCCB, for its part, does not interfere with umpires in the course of their duties. It discusses problems with them at the start of the season and the secretary, Donald Carr, is always available for consultation. But the Board did not consider it fair to ask players and umpires in advance to relax the playing conditions and their approach for this one match. It did not, of course, know that the late August weather would play such a part.

MCC, the ground authority, did not intervene because it was the TCCB which was responsible for the participants and for the regulations under which the match was played.

So nothing happened and the waiting went on with the crowd increasingly restless, until Billy Griffith, the President of MCC, could stand it no longer.

A President during Test matches has a heavy day in his box, for he has to entertain official guests who may include prime ministers, ambassadors, archbishops, as well as distinguished visitors from overseas, of whom there was no shortage on this occasion. But Billy, a very sick man at the time, struggled downstairs, across to the pavilion and up to the umpires' room where he ordered them to start play. To spare them embarrassment he told them to go out, look and decide to play at once. He said that he would take full responsibility for any consequences.

While this was going on, I arrived on the scene, prompted by what Billy later referred to as 'the increasing misery of what should have been a great occasion' and was able to give Billy full support. Billy told the umpires that he had absolutely no right to give them the order. I also had no business to interfere. But we both felt that something had to be done urgently and, partly as a result of Billy's intervention, the match was restarted by the umpires.

Protecting the square at Lord's with its nine-foot slope is, of course, always difficult, but covering, in quality and quantity, is improving all the time and I am sure that this sort of thing could not happen again.

When I succeeded Doug Insole as chairman of the cricket subcommittee of the TCCB in the late 1970s I was especially interested in the end-of-season reports by the captains and umpires. In early October we have a meeting of each at Lord's, inviting comments on all sorts of events which had taken place during the season, on how new playing conditions had worked out and so on. Our committee then reported to the Board with recommendations which were considered at the Board meeting in December.

I cannot believe that current players and officials of any other game are more thoroughly consulted on its conduct than those active in English first-class cricket. The Board has made few decisions involving players without consulting the Cricketers' Association. The views of the captains carry often decisive weight when changes in playing conditions are under consideration. The picture which one still sometimes sees painted of cricket being run by a lot of pompous, potbellied, aristocratic reactionaries is an old and feeble joke.

I am often asked if I find the highly paid modern Test player very different from my own contemporaries. My answer is that if they can make a lot of money out of cricket while promoting its interests, good luck to them. But it is important for them to realize that they do have enormous responsibilities. They are watched more closely than we were, on and off the field. The way they play, the way they behave and the lives they lead all reflect on the game. The more they make out of it, the greater their responsibility. I like to think that most of them realize that they have a price to pay for their success. They can hardly have failed to notice the huge popularity in the age of television of golf in which the world's great players are immaculately mannered – and always smartly dressed.

First-class cricket is just the harshly exposed tip of the iceberg and one must never forget that the game originated in this country and is still played for fun and nothing else by thousands in cities, towns and villages. I never cease to delight in the sight of white-flannelled figures on a green village ground and when possible always stop and watch a few overs.

When I talk to club, village and school cricketers, I am frequently struck by how much it matters to them that England should play well and do well. It matters to me, too, and it mattered a great deal to the old type of professional who earned little from the game but believed passionately in what it stood for. The traditions of the game are so deeply embedded that I doubt that the modern player is very different in this respect, even in the age of agents, sponsors and, at the top, high incomes from fringe benefits.

I sometimes sense that when a batsman is out nowadays he is less bothered by it than we were. Perhaps this is a result of the plethora of limited-over innings which he plays and in which to be out for 20 may be infinitely worthier than to be not out for 15.

I always used to sit down in the dressing room, thinking about my dismissal and analysing it. Could I have prevented it? How should I avoid being out in the same way again? I was always disappointed when I got out, for the team as well as for myself. I am therefore not in favour of the batsman who walks off with a couldn't-care-less look. Or, incidentally, of one who departs without having the courtesy to make a clear acknowledgement of the crowd's applause.

For as long as I can remember, cricket has been said to be in a crisis or at a crossroads. On the whole, I think that it has adapted rather well to changed times – with the help of sponsorship and television. Nobody is complacent about that. Among the good years there are always bad wet years which quickly douse complacency. Certainly we have problems but no system is ever going to be perfect.

We do have an excessive financial reliance on sponsorship and Test receipts but we are not unique in that. The advent of television has meant that in nearly all games the big events have grown in popularity at the expense of competitions at lower levels. People see the best players on television in their homes and are less inclined to pay to watch their local side, however much they support them in spirit.

I have touched on the difficulties under which a chairman of selectors works in an age when so much limited-over cricket is played, but there are no facile solutions to this or any other problems. If there were, they would have been found by now. I have watched and been a member of numerous committees looking into the future of the game and I have nothing new to add to what has already been considered in great detail – and either adopted or discarded.

We have experimented a lot over the years, for example with minor alterations to the playing conditions such as the limitation on first innings in the county championship and the abolition of the follow-on. These could be dropped when they did not work, but for any major change in the structure of cricket one would have to be as sure as possible that it would be an all-round improvement on what exists at present.

I believe that one of the most difficult decisions to be made by cricket administrators in the 1980s is to what extent they should try to educate the public about the game and to what extent they should allow the public to influence them.

Test matches apart, more people go to watch an inferior form of cricket with negative bowling, defensive field settings and batsmen playing crude cross-batted strokes than watch the conventional game of charm and variety which has developed over the centuries. As in golf, there is a market for matches in which 'celebrities' from other walks of life take part. Unlike golf, cricket is not an easy game to handicap.

In small doses these matches are harmless and profitable. But in the long term will the game – and its finances – benefit if a generation grows up to believe that cricket is just slogging and not the age-old duel between bowlers and batsmen?

I appreciate the special problems of modern cricket in Australia and of our Board's difficult position when England teams tour there. But I was still shaken by the sight of England playing daylight one-day internationals in New Zealand in coloured clothes. The TCCB are totally opposed to playing in coloured clothing in this country but on overseas tours they fall in with the wishes of the host country in most matters. The New Zealand Board and its sponsors wanted to associate the series in the minds of a new cricket public with the popular televised cricket which it had been seeing from Australia.

This is a trivial matter in itself – the cricket is the same however garish the cricketers – but not without significance. If players have to be dressed in different colours to persuade people to watch, what hope is there of making spectators grapple with the more subtle and less spectacular skills of real cricket?

The answer probably is that at present nobody knows. It may well prove that a percentage of those drawn to the game by gimmicks will go on to learn and appreciate its finer points.

How to modernize while retaining precious traditions, how to move with the times without lowering standards, how to balance the books without allowing sponsors too much say, how to keep players employed without overtaxing their talents. These are the issues facing the administrators of the 1980s.

Yet their deliberations concern only cricket at the top. First-class cricket is immensely important for the examples set and the pleasure given to countless followers near and far. But it is not the whole game.

I know the difficulties that modern first-class players have in changing their methods to suit the particular type of cricket which they are asked to play. I wonder what they will remember in later years of this hotchpotch. However close and exciting the finishes, there is a sameness about limited-over matches which makes them swiftly forgettable, especially when they are played in such abundance. I recognize that modern international cricketers, playing almost full time and dependent on the game for a substantial income, must look at it in a different way from most players of my generation. That is inevitable.

But there are hundreds of thousands of other cricketers of all races throughout the world who are not dependent on the game for their bread and butter, and if, as I believe, they derive much the same pleasure from it as I have, cricket's place in society is as assured as ever.

Peter May in First-Class Cricket

In England

Season	Matches	Inns.	Not Outs	Runs	Highest Score	100's	50's	Average	Catches
1948	1	2	0	5	3	0	0	2.50	0
1949	6	12	1	695	175	1	5	63.18	2
1950	27	38	3	1,187	227*	2	4	33.91	10
1951	26	43	9	2,339	178*	9	9	68.79	17
1952	27	47	7	2,498	197	10	7	62.45	15
1953	34	59	9	2,554	159	8	11	51.08	21
1954	29	41	7	1,702	211*	6	6	50.05	26
1955	25	42	5	1,902	125	5	12	51.40	33
1956	30	50	7	1,631	128*	3	8	37.93	31
1957	29	41	3	2,347	285*	7	15	61.76	29
1958	29	41	6	2,231	174	8	9	63.74	27
1959	11	16	2	663	143	2	4	47.35	12
1961	22	42	5	1,499	153*	2	10	40.51	16
1962	20	31	5	1,352	135	3	8	52.00	16
1963	3	4	0	90	85	0	1	22.50	1

In Australia

1954–55	14	23	3	931	129	4	3	46.55	13
1958–59	13	22	1	1,197	140	5	5	57.00	4

In New Zealand

1954–55	4	6	0	165	48	0	0	27.50	3
1958–59	4	4	1	315	124*	1	2	105.00	1

In West Indies

1953–54	10	18	2	630	135	2	3	39.37	0
1959–60	9	12	0	389	124	1	1	32.41	1

In South Africa

1956–57	16	24	1	1,270	206	6	4	55.21	4

All First-Class Matches

	389	618	77	27,592	285*	85	127	51.00	282

TEST CRICKET

Matches	Inns.	Not Outs	Runs	Highest Score	100's	50's	Average	Catches
66	106	9	4,537	285*	13	22	46.77	42

COUNTY CHAMPIONSHIP

Matches	Inns.	Not Outs	Runs	Highest Score	100's	50's	Average	Catches
175	278	42	11,440	211*	30	59	48.47	153

FOR CAMBRIDGE UNIVERSITY

Matches	Inns.	Not Outs	Runs	Highest Score	100's	50's	Average	Catches
38	58	12	2,861	227*	9	9	62.19	26

CENTURIES (85)
for England (13)

v. Australia (3) 113, 104, 101
v. South Africa (3) 138, 117, 112
v. West Indies (3) 285*, 135, 104
v. New Zealand (3) 124*, 113*, 101
v. India (1) 106

For Surrey (39)

v. Kent (6) 143, 128*, 124, 116, 107, 102
v. Cambridge University (3) 207, 137, 102*
v. Lancashire (3) 174, 122*, 100
v. Middlesex (3) 159, 123*, 121
v. Nottinghamshire (3) 211*, 163, 135*
v. Essex (2) 167 103*
v. Hampshire (2) 123*, 117*
v. Northamptonshire (2) 169, 136
v. Somerset (2) 153*, 107*
v. Sussex (2) 136*, 117
v. Yorkshire (2) 155, 125
v. New Zealand (2) 165, 112*
v. Leicestershire (1) 197
v. Warwickshire (1) 135
v. Worcestershire (1) 118
v. M.C.C. (1) 151
v. The Rest (1) 125
v. India (1) 143
v. Pakistan (1) 119

For Cambridge University (9)

v. Hampshire (2) 227* 178*
v. Sussex (2) 167, 120
v. Essex (1) 104*
v. Lancashire (1) 139*
v. Middlesex (1) 120
v. Warwickshire (1) 156*
v. Yorkshire (1) 171

Other matches (24)

M.C.C. v. Yorkshire (2) 174, 100*
M.C.C. v. Combined XI (2) 129, 113
M.C.C. V. Australian XI (2) 140, 114
M.C.C. v. Western Province (2), 162, 116
M.C.C. v. Rhodesia (2) 206, 124*
M.C.C. v. Jamaica (2) 124, 124
M.C.C. v. New South Wales (1) 136
M.C.C. v. South Australia (1) 114
M.C.C. v. Victoria (1) 105*
M.C.C. v. Eastern Province (1) 118
M.C.C. v. Natal (1): 107
Gentlemen v. Players (3) 157, 119*, 112*
T. N. Pearce's XI v. Australians (1) 100
T. N. Pearce's XI v. West Indians (1) 119
T. N. Pearce's XI v. New Zealanders (1) 131
Combined Services v. Worcestershire (1) 175

Index